I0896127

AMERICA IN THE TEENS

America in the Twentieth Century
John Robert Greene, *Series Editor*

Other titles in America in the Twentieth Century

America in the Twenties
Ronald Allen Goldberg

America in the Thirties
John Olszowka, Marnie M. Sullivan,
Brian R. Sheridan, and Dennis Hickey

America in the Forties
Ronald Allen Goldberg

America in the Fifties
Andrew J. Dunar

America in the Sixties
John Robert Greene

America in the Seventies
Stephanie A. Slocum-Schaffer

America in the Nineties
Nina Esperanza Serrianne

AMERICA IN THE TEENS

Andrew J. Dunar

Syracuse University Press

Syracuse University Press
Syracuse, New York 13244-5290

First Edition 2016

16 17 18 19 20 21 6 5 4 3 2 1

∞ The paper used in this publication meets the minimum requirements of the American National Standard for Information Sciences—Permanence of Paper for Printed Library Materials, ANSI Z39.48-1992.

For a listing of books published and distributed by Syracuse University Press, visit www.SyracuseUniversityPress.syr.edu.

ISBN: 978-0-8156-3480-5 (hardcover)
978-0-8156-3465-2 (paperback)
978-0-8156-5377-6 (e-book)

Library of Congress Cataloging-in-Publication Data

Names: Dunar, Andrew J., author.
Title: America in the Teens / Andrew J. Dunar.
Description: First edition. | Syracuse, New York : Syracuse University Press, 2016. | Series: America in the Twentieth Century | Includes index.
Identifiers: LCCN 2016021453 (print) | LCCN 2016024275 (ebook) | ISBN 9780815634805 (hardcover : alk. paper) | ISBN 9780815634652 (pbk. : alk. paper) | ISBN 9780815653776 (e-book)
Subjects: LCSH: United States—History—1913–1921. | United States—History—1909–1913.
Classification: LCC E766 .D86 2016 (print) | LCC E766 (ebook) | DDC 973.91—dc23
LC record available at https://lccn.loc.gov/2016021453

Manufactured in the United States of America

To the memory of my parents

ANDREW DUNAR

MARION ELIZABETH DUNAR

Contents

Illustrations

Foreword

"There just never seems to be enough time." "The textbook is so bland, the students won't read it." "Don't *teachers* ever write?" "If I could only find more than one book that I feel good about assigning." These complaints are endemic to those of us who teach survey American history courses. The series America in the Twentieth Century was designed to address these issues in a novel fashion that attempts to meet the needs of both student and instructor alike.

It uses decades for its organizational schema (admittedly a debatable choice, but it is our experience that chronology, not theme, makes for a better survey course), and each book tackles the main issues of a particular decade in a fashion at once readable and scholarly in nature. The series editor has chosen authors primarily for their teaching skills—indeed, each book proposal was accompanied by syllabi that show the prospective author's course pedagogy. In fact, contributors have been urged to write these books from their lecture notes and to limit footnote references, which can often distract or intimidate the student reader. In a departure from virtually every textbook series of note, one member of our editorial board is a presently sitting college student, whose comments on the manuscript may well be the most helpful of all. Each chapter ends with a recommended reading list of the authors' favorite books. The list is, admittedly, not exhaustive, but no list of our favorite works ever is.

The result is a readable, concise, and scholarly series of books from master teachers who know what works in the college classroom. We offer it to college instructors and their students in hopes that they will, in the words of the Latin maxim, do the one thing that we all in the academy hope that professor and student will do together: "Tolle et lege" (Take and read).

John Robert Greene

Acknowledgments

Thanks first to series editor Bob Greene, who founded this series and nurtured it. Bob gave me the opportunity to write two of the books in the series, one on the fifties and another on the teens, and offered advice and encouragement throughout. Everyone at Syracuse University Press was helpful, professional, and responsive. Deanna McCay, Suzanne Guiod, Kelly Balenske, Mona Hamlin, and Kay Steinmetz especially offered assistance at key points. I was fortunate to have the meticulous Annette Wenda as a copyeditor; it would be hard to imagine anyone better at her craft. In thirty years of teaching at the University of Alabama in Huntsville, I benefited in countless ways from having extraordinary Americanists as colleagues, including Johanna Shields, Stephen Waring, Lee Williams, Christine Sears, James Isbell, and John Kvach. Although Jack Ellis is a Europeanist, our work overlapped in ways that were mutually beneficial, and his encouragement was always welcomed. Beverley Gentry provided support in countless ways. Students may not realize how much they influence professors, and I was fortunate to have excellent students in my foreign relations and twentieth-century American history courses. Cathie, Jamie, Kim, and Michael provided unstinting support on the home front. I dedicate this book to the memory of my parents, Andrew and Marion Dunar, both of whom were born during the years described in this book.

AMERICA IN THE TEENS

Introduction

For Americans, the second decade of the twentieth century began in optimism and ended in disillusion. By 1910 the United States had emerged as one of the most dynamic nations in the world, an economic powerhouse that could compete on equal footing with the leading European nations. In the midst of a regenerative reform movement known as Progressivism, its cities, institutions, and government had undergone modernization stimulated by industrialization and urbanization. The second half of the decade, however, dominated as it was by the First World War, witnessed unprecedented destruction and death—as a result not only of the war, but also of a worldwide influenza epidemic. The war underscored fissures in American society that had been obscured or minimized by economic prosperity at the beginning of the decade. These problems included racial divisions, labor-management issues, and ethnic strife stirred by immigration. It was in this atmosphere that the nation experienced one of the most unsettling decades of the twentieth century, and it is the context of this book.

The first two chapters examine the political situation in the early years of the decade. Several factors made it one of the most competitive and important periods in American politics since the Civil War. It was competitive because the dominant Republican Party experienced deep divisions that gave the Democrats a chance to win the presidency for the first time since Grover Cleveland held the office. Republicans split into two camps, the conservative Old Guard, led by President William Howard Taft, and the Progressives, led by former president Theodore Roosevelt. Thus, the election of 1912 matched the previous president (Roosevelt) against the current president (Taft) and the future president (Woodrow Wilson). Further complicating this competition was the fact that all three men claimed to be Progressives.

The politics of the era were also important to the future of the nation. The election of 1912 witnessed a genuine intellectual debate between two intellectuals, political scientist Woodrow Wilson and historian Theodore Roosevelt. But the importance of the politics of the era extends far beyond the issues of the day. Of the three men who occupied the office, two of them—Roosevelt and Wilson—took steps that greatly expanded the powers of the presidency, thus beginning a trend that continued throughout the century, leading to what historian Arthur M. Schlesinger would later call the "imperial presidency."

The next four chapters examine other aspects of the decade: foreign policy, financial and economic issues as well as technological developments, society, and culture. Prior to World War I, American foreign policy focused particularly on Latin America, which is the subject of chapter 3. Taft's policy toward the region, which came to be called dollar diplomacy, sought to supplant military intervention with investment, with at best a mixed record. Wilson, who intended to concentrate on domestic affairs, found himself intervening in the Caribbean Basin frequently. His intervention in Mexico in response to the Mexican Revolution was his most important foreign policy decision prior to World War I.

Chapter 4 deals with two aspects of the rapid expansion of the American economy in the early twentieth century. The first is financial reform, the most important aspect of which was the creation of the Federal Reserve System, the most significant development in banking since the battle over the Bank of the United States during Andrew Jackson's presidency. Another aspect of economic growth was the development of new technology, and here the United States moved into a position of international leadership. The chapter focuses on the development of Ford Motor Company as an example of American enterprise and entrepreneurship.

The 1910s was a decade of social change across a broad spectrum, a phenomenon examined in chapter 5. Immigrants continued to come to the United States in large numbers in the early years of the decade, providing a workforce for developing industry, but also experiencing opposition in industrial centers. African Americans began leaving the South in large numbers, seeking jobs in industrial cities of the North and Midwest. This African American diaspora continued for decades and brought about more tensions to industrial cities.

Chapter 6 examines the rich culture that characterized the decade. In the visual arts, Americans endeavored to break from European artistic leadership and to establish an independent American artistic vision. This innovation was more clearly the case in music, where African roots influenced the development of jazz and ragtime, both uniquely American. The motion picture industry, particularly the pioneering work of director D. W. Griffith and the emerging star system that propelled actors to international fame, allowed American movies to compete with European films.

The last five chapters investigate the many and varied ways in which American participation in World War I affected the United States. Chapter 7 traces efforts by President Wilson to keep the United States out of the war and the complex interplay of international events and internal pressures that eventually brought the nation into the conflict. Once the nation entered the war, its participation had a profound effect on domestic affairs, and chapter 8 charts the war's impact at home. Chapter 9 turns to the US military involvement in the Allied war effort. It examines the task of raising an army and then follows the US military contribution to the Allied victory. After the war ended in November 1918, President Wilson spent several months in Europe, participating in the Versailles Peace Conference, which made crucial decisions about postwar agreements and territorial shifts that stretched from Western Europe to the Middle East and had a profound effect that echoed throughout the twentieth century. Chapter 10 considers these crucial discussions but focuses especially on President Wilson's dream of forming a League of Nations that would seek to resolve disputes peacefully through negotiation instead of war. Ultimately, the US Congress rejected membership in the League of Nations, a decision that was one of the developments that led to postwar disillusionment.

Chapter 11 looks forward into the 1920s. It does so by going back to the end of the war and discussing how the war and its aftermath created the circumstances that shaped the 1920s. Elements of disillusionment dominate this discussion: disappointment with the failure of the war to eradicate sources of international discord and the failure of the League of Nations, renewed racial strife, labor strikes, distrust of recent immigrants and ethnic minorities, and a recession at the beginning of the 1920s.

The United States entered the second decade of the twentieth century as a very different nation than it had been a generation earlier. Complex economic and social forces had been transformative. Industrialization and urbanization were merely the most apparent forces, altering ways in which Americans lived and worked.

The new industrial cities of the Northeast and Midwest were crowded, unplanned, and often contentious. Immigration patterns had changed in the early 1890s; under the pattern prevalent prior to 1890, most immigrants arrived from northern and western Europe. Most of them were literate, Protestant, and spoke English. The "new immigrants" arriving after 1890 came mainly from southern, eastern, or central Europe. Many of them came to take industrial jobs. They were mainly Catholic or Jewish. Few of them spoke English, and they had received less education than previous arrivals. Thus, ethnic, class, and religious differences often spawned clashes in the developing industrial cities. Some of the most violent labor strikes in American history occurred during the 1890s.

Economic changes had been as dramatic as the social changes. The surge of industrialization in the late nineteenth century prompted the emergence of more complex forms of business organization, and developing corporate capitalism spawned great wealth for industrial magnates and wrenching poverty for their workers. Cutthroat competition eliminated small businesses and created an incentive for mergers, creating large firms that dominated industries. Ineffective regulation and court decisions in the mid-1890s made corporate mergers even more attractive, so much so that the last years of the nineteenth century and the first years of the twentieth witnessed a flurry of business combinations known collectively as the Great Merger movement.

The rapidity of these changes prompted a variety of responses, including calls for government action, the creation of labor unions, and the emergence of reform movements. Among the earliest demands for governmental action came from rural areas, where farmers believed that the government had favored industry in passing tariffs, that railroads had discriminated against small shippers, and that banks, monetary policy, and the federal government favored industry over farming. The federal government's most significant response was the establishment of the nation's first regulatory agency, the Interstate Commerce Commission (ICC), designed to regulate the railroads. The government staffed the agency with former railroad men, since only those individuals who had worked in the industry could understand what had to be done to regulate it. Unfortunately, the commission's members shared the perspective of railroad men and consistently ruled in favor of the railroads. The same problem would plague other regulatory agencies, leading to the pejorative term *captive agencies.*

By 1910 the United States had established itself as among the first rank of world powers. In the preceding twenty-five years, urbanization and industrialization had transformed the nation, and by the end of the decade the US Census revealed that for the first time the majority of Americans lived in cities. After the election of 1896, the United States became an industrial power under Republican domination in Congress and in the White House. An aggressive capitalism dominated by large firms ruled the economy, leaving unions and small companies to fend for themselves. This tendency had been tempered by Roosevelt's "trust busting," but he had been selective in the trusts he busted and still supported big capitalism. Not only unions but also ethnic and racial minorities suffered under this system. European immigrants found jobs in industry but under adverse working conditions, Asian immigration dwindled under exclusionary policies, and African Americans had seen their social and economic standing erode steadily after the end of Reconstruction in 1877. The growth of cities prompted a wide-ranging reform movement called Progressivism that centered on urban reform and included both major political parties and the first three presidents of the new century, two of whom were Republicans and one a Democrat. The nation had asserted its emerging power in world affairs in the 1898 war with Spain, and that power had only grown under the presidency of the nationalistic Theodore Roosevelt, who in particular demonstrated US influence in Latin America.

As the new decade began, the United States was on the brink of becoming a major world power, and by many economic measures it had already achieved this status. The rise in power, however, came with new challenges. How would the country handle its new international role? Would it fulfill its self-proclaimed destiny as an exceptional nation, a beacon to the world? How would it deal with the demands of marginalized minorities, particularly African Americans and ethnic immigrants? Would it be able to resolve conflicts between labor and the captains of industry? Would the nation be able to sustain its impressive rate of economic growth and its zeal for reform? How would its identity change as cultural forms such as jazz and motion pictures emerged as particularly American art forms? Americans in 1910 looked forward to meeting these challenges.

1

The Taft Presidency, the Republican Insurgency, and the Progressive Movement

Two men, Theodore Roosevelt and Woodrow Wilson, dominated American politics in the first two decades of the twentieth century. Both men transformed the office of the presidency, fostering the expansion of the powers of the office. By increasing presidential power at the expense of Congress, they initiated a trend that continued throughout the twentieth century. Their administrations were separated by the presidency of William Howard Taft, who never fully escaped the shadow of his predecessor and whose split with Roosevelt made possible Wilson's election in 1912.

THE PROGRESSIVE MOVEMENT

President Taft and former president Roosevelt agreed in many respects on the problems that the United States faced in the early years of the twentieth century. They had worked together exceptionally well, with Taft accepting and executing several assignments under Roosevelt, earning Roosevelt's confidence to the point that Roosevelt wanted Taft to succeed him as president. It was in this era that the Progressive movement defined much of the debate over domestic policy, and both presidents considered themselves Progressives. Yet ultimately, the friendship foundered over domestic policy and Progressive reforms, issues that had not affected their relationship during Roosevelt's presidency, since Taft's role as a member of Roosevelt's administration focused exclusively on foreign policy. But Progressivism was not solely a policy of the Republican Party, and in fact Woodrow Wilson, the Democrat who succeeded Taft, also considered himself a Progressive.

To understand developments in American society, politics, and the economy in the early twentieth century, it is essential to examine Progressivism and the Progressive movement. Progressivism emerged in the late nineteenth and early twentieth centuries during one of the most vital eras of reform in American history. The push for reform involved—in addition to Progressivism—the rural reform movement known as Populism and labor reform, including moderate unions such as the American Federation of Labor (AFL) and more radical unions such as the Industrial Workers of the World (IWW). Both major political parties supported some of these reforms, as did the Socialist Party. These reform movements to a great extent developed in reaction to the problems emerging in American society as a result of the pressures of rapid industrialization and urbanization. The capitalist economy was expanding rapidly and spawning businesses, organizations, and governmental institutions of its own that had the resources and political power to stave off many of the proposed reforms or modify them in ways that limited their impact.

Progressivism was mainly an urban movement that developed in response to problems that were emerging in American cities. Historians generally date Progressivism as extending from 1890 to 1920, and during those three decades the United States moved from being a predominantly rural nation to a nation in which more than half its people lived in cities. The US Census of 1920 was the first in which the majority of Americans lived in cities. In 1890 58 cities had a population of more than fifty thousand; by 1920 that number had risen to 144. Industrial cities were the engines of economic development, but they also spawned poverty and disease in overcrowded slums that arose near industrial factories. Progressives blamed these problems on owners of the new industries, whom they considered to be interested solely in profits, caring little about how their workers lived or what their conditions were on the job. They pointed to industrial violence, strikes, unemployment, and economic depression as the by-products of their style of management and competition.

The term *Progressivism* encompassed a wide range of solutions for the ills of modern society, and as such it came to have a variety of meanings. To some, it meant correcting flaws in the practice of politics, to bring democracy closer to the people. To others, it meant attacking corruption and curbing abuses of power. To professionals, it meant establishing standards of conduct within their chosen field. To leaders in targeted areas of social reform, it meant instituting humanitarian reforms for the benefit of the poor, the downtrodden—people who had nowhere to turn. What united them was an optimistic faith in progress and in the power of government to promote it. Despite the problems they observed in the world around them, they believed that corrections could be made. They believed that government could be used to make such adjustments, that organization, efficiency, and persistence could overcome the inertia that had resisted such reform in previous generations.

The Progressives were generally young men and women who had college degrees or had at least attended college. Many of them were professionals, engaged in fields such as law, teaching, medicine, social work, or religion. They had a commitment to improving society and a belief that society could be improved. They approached reform by organizing and formed groups that in many cases are still active and well established. They formed occupational or professional organizations such as the American Medical Association, which was one of the earliest. Other such groups included the American Bar Association for lawyers, the American Public Health Association, and the American Historical Association, of which both Theodore Roosevelt and Woodrow Wilson served as president. They formed interest groups with a wide range of concerns: the National Association for the Advancement of Colored People (NAACP), a biracial organization; the US Chamber of Commerce; and the National Consumers League. Other organizations centered on one specific reform or a package of reforms related to one particular problem, such as the National Child Labor Committee, the National Municipal League, or the National Housing

Association. In other cases, Progressives strengthened reform campaigns that had been active for decades, such as prison reform, Prohibition, and women's suffrage.

Progressives used many tactics, including protest parades, petitions, and speeches. Best known of their tactics came to be called muckraking, and the practitioners became known as muckrakers, who would today be called investigative journalists. The muckrakers wrote for magazines that sought to expose corruption through long, often serialized investigative articles. Among the most popular of these magazines were *McClure's*, the *American Magazine*, and *Hampton's*. The writers included seasoned journalists who welcomed the opportunity provided by these journals and young reporters getting started in their careers. The term *muckrakers* came from a speech by Theodore Roosevelt, who referred to a character from John Bunyan's *Pilgrim's Progress*, the Man with a Muck Rake. Roosevelt acknowledged that such people filled a useful role but had to know when to stop raking the muck. He suggested that the point to desist came when critics became more concerned with exposing problems than with fixing them and that it was easy to criticize but more difficult to offer solutions. Roosevelt's comments gave many critics pause, but they regained their footing by aligning themselves with the Progressive movement after TR left office. Muckraking later faded when Progressivism declined.

The muckrakers showed an interest in a wide variety of social and economic issues, and a number of them became involved in politics. Ray Stannard Baker wrote *Following the Color Line* (1908), considered the first exposé of American racial problems. A graduate of Michigan Agricultural College (now Michigan State University), he wrote for *McClure's* but in 1908 joined with fellow muckrakers Lincoln Steffens and Ida Tarbell (best known for exposing the business tactics of John D. Rockefeller and Standard Oil) to begin the *American Magazine*. Baker assisted Woodrow Wilson's presidential campaign in 1912 and became one of Wilson's advisers. He served as Wilson's secretary at the Paris Peace Conference and later accepted Wilson's offer to be his official biographer. The last two volumes of his eight-volume biography won the Pulitzer Prize in 1940.

Lincoln Steffens, cofounder of the *American Magazine* with Baker, wrote an exposé on one of the central Progressive themes in his book *The Shame of the Cities*. He attended several European universities. He wrote for *McClure's* before moving on to the *American Magazine*. He traveled widely in the 1910s. In 1914 he went to Mexico during the revolution and served for a time as a liaison between the Wilson administration and the Carranza government. In 1917 he went to Russia during the revolution, and his experiences there were the source of his famous statement "I have seen the future and it works." When he wrote his autobiography in the 1930s, he discussed the quotation and his later disenchantment with communism.

Upton Sinclair, another politically active muckraker and the author of nearly one hundred books, is remembered for his novel *The Jungle* (1904). Sinclair, who graduated from the City College of New York, joined the Socialist Party and wrote *The Jungle* as a socialist tract. Instead, President Roosevelt called him in and used the novel as the basis for bills that became the Meat Inspection Act and the Pure Food and Drug Act. Sinclair was a man of many talents and wrote and produced movies during the 1910s. He later went to California, where he ran for the US House, for the US Senate, and for governor of California, all as a Socialist, and lost all races. In 1934 he ran again for governor, this time as a Democrat, with a campaign goal expressed as EPIC (End Poverty in California). Socialists didn't support him because he had deserted them, and Democrats were reluctant as well because he had been a Socialist. He lost again, but his EPIC campaign was one of the contributing factors that pushed President Franklin Roosevelt to initiate Social Security.

Broad reform movements that had begun in earlier decades gained impetus under the umbrella of Progressivism during the 1910s. The campaign for women's suffrage was one of them. Women had long been involved in reform movements and had taken leadership roles in movements such as child labor, temperance, prison reform, and suffrage for African Americans. At a monumental meeting at Seneca Falls, New York, in 1850, women recognized the importance of the vote in influencing social reform and began to organize a campaign to win the vote for women. For decades the movement suffered from internal divisions, with some women wanting to proceed state by state, others seeking a national amendment, and still others opposed to the movement, believing that women would sacrifice the moral high ground if they became involved in the nasty give-and-take of politics. The movement coalesced in the 1910s and won the passage of the Nineteenth Amendment to the Constitution, securing the vote for women.

Prohibition was another social movement that benefited from the reforming zeal of Progressivism, although not all prohibitionists were Progressives and all Progressives certainly were not prohibitionists. The cry for temperance (the more common term for opposing the consumption of alcohol during the nineteenth century) was another goal attracting the support of women reformers, and like suffrage it gained traction during the 1910s, culminating in the adoption of Prohibition as the Eighteenth Amendment. This noble (some would say misguided) experiment came to an end in 1933 when the adoption of the Twenty-First Amendment repealed the Eighteenth. (See chapter 5 for more a more detailed discussion of both women's suffrage and Prohibition.)

Progressives were also active in cities, where they pushed for public ownership of utilities. They also attacked the boss system that dominated many northeastern and midwestern cities, proposing instead systems such as city managers that would be less susceptible to control by political machines such as Tammany Hall in New York.

At the state level, Progressive governors—Republicans and Democrats—sought a variety of reforms. In Wisconsin Governor Robert La Follette worked with professors from the University of Wisconsin to devise reforms that other states adopted, so much so that Wisconsin became known as the "laboratory of democracy." Among these reforms were direct primaries, in which voters selected the party's candidates for office; the regulation of railroad rates; and state laws that prevented corporations from unfair advantages over competitors. Many states adopted the initiative (so that citizens could petition for state laws rather than waiting for legislatures to do so), referendum (a direct vote by the citizens on a specific political issue), and recall (to allow for the recall of a public official by petition followed by a vote of the citizens). Many states had moved toward the direct election of senators, a process previously reserved for state legislatures. Congress approved the proposed amendment in 1912, and in April 1913, after the legislatures of three-fourths of the states approved, direct election of senators became the Seventeenth Amendment to the Constitution.

States also took action on social welfare issues promoted by Progressives. By 1916 nearly two-thirds of the states had passed factory inspection laws and legislation requiring accident insurance. The National Labor Committee proposed laws regulating child labor, and many states supported such action. Typically, these laws specified a minimum age for children to work (twelve to sixteen in most states) and a maximum number of hours that they could work (usually eight to ten). These laws proved difficult to enforce, and child labor continued to be an issue into the 1920s. States passed laws to protect women employees on the job. States also passed laws that were the forerunners of old-age pensions.

Opposition arose from many quarters; these laws were far from universally popular. While many women advocated protective legislation for women workers, others opposed it, believing that such laws made women second-class employees and gave employers a rationale for lowering their pay; they argued that women could compete with men in the workplace on a basis of equality. When the federal government considered child labor legislation, southern states opposed such action, arguing that it should be a state issue—code for the fact that they would not pass laws that would make their states unpopular with employers. The National Association of Manufacturers opposed child labor laws as an infringement on the free-enterprise system. And some believed that social reform was not the business of the government at all and ought to be left to the churches.

This last idea is representative of the times, when the roles of churches and of the government were undergoing change and attitudes toward both were in a period of transition. The Social Gospel, a popular movement in Protestant churches in the late nineteenth and early twentieth centuries, urged churches to shoulder more responsibility for social problems emerging in industrial society. It developed in the late nineteenth century in response to several social trends: churches experienced declining attendance, leading some to question their relevance; labor leaders criticized religious leaders for siding with capitalist leaders and ignoring the concerns of the people in industrial cities; and, finally, religious leaders themselves realized the desperate plight of people living in poverty.

Charles Sheldon, a Congregationalist minister, was one of the prominent leaders of the movement. His novel *In His Steps*, first published in 1896, was a phenomenal best seller and an accessible means of promoting the Social Gospel. Sheldon expressed the novel's theme succinctly in its subtitle, *What Would Jesus Do?* The book sold some thirty million copies, making it one of the best-selling books of all time. Walter Rauschenbusch, a Baptist minister in New York City, came to his interest in the Social Gospel by observing the desperation of his parishioners trying to provide for their families. Considered by historians to be one of the leading architects of the Social Gospel, Rauschenbusch wrote several books elaborating its fundamental beliefs, including *A Theology for the Social Gospel* (1917).

While the Social Gospel movement called for nongovernmental action, it was not antigovernment; it simply operated in a different realm. Both Roosevelt and Wilson supported the Social Gospel, and neither of them believed that it infringed on governmental responsibilities. And because it supported the concept of collective action to deal with a new set of social problems developing in industrial cities, it had the effect of influencing people to accept the need for collective action itself and made governmental decisions to initiate new kinds of social programs more acceptable. At the same time, Populism, Progressivism, and the labor movement were all challenging government at all levels to respond to the forces unleashed by industrialization and rapid urbanization.

Taft's presidency was shaped in the maelstrom of a debate over Progressivism within the ranks of the Republican Party. The leading congressional proponents of Progressivism were staunch supporters of Theodore Roosevelt, and during Taft's presidency they became known as insurgents. As such they were opponents of the Republican Old Guard, conservatives who often opposed Roosevelt's Progressive supporters within the party. Taft's principal political challenge was to negotiate between these two factions within his party; it was a challenge that he faced in the early months of his presidency, and he lacked the instincts that had enabled Roosevelt to deal with internal party squabbles.

TAFT, THE REPUBLICAN PARTY, AND THE PRESIDENCY

By temperament, character, and experience, Taft was an excellent jurist. Before and after his years in the White House, Taft served in appointive judicial positions, including service as chief justice of the Supreme Court in the 1920s. He came to political office not as a candidate who relished the give-and-take of politics but as one who had held appointive offices and served them well. Taft inherited his interest in the law from his father, Alphonso Taft, who served as President Grant's last attorney general. The younger Taft, born in Cincinnati on September 15, 1857, graduated from Yale and from the Cincinnati Law School. Admitted to the Ohio Bar in 1881, he served on the superior court of Ohio, and in 1890 President Benjamin Harrison appointed him solicitor general, the second-ranking position in the Justice Department. While serving in Washington, he met Theodore Roosevelt, who then held a position with the US Civil Service Commission, and the two became friends. After two years he returned to Ohio, where he served on the Federal Court of Appeals, representing the Sixth District, which included Ohio, Kentucky, Michigan, and Tennessee.

Taft's next call to Washington came from President William McKinley. In the aftermath of the war with Spain at the end of the nineteenth century, the United States had acquired control of the Philippines. The transition from Spanish control to American control did not go smoothly; while the Philippines welcomed American support in ridding the islands of Spanish imperialism, rebels had no interest in exchanging one colonial master for another and opposed

American involvement beyond liberation. General Arthur MacArthur headed US military forces fighting the rebels, but McKinley wanted to appoint a civilian commission to govern the Philippines and asked Taft to head the commission as governor-general. Taft had opposed acquisition of the Philippines and thought he should not accept, but when McKinley persisted, Taft agreed. His administration of the islands was effective, particularly in establishing a civilian government with significant Filipino participation. It was a high-profile position, and Taft's name became familiar to Americans.

After the assassination of President William McKinley in September 1901, Vice President Theodore Roosevelt became president. Roosevelt anticipated appointing Taft to the Supreme Court, but when the next vacancy occurred in 1902, Taft turned it down, not because he was not interested, but because he believed he needed to complete his responsibilities in the Philippines. When Elihu Root asked to step down as secretary of war in 1904, Roosevelt again reached out to Taft. The president flattered Taft, saying, "If only there were three of you," meaning that he could have one in the Philippines, one on the Supreme Court, and another as secretary of war. Taft could not turn down the president, whose request received support from the outgoing secretary of war and Taft's ambitious wife, Nellie.

Taft served as secretary of war for the remaining years of Roosevelt's presidency and served as the president's confidant and adviser, particularly on foreign policy issues. Taft's biographer Lewis Gould referred to him as an "all-purpose troubleshooter," and indeed he had a hand in several foreign policy initiatives. Roosevelt dispatched him to Panama, where he supervised planning and construction of the canal. In July 1905 Taft led a congressional delegation to Asia, where he met with the Japanese foreign minister and struck an agreement in which Japan recognized American rights to the Philippines in return for a reciprocal recognition of the Japanese occupation of Korea.

Taft performed well in each assignment, and his relationship with Roosevelt matured in a spirit of pragmatic cooperation. Taft was a loyal subordinate, and political scientist Peri Arnold suggested that his "hypersensitivity about approval by superiors" made him an ideal subordinate.[1] When another opening occurred on the Supreme Court, Roosevelt again offered it to Taft, who with Nellie's encouragement again turned down the offer in order to stay in the administration. Nellie hoped her husband might become president, and indeed Roosevelt had begun to consider Taft as a possible successor, since during Roosevelt's presidency Taft supported him loyally. Taft's major responsibilities dealt with foreign policy, and since the most divisive issues in the early years of the twentieth century were domestic matters defined by the Progressive movement, he made few enemies. Roosevelt charted policy, and Elihu Root, who became secretary of state in 1905, helped to craft the American position on foreign affairs. Taft thus administered policies devised by Roosevelt and Root, and he did so effectively.

Roosevelt had declared in 1904 that he did not intend to seek reelection in 1908, although his enjoyment of the office was so palpable that it would have surprised no one if he had changed his mind. Even after he announced his support for Taft as his successor early in 1907, many suspected that Roosevelt still might run. When he stuck to his promise, the endorsement of such a popular president made Taft a clear front-runner for the Republican nomination. He had challengers, including powerful Speaker of the House of Representatives Joe Cannon and influential Progressive senator from Wisconsin Robert La Follette. Neither was able to mount a formidable challenge to Taft, who won the nomination in June on the first ballot at the Republican National Convention in Chicago.

In July the Democrats met in Denver and nominated William Jennings Bryan, who had also been the party's candidate in 1896 and 1900, losing both times to William McKinley. Bryan, a liberal Democrat with a reputation as one of the nation's leading orators of the age, had energized the 1896 election with his "Cross of Gold" speech against the gold standard and the moneyed interests of the Northeast,

1. Peri E. Arnold, *Remaking the Presidency: Roosevelt, Taft, and Wilson, 1901–1916* (Lawrence: Univ. Press of Kansas, 2009), 95.

one of the most famous speeches in American political history. But that election had led to realignment: Republicans had emerged as the dominant party and would maintain that edge until the Great Depression began in 1929, a stretch during which only one Democrat, Woodrow Wilson, won the presidency. Bryan now faced longer odds: Republican political dominance and the shadow of the popular Theodore Roosevelt, who campaigned for Taft. Yet Bryan believed that he had a realistic chance to win and had reasons for his optimism. The Democrats were united, as they had not been in recent elections, and there were deep divisions in the Republican Party. Reform was the key issue of the day. Bryan called for lower tariffs and railroad regulation, reforms that Democrats had promoted without success in recent elections. But tariff reform resonated in rural regions, and indeed with the general public. Farmers believed that the government had unduly favored industry at their expense, and consumers understood that tariffs increased the price of many of their purchases.

Bryan was able to hold the South, a Democratic region since the Civil War, but Taft dominated in the rest of the nation. Taft won the popular vote by a margin of 1.2 million votes and nearly doubled Bryan's electoral vote, 321 to 162.

The new president was a large man, weighing in the vicinity of three hundred pounds throughout his presidency. He had a rumbling laugh and seemed a congenial man. Although he did not tell jokes, he often chuckled as he spoke, and his enjoyment of the moment was infectious. Yet this appearance of joviality hid an unpleasant aspect of his character. He bore grudges, and Roosevelt once said that he considered Taft one of the "best haters" he knew. Taft could be indiscreet and often made remarks without thinking of their consequences.

Despite his convincing victory, Taft began his presidency with several obstacles before him. The first, and in the long run the most critical, was his relationship with his predecessor. Taft and Roosevelt had been friends for many years, and that Taft had served him loyally is beyond question. Roosevelt had endorsed him, and while that helped Taft win the Republican nomination, Roosevelt believed that it also carried certain obligations, particularly a commitment to Roosevelt's agenda. That quickly became problematic, and Taft unwittingly made matters worse even before his election. Taft and Roosevelt talked often, and in one of their conversations TR asked Taft if he planned to keep Roosevelt's cabinet. Without thinking through the implications of his response, Taft agreed that he planned to do so and even suggested that Roosevelt could inform the cabinet of his intentions. While the cabinet included outstanding men such as Secretary of State Elihu Root, Taft had doubts about some of the others and eventually retained only two.

Taft's conception of the nature of the presidency differed fundamentally from the beliefs of his predecessor. Roosevelt stretched the powers of his office unrelentingly, beginning a twentieth-century trend that transformed the presidency. Taft conceived the powers of the presidency in narrower terms. Although he had been loyal to Roosevelt, Taft did not accept everything his predecessor did without question, and indeed some of those differences would contribute to the erosion of their relationship. Roosevelt was an unabashed self-promoter, and Taft did not approve of the way in which Roosevelt had dealt with the press. Roosevelt had given scant attention to expenditures and had increased the national debt, particularly in his last two years in office. Taft's fiscal conservatism led him to look for ways to make government more efficient and smaller.

Another challenge Taft faced was the nature of his relationship with the Republican Party. The party had fissures that resulted from the emergence of Progressivism as a force in American politics. Progressivism was a broad movement—so broad, in fact, that some historians have argued that it shouldn't be considered a movement at all, since most movements (such as civil rights) have specific goals organized around a discrete theme and Progressivism ranged across a vast aggregation of reforms, unified only by the fact that many of them dealt with urban issues. As a result, Progressivism crossed party lines. There were supporters and critics of Progressives in both parties, and ultimately all three major candidates for the presidency in 1912 (Roosevelt, Taft, and Wilson) had a claim to Progressive credentials.

But if Roosevelt's Progressive credentials were impeccable, Taft's were suspect among the Roosevelt wing of the Republican Party, and Taft lacked the political instincts that had enabled his predecessor to navigate the treacherous waters that divided the party. On two crucial issues—the tariff and a clash over the concepts of conservation and development—Taft alienated Republican Progressives and, without intending to do so, provoked an irrevocable breach with Roosevelt. Had it been only a matter of the tariff, the relationship with Roosevelt may have been strained but not broken. However, both occurred within the first year of Taft's presidency, seemingly cascading over one another. And because of the people involved, the conservation issue was more personal, its implications more hurtful.

THE PAYNE-ALDRICH TARIFF AND A SPLIT AMONG REPUBLICANS

The first issue that divided Republicans emerged in the early months of Taft's presidency and remained controversial throughout. The tariff had long been a winning issue for the Republicans, and as they pushed tariff rates ever higher, it won them the support of big business. As Roosevelt's presidency neared its end, however, a split emerged among Republicans, some of whom believed there should be reductions in some rates to satisfy disgruntled consumers. Roosevelt recognized political danger and dodged the issue. By the time Taft became president, the issue could no longer be ignored, and Taft demonstrated his commitment to reform by calling for tariff reduction in his inaugural address.

Even before the tariff battle itself took place, it triggered a related issue that became one of several matters that contributed to the disenchantment between Taft and the Republican insurgents—the Republican Progressives who were staunch Roosevelt supporters. Speaker of the House Joe Cannon, a Republican conservative, wielded enormous power. He scheduled debate in the House, in effect deciding if and when bills would come to the floor. He selected chairs of House committees, including the powerful Rules Committee. With a tight grip on the House and the support of conservative Republicans, he was entrenched, seemingly beyond challenge. Yet the Republican insurgents considered him such an impediment to their agenda—on the tariff and other matters—that they decided to attack him indirectly by trying to expand the Rules Committee and put some positions beyond his appointment authority. This idea was a long shot, and even Roosevelt advised Taft that it was more prudent to work with Cannon than to challenge his authority. Taft took this advice and as a result earned the distrust of the insurgents. Thus, before the tariff debate even began, Taft found himself caught in an intraparty squabble that would impact the rest of his presidency. So at the beginning of the most critical issue of his presidency, he was already in a difficult position.

But tariff policy was complex, since it was not a straightforward matter of industry wanting higher rates and consumers wanting them lowered. Because tariff bills enumerated rates on specific items, most congressional districts had some items—be they industrial or agricultural—that they wanted protected, and of course consumers wanted wholesale reduction of rates. Furthermore, tariffs produced revenue, and if rates went down, revenue had to be made up elsewhere. Congress had passed a bill supporting an income tax, but the Supreme Court struck it down. (The income tax would finally be achieved by constitutional amendment.)

Taft had no experience in the complicated politics of the tariff, while members of Congress had been playing this game for years and knew their moves. Thus, Taft was at a disadvantage in a debate that began the month after his inauguration, when he was still adjusting to his new role. Unfortunately, the debate was critical, so much so that Taft's biographer Lewis Gould called it "the defining moment of [his] presidency."[2] The president was pulled in two directions, by conservative party leaders who wanted to retain or even increase the tariff, on one side, and insurgent Progressives urging tariff reduction,

2. Lewis L. Gould, *The William Howard Taft Presidency* (Lawrence: Univ. Press of Kansas, 2009), 51.

on the other. Speaker of the House Joe Cannon of Illinois controlled business in the lower chamber as a virtual dictator (some even called him a czar) by assigning bills to committees chaired by political allies and by scheduling (or *not* scheduling) bills for debate on the floor. The battle originated in the House, where New York Republican Sereno E. Payne introduced a bill that increased rates on seventy-five items and made modest reductions on four hundred others, too little to satisfy Progressives.

In the Senate, Republican Progressive insurgents—Robert La Follette of Wisconsin and Albert Beveridge of Indiana in particular—pushed Taft to support their position of advocating substantial tariff reduction. But shortly after Taft's inauguration, Cannon met with the president and warned that he would never get insurgent cuts through the House. Other Republican leaders, Roosevelt among them, conceded that Taft had little choice but to accede to Cannon. Taft did so, prompting charges of betrayal from the insurgents. Payne's bill won House approval and went to the Senate, where matters were more complicated.

The Senate was unrulier than the House. Even though Republicans held a thirty-seat majority, Senate Republicans split over the tariff. The insurgent Progressives were smaller in number, but they represented the Roosevelt legacy and increased their numbers by reaching across the aisle to antitariff Democrats. Thus, Senator Nelson Aldrich of Rhode Island, a leader of the Republican conservatives in the Senate, had a more formidable task in trying to maintain cohesion among Senate Republicans.

After approval in the House, the tariff bill passed to the Senate, where Senator Aldrich substituted his own version, which reduced cuts and introduced increases. Congressional leaders had suggested that Taft could enter the debate when the bill went to conference, where differences between the House and Senate versions would be resolved. Taft agreed to do so, but it left him in a corner. The Senate and House conferees negotiated between rates set in each chamber, leaving little possibility for major changes of the sort Taft hoped to achieve. The final version after a Senate-House conference became known as the Payne-Aldrich tariff, the first substantial modification in tariff policy since the 1897 Dingley tariff.

The bill failed to satisfy Progressives, who blamed Aldrich for sabotaging their efforts at tariff reform. They urged Taft to support their advocacy of genuine tariff cuts. Taft now plunged into the fray, which in July shifted to debates over specific commodities. Taft sought specific cuts on oil and cattle hides, the latter of which became perhaps the most divisive issue. The insurgents pushed for cuts on other items, including cotton and wool. Taft realized that to support insurgent demands would be to jeopardize tariff reform altogether. Ultimately, he stood with conservatives, even as the insurgents pushed him to institute more cuts. Until this juncture Taft had stayed on the sidelines. By doing so, however, he had simply postponed a problem, for he now had to take a stand on a bill that contained little to please the insurgents, who wanted him to oppose the bill or even veto it.

In the end, it had become a test of Taft's leadership more than just another tariff bill. Taft demanded elimination of provisions included as favors to some of Cannon's allies, but otherwise he accepted an essentially conservative bill. He defended the law as the best tariff bill the Republicans had ever passed, even though the common perception was that once again, the wealthy elite had been the beneficiaries of a tariff revision. The insurgents felt betrayed and let Roosevelt know it. Roosevelt was abroad, on a safari in Africa, a trip undertaken in part to remove himself from politics and give Taft an opportunity to shape his administration without the large shadow that Roosevelt would inevitably cast. But Roosevelt's lieutenants and political allies kept him posted, and he heard their side of the story unfiltered by Taft. All of it had taken place within the first six months of Taft's tenure, yet, as Louis Gould concluded, it became "a self-inflicted wound that shaped the rest of his presidency."[3]

3. Ibid., 51.

THE BALLINGER-PINCHOT CONTROVERSY

The other major controversy involved an issue that frequently came up during presidencies of the twentieth century: the stewardship of the nation's natural resources. Was it the government's responsibility to preserve natural resources such as national forests, minerals, and oil reserves, or should the government encourage their development? Under Taft this question became more than a policy debate because the central figures in the argument were high-ranking officials, one of whom was a Roosevelt appointee and a close friend of TR as well, while the other was a member of Taft's cabinet. The timing could hardly have been worse for Taft, as the story broke in September 1909, in the immediate aftermath of the tariff controversy, and led to a second self-inflicted wound. The two issues combined spurred criticism of Taft for a lack of political acuity.

Gifford Pinchot had served as chief forester of the United States under Roosevelt, head of the newly created Forest Service. At the time of his appointment in 1905, protection of the nation's forests moved from the Department of the Interior to the Department of Agriculture. Pinchot was one of the carryovers into the Taft administration. Pinchot professionalized the management of the national forests and more than tripled the land reserved as part of national forests, from 56 million acres to 172 million acres. No one had a better claim to having helped shape the conservation achievements of the Roosevelt administration, one of its most lasting legacies.

Pinchot's antagonist in a very public row was Richard Ballinger, Taft's secretary of the interior. Ballinger had also served in the Roosevelt administration. He had served as mayor of Seattle before TR appointed him as commissioner of the General Land Office, which resided in the Department of the Interior, headed by James Garfield. Both Pinchot and Ballinger considered themselves loyal Roosevelt conservationists, but as a westerner Ballinger was more tolerant of development. These categories were not rigid, and while Pinchot was wholly committed to protection of the forests, Ballinger was more of a moderate who did not want to foreclose all development.

Until Ballinger's arrival, Pinchot was able to exert influence over land policy in the Department of the Interior, despite the fact that his Forestry Service was under the Department of Agriculture. Ballinger's appointment thus put limits on Pinchot's freedom of action, and because their responsibilities overlapped and they had different views of the role of government in the environment, they clashed even before the allegations that constituted the Ballinger-Pinchot controversy surfaced. In one case, Pinchot had developed cooperative arrangements between the Departments of Agriculture and the Interior regarding irrigation that Ballinger considered illegal, and he ordered them reversed.

So Pinchot took delight when an issue emerged that gave him an opportunity to strike at his adversary. Louis Glavis, a federal investigator in Portland, Oregon, for the General Land Office, believed that land claims for coal land in Alaska contained irregularities and that Ballinger was guilty at least of a conflict of interest and complicit in allegedly illegally handling the claims. According to Glavis, the claims, registered in the name of Clarence Cunningham, were to be combined with other claims and in fact were a cover for Morgan-Guggenheim interests. Pinchot told Glavis to present his information to the president and gave Glavis the necessary introduction to arrange a meeting with Taft. The most glaring allegation appeared to be that Ballinger had accepted a $250 fee to represent Cunningham's claim—but he had done so while he was a lawyer in private practice, before he accepted the position at Interior. Ultimately, Congress cleared Ballinger of all charges, but the importance of the controversy rested not in Ballinger's guilt or innocence, but rather in the way in which Taft handled the case.

After receiving Glavis's report, Taft met with Ballinger and Oscar Lawler, an attorney in the Department of the Interior and a Ballinger supporter. He asked Lawler to prepare a report and used that report as the basis for his response. This tactic was certainly not illegal and in fact is a common practice. Taft sided with Ballinger and argued that his secretary of the interior had been cleared of charges. Taft asked Pinchot to stay in office but approved the dismissal of Glavis. Taft pursued a legal approach to the charges and sought to do so with a minimum of publicity.

Unfortunately, his adversaries were not following the same guidelines, and they took their case to the public. In *Collier's Weekly*, a magazine sympathetic to Progressive causes, Glavis attacked Ballinger in an article titled "The Whitewash of Ballinger." In muckraking journals such as *Collier's* and *McClure's* that flourished with stories of corruption in high places, Pinchot and Glavis, with assistance from prominent attorney Louis Brandeis, shifted the nature of the debate. They put Ballinger on the defensive, attacked the Guggenheims, and criticized Taft's handling of the controversy, using innuendo where facts were sparse. Even though Taft had done nothing improper, there was at least an appearance of a lack of transparency in the way in which he had defended Ballinger.

Pinchot had agreed to stay on as chief forester, but he would not let go of the controversy. The next opportunity to strike came in December, when Congress came back into session. Pinchot wrote a letter to Senator Jonathan P. Dolliver, the nominal leader of the insurgent Republicans, knowing that the letter would be publicized—as it was when Dolliver read it before the Senate. Pinchot admitted that he had released information about Ballinger after the president had ordered that no more information about the case be circulated but said that he had done so because Taft had fired Glavis without understanding the facts of the case. Taft consulted his cabinet and Elihu Root, who had served under Roosevelt as both secretary of war and secretary of state. All agreed that he had to fire Pinchot, and Root said it should be done immediately. Pinchot had prompted the crisis and left Taft little choice. Even Senator Henry Cabot Lodge, a close friend of Roosevelt, acknowledged that "no President could have tolerated such a letter as Pinchot sent to Dolliver."

Taft now compounded his political circumstances by failing to write to Roosevelt and explain his side of the story. It left the narrative in the hands of Pinchot once again, and Taft lost the chance he might have had to keep his relationship with Roosevelt intact. Even with Lodge's admission that Taft had no choice but to dismiss Pinchot, Roosevelt heard mainly Pinchot's point of view, and, coming so shortly after the tariff dispute, it distressed Roosevelt and aggravated their relationship, which increasingly came to represent a microcosm of the division that had been developing in the Republican Party between Old Guard conservatives and the Progressive insurgents.

TAFT: PROGRESSIVE OR CONSERVATIVE?

By the end of 1909, the Payne-Aldrich tariff and the Ballinger-Pinchot controversy had defined the Taft presidency and set the stage for a rift between the president and former president Roosevelt. Taft's handling of those issues left him aligned with the Republican Old Guard and in opposition to the Republican Progressives, despite the fact Taft had not abandoned Progressivism. Taft sought party unity, but to Roosevelt supporters in the party pleas for unity rang hollow. Attorney General George Wickersham widened the breach when he said that Republicans needed to decide if they were for the president and the party, accusing those individuals who were not of giving aid and comfort to the enemy, which he suggested defined treason. This accusation provoked only further disunion and countercharges by insurgents in the months leading to the election.

Taft's legislative record was one of modest success, and it contained elements of Progressivism that often reflected more on the leverage of the Progressive Republicans in Congress than it did on Taft's own inclinations. Such was the case with the Mann-Elkins Act, one of the signal legislative achievements of the first half of Taft's term. Taft had successfully convinced the railroads to revoke rate increases, and in one sense the act achieved some of the goals regarding railroad regulation that the Roosevelt administration had not been able to get through Congress. However, by increasing the power of the Interstate Commerce Commission to a greater degree than Taft would have preferred, it demonstrated the influence of the congressional insurgents. The act allowed the ICC authority to regulate rates and extended its authority to include communications—telephone, telegraph, and radio.

Taft also achieved one of his pet projects, a postal savings system that allowed post offices to serve as savings institutions for individuals, even in very small amounts. The system remained in effect for more than a half century, canceled only in 1966 because banks had assumed this function. He extended civil service to include postmasters and civil servants working for the navy.

Despite these achievements, the off-year election in 1910 widened the growing gulf between Roosevelt and Taft. Roosevelt returned from his African safari and a tour of Europe in time to participate in the campaign. He went on a speaking tour in the West, and while he didn't say anything critical of Taft, he didn't say anything supporting him, either. Tussles between the two men emerged in the thick of the campaign. Taft supporters kept Roosevelt from being selected as chair of the New York Republican convention, fearing that TR would use the position to promote a possible presidential candidacy in 1912. Taft wrote saying that he had not opposed Roosevelt, but Roosevelt was irked that the letter was too little and too late. Taft edged back from throwing his lot in with the Old Guard, knowing it could destroy the last two years of his presidency if he had an open break with TR. But it was clear that the old camaraderie was no longer there. When the two men finally met in September, the press concentrated more on the question of who had initiated the meeting than on its substance—which did not amount to much in any case.

The election was a disaster for the Republicans, which did nothing to mend the rift. Democrats captured control of the House, something they had not been able to do since 1894. The Republicans lost ten seats in the Senate but maintained a majority. Republicans remained a house divided, with little hope that they could reunite for the election of 1912. Taft faced a difficult situation heading into the second half of his presidency. Republican Progressives opposed him, and many of them were openly supporting Roosevelt for the Republican nomination in 1912. With the House in Democratic hands, the prognosis was not positive.

Nonetheless, Taft was able to make a record, and some of his achievements reflected Progressive tenets. One area in which he had an unusual opportunity to leave his imprint unfortunately yielded disappointing results. In 1909 Justice Edward White urged Attorney General George Wickersham not to give the Supreme Court any difficult cases, as several of the justices were too old, ill, or senile to rule effectively. Later that year one of the justices died, two more died in 1910 and another resigned, and a fifth justice died in 1911. Thus, Taft filled five vacancies on the Supreme Court and an additional vacancy as chief justice, which he filled by promoting Justice White to chief justice. No president since George Washington had filled more vacancies, and only Franklin Roosevelt, who was elected four times, filled more afterward. Taft had experience as a judge, and while circumstances had prevented Theodore Roosevelt from appointing him, Taft had hoped that he might be chief justice himself; some suggest that by appointing the sixty-five-year-old White to chief justice, Taft thought he might still have a chance to be appointed chief justice after White. Taft's appointments, with one exception, were not exceptional. The exception was Charles Evans Hughes, and Hughes stayed on the Court for a brief time before resigning in 1916 in order to seek the Republican nomination for president; he won the nomination but lost the general election to Woodrow Wilson. Ironically, Taft eventually did become chief justice, nominated by Warren Harding in 1921; when Taft retired in 1930, Herbert Hoover nominated Charles Evans Hughes to replace him.

Taft's appointments to the Court were conservatives, and because he appointed so many of them, he did help to shape the Court for a generation. The conservative orientation of the Court remained intact until Franklin D. Roosevelt began to fashion a liberal Court in his second term. Roosevelt responded to Supreme Court action declaring key New Deal programs to be unconstitutional, a movement within the Court led by four staunch anti–New Deal conservatives who became known as the "Four Horsemen." Only one of them, Willis Van Devanter, was a Taft appointee. Of the other three, Wilson appointed one and Harding two.

Despite his conservative inclinations, Taft did not turn his back on reform. Even though Theodore Roosevelt earned the nickname "Teddy the Trust Buster," Taft in his one term prosecuted more trusts than Roosevelt did in nearly two terms, yet Taft received less credit than TR for his antitrust actions. Roosevelt's management style meant that he was more directly involved in antitrust decisions, whereas Taft tended to delegate more authority to his cabinet members, and in this case he had confidence in his attorney general, George W. Wickersham. Furthermore, Roosevelt carefully selected the cases he prosecuted, and in doing so he chose high-profile cases, such as the Northern Securities case, that generated a lot of publicity.

Nonetheless, Taft did not shy away from high-profile cases and in fact inherited two of them from the Roosevelt administration, against Standard Oil and the American Tobacco Company. The Court handed down both decisions on the same day in 1911. In the case of Standard Oil, the Supreme Court upheld the lower court decision ordering the dissolution of the company. Standard Oil broke into thirty-four companies worldwide, and today many of the largest oil companies are descendants of the original Standard Oil, including Chevron and ExxonMobil. The decision in the case of the American Tobacco Company was similar: the company broke into four smaller companies.

The importance of these decisions, however, is told only in part by the dissolution of the trusts. Chief Justice White wrote the Court's decision in the Standard Oil case, and the reasoning in the decision had the effect of limiting the Sherman Anti-Trust Act, which was the basis for the antitrust cases prosecuted under Roosevelt and Taft. White used common law and case law to establish that the Sherman Act applied only to unreasonable restraint of trade. He established what became known as the "standard of reasonableness," or the "rule of reason," in the interpretation of antitrust cases, limiting the cases in which antitrust could apply. Even after the Clayton Antitrust Act and the establishment of the Federal Trade Commission (FTC) during the Wilson administration, the "rule of reason" remained as a test in antitrust cases.

Taft and Wickersham also took on the beef trust and the electrical trust. Ultimately, one of Taft's antitrust cases led to another blow to the already rocky relationship with Roosevelt. In 1911 Attorney General Wickersham filed an antitrust suit against US Steel. The suit discussed a prior suit filed by the Roosevelt administration in 1907, suggesting that President Roosevelt had dismissed the case based on inadequate information, a charge that Roosevelt had earlier vigorously denied. At the time, the nation had been experiencing a recession, and J. P. Morgan had appealed to President Roosevelt, telling him that US Steel had to be able to purchase stock in the Tennessee Coal and Iron Company to help avert a further economic decline. Roosevelt had agreed, and the 1911 suit claimed that he had been deceived. It did not accuse him of any impropriety, but it was nonetheless embarrassing because of his insistence since 1907 that he had done what had been necessary. Taft had not seen the suit before it was filed, but it was another case of a lack of political acuity on his part—and on the part of Wickersham as well—but of course it was Taft who took the blame.

SUGGESTED READINGS

A good starting point for examining any presidency is the fine series on each of the presidents published by the University Press of Kansas. The volume on Taft is Lewis L. Gould's *The William Howard Taft Presidency* (Lawrence: Univ. Press of Kansas, 2009). Peri Arnold's *Remaking of the Presidency: Roosevelt, Taft, and Wilson, 1901–1916* (Lawrence: Univ. Press of Kansas, 2009) examines the ways in which the nature of the presidency changed in the period covered in this book. Theodore Roosevelt remained a potent political presence after the end of his presidency, not only during the Taft administration but during Wilson's presidency as well. There are many good biographies of Roosevelt, but one that is particularly useful for the period covered in this book is the concluding volume of Edmund Morris's three-volume biography of TR, *Colonel Roosevelt* (New York: Random House, 2010).

On Progressivism, see Arthur S. Link and Richard L. McCormick's *Progressivism* (Hoboken, NJ: Wiley-Blackwell, 1983), Steven Diner's *A Very Different Age: Americans of the Progressive Era* (New York: Hill and Wang, 1998), and Michael McGerr's *A Fierce Discontent: The Rise and Fall of the Progressive Movement in America* (New York: Oxford Univ. Press, 2003).

2

The Election of 1912

The election of 1912 was one of the key elections of the twentieth century. In a race unprecedented in American history, it pitted three presidents (former president Theodore Roosevelt, incumbent William Howard Taft, and future president Woodrow Wilson) against one another. The three of them would hold the presidency for nearly five full terms. It featured the most competitive third-party candidate in American history and a deep rift in the dominant party. All three candidates claimed the mantle of Progressive reformer, and each had a legitimate claim to the label—which makes this election particularly revealing about the nature of Progressivism. And there was a fourth candidate, Eugene Debs, a radical labor leader who ran as the candidate for the Socialist Party and spoke to many Americans who felt neglected by the major parties, both of which accepted capitalism as the engine that drove the American economy, even if it needed some adjustment. Debs's campaign never envisioned victory, but it spoke to and for a long-neglected constituency, and his showing demonstrated that it was a growing sector of the electorate.

The election was the first truly competitive presidential election in nearly a generation. Elections after Reconstruction were close, with Republicans and Democrats contesting for spoils and with neither party dominating either the presidency or control of Congress. That situation had changed with the election of 1896, one of the pivotal elections of realignment in American history, in which the Republicans swept the board, winning the presidency for William McKinley, who soundly defeated William Jennings Bryan, the candidate of both the Democrats and the Populists. The election virtually destroyed the

Populist Party and weakened the political power of the rural areas it represented. The Republican victory was also a victory for a nationalistic imperialism that dominated American foreign policy into the twentieth century. It marked a triumph of rising cities over declining rural areas, for industrialization over agriculture, for high tariffs over tariff reduction, and for the creditor sections of the country in the Northeast over debtors in the South and the West. Republicans dominated American politics from 1896 until 1932—with the exception of the 1910s.

The off-year elections of 1910 gave the Democrats hope. The Republican split between the insurgent Progressives and the conservatives, who backed President Taft, was a political reality that spawned Democratic optimism. The Democrats exploited Republican divisions and captured the House by gaining 56 seats, giving them a 228–161 margin, with 1 seat going to Socialist Victor Berger from Milwaukee. The Republicans lost 10 seats in the Senate but still held a 51–41 margin over the Democrats. The Democrats gained 4 governor seats to reverse the Republican 25–21 lead. Democrats had every reason to be optimistic about winning the White House for the first time in twenty years.

All four candidates in 1912 were of the same generation, nearly the same age, born in consecutive years in the 1850s. Thus, all were born in the decade before the Civil War, and none had reached the age of ten when the war ended. Debs was the oldest, born in November 1855. Wilson was born in 1856, Taft in 1857, and Roosevelt in 1858. Wilson was the only southerner, born in Staunton, Virginia. The family lived in Augusta, Georgia, during the war, and Confederate soldiers occasionally camped on the grounds of his father's church. But Roosevelt bore the heaviest burden of the war. Roosevelt's family was one of many divided by the war. His father, Theodore Sr., a New Yorker, bought a substitute rather than enlist in the Union army. It was a common-enough practice among men of his social standing, but some of his son's biographers believe that TR's proclivity for physical activity, his desire to prove himself, and his pursuit of military action came from guilt over his father's decision. His mother's immediate family included brothers committed to the Confederate cause. Martha Bulloch's brothers James and Irvine both figured prominently in the purchase of the famous Laird rams, Confederate raiders bought from Britain that harassed Union shipping to great effect and led to the most significant diplomatic clash between the Lincoln administration and Britain during the war. James negotiated the purchase of several of the raiders, including the most notorious of the fleet, the CSS *Alabama*, and Irvine served on the *Alabama*.

The race in 1912 was one of the more fascinating presidential contests in American history. The excitement it generated at the time owed to the fact that it was the first truly competitive presidential election in many years. Many factors combined to fascinate Americans at the time and intrigue them ever since: the reentry of Theodore Roosevelt into the political arena and the consternation it caused among Republicans, the use of state primaries for the first time to select some of the delegates to the national conventions, the Republican "split ticket," the emergence of a third party that was genuinely competitive, the tight Democratic convention that took forty-six ballots to name a candidate, the presence of a dynamic Socialist candidate, and a campaign that featured two intellectual candidates debating the crucial issues of the day. There are many angles to examine in this election, and perhaps the most straightforward approach is to examine each of the four contending party campaigns in the order in which their conventions took place and then consider the general election campaign.

THE SOCIALISTS: EUGENE DEBS AND THE LABOR VOTE

Many workers believed that neither major party spoke to their concerns. The Socialist Party sought to fill that void. Socialists were not a cohesive group, and the term *socialism* had different meanings to different people. Adherents to socialism ranged from Marxists, who considered capitalism to be the root of social ills and whose ultimate goal was to overthrow the system, to those individuals who wanted to reform the system by participating in it and running candidates for office. Part of the confusion came from different American political parties that bore the name "Socialist." The Socialist Labor Party of the late nineteenth century was indeed a radical party dedicated to revolution and class conflict. Led by Daniel De Leon at the turn of the century, it had always been a small group without mass appeal. In contrast, the Socialist Party of America, founded by veteran leader of the American Railway Union (and the Pullman Strike in Chicago in 1894) Eugene V. Debs, Milwaukee Socialist editor and politician Victor Berger, and others in 1901, sought influence by electing public officials.

The lines demarking these parties were more fluid than these definitions make them seem, and members moved from one to the other and to and from smaller Socialist organizations, almost seamlessly. Berger belonged to the Socialist Labor Party, for example, before cofounding the Socialist Party of America. And Debs had earlier cooperated with Bill Haywood, the most radical of the early-twentieth-century labor leaders, in forming the Industrial Workers of the World. The diversity of the Socialist Party of America made possible its increasing influence. By 1912 it claimed a dues-paying membership of 118,000, and its claim that it could muster a million votes in the presidential election was no idle threat.

Women played a central role in the Socialist Party's newfound viability. Women constituted about 10 percent of its membership. Among the women prominent in the movement were Hull House reformers Florence Kelley and Ellen Gates Starr, writer and social activist Charlotte Perkins Gilman, and birth control advocate Margaret Sanger. Frances Willard, founder of the Women's Christian Temperance Union (WCTU) and a suffragist, had died in 1898, but her calls for Prohibition and the women's vote were very much alive in 1912.

Getting a head start on the major parties, the Socialists held their convention in May in Indianapolis, the capital of Debs's home state. Debs, a popular lecturer often described as charismatic, had run for the presidency as a Socialist in 1900, 1904, and 1908. In 1900, as the Social Democratic candidate, he received 87,945 votes, finishing fourth (behind the major party candidates and the candidate for the Prohibition Party). In 1904 and 1908, as the candidate for the Socialist Party of America, he received more than 400,000 votes in each election. The party nominated him again. Emil Seidel, the Socialist mayor of Milwaukee, became his running mate. Factional disputes, which had become common among Socialists, erupted again at the convention. The controversial Bill Haywood won a seat on the executive committee, but members who were more conservative pushed through a reform to expel members who supported industrial sabotage, a measure aimed at embarrassing Haywood. The Socialists' issues included a demand that railroads and utilities be nationalized and support for a number of Progressive reforms. Haywood's radicalism went further than most Socialists were willing to venture, and the reforms that they endorsed were moderate and mainstream.

REPUBLICAN HEAVYWEIGHTS: TAFT VERSUS ROOSEVELT

Much was at stake on the Republican side. The Republicans remained the dominant party: the coalition they had fashioned in 1896 remained in place, although its contours had changed. In 1896 the United States was an energetic country riding a surge of nationalism and industrial growth. The Republicans—and indeed the nation—had made choices in the previous sixteen years that had brought the party to a crossroads between reforming Progressives and conservatives that threatened to wrench the party apart. Their differences were fundamental, touching on conflicting views of the responsibility of government and of the majority party. But problems that the three Republican presidents since 1896—McKinley, Roosevelt, and Taft—faced had required the party to consider the implications of its policies. The Republicans were the party of business. But should big business be regulated, and, if so, how? What was the party's responsibility to labor? Rebellions in American protectorates in Cuba and the Philippines challenged the American conviction that it was a more responsible and benevolent manager of its protectorates than Europeans had been of their empires. Strains of urban growth posed a wide range of problems of modern cities that were more complex than they had seemed in 1896.

Two strong-willed warhorses battled for the Republican nomination and for the soul of the Republican Party, the only time in American history in which a sitting president and a former president fought for their party's nomination. Ever since Theodore Roosevelt named his trusted friend and adviser William Howard Taft as his preference to succeed him during the 1908 campaign, their friendship had deteriorated to a bitter rivalry that tested party leaders. That relationship was the pivot upon which the Republican nomination hinged.

In the early months of the Taft administration, Roosevelt gave Taft latitude to establish his own record. Roosevelt's famous African safari departed in April 1909, a month after Taft's inauguration, and although Roosevelt's friends and supporters—most notably Henry Cabot Lodge—kept the former president informed of Taft decisions that Progressive Republicans believed ran counter to the Roosevelt legacy, TR concentrated on the hunt. Sixty years later E. L. Doctorow noted in his novel *Ragtime*, "The great conservationist had bagged seventeen lions, eleven elephants, twenty-one rhinos, eight hippos, nine giraffes, forty-seven gazelles, twenty-nine zebras, and kudu, wildebeest, impala, eland, waterbuck, wart hog and bushbuck, beyond number."[1] As far removed as he was from American politics, Roosevelt found it easy to refrain from comment on the reports he received. After the safari ended, Roosevelt returned home via Norway, where he received the Nobel Peace Prize for his role in mediating the peace after the Russo-Japanese War.

In June 1910 Roosevelt returned to the United States, and once on American soil it became difficult to remain uninvolved. Then perceived slights—both political and personal—began to erode the friendship between Taft and Roosevelt. Innocent comments could be misinterpreted and fester. Just days after his election, Taft sent a letter to Roosevelt thanking him for his help during the campaign and said that without the support of Taft's brother Charley (who handled

1. E. L. Doctorow, *Ragtime* (New York: Random House Trade Paperbacks, 2007), 112.

campaign finances) and Roosevelt, the outcome of the election might have been different. Roosevelt bridled at being placed in the same category as Taft's wealthy half brother, but Taft had no way of knowing that Roosevelt had taken the letter as an insult.

Incumbency ordinarily gives a sitting president significant advantages during an election campaign. A president's actions automatically garner attention, and he can often trump his opponents' attempts to make news. For Taft, however, those advantages were limited. Roosevelt remained enormously popular, and after all he had been Taft's mentor. Furthermore, few challengers have the notoriety that followed Roosevelt's every move, and fewer still are able to upstage an incumbent by accepting the Nobel Peace Prize. And whenever President Taft did anything, reporters were sure to seek Roosevelt's response.

Nonetheless, Taft's incumbency did give him advantages, the most important of which was control of the Republican Party. The issues that provoked the Taft-Roosevelt split had driven Taft to the party regulars, the conservatives. In effect, he had cast his lot with them and they with him. These party regulars did battle with the Republican insurgents in Congress and in political contests around the nation as the election of 1912 approached. Taft and Roosevelt avoided confrontation and never met to discuss their differences. As a result, those differences simmered—to the detriment of the prospects of either man to win the presidency.

After the Taft administration reached its halfway point, one political contest in particular foreshadowed this intraparty contention, and it occurred in Roosevelt's home state of New York. Taft offered a seat on the Supreme Court to New York governor Charles Evans Hughes, who accepted. Hughes had been a strong supporter of the direct primary to nominate candidates for office and wanted to ensure support for that legislation. He approached Roosevelt, who agreed with the bill. Roosevelt had said that he did not want to become involved in politics, but this issue seemed to be a safe one since Taft also supported direct primaries. So Roosevelt put his name forward to be temporary chairman of the state convention in order to have a role in selecting the party's gubernatorial nominee. But the Republican regulars balked, concerned that the convention might not fully support Taft's reelection. Without conferring with Taft, they put forth Vice President James Sherman to challenge Roosevelt, and Sherman prevailed, 20–15. Privately, Taft was delighted that "they have defeated Theodore," but he wrote a letter expressing his hope that the Republicans would work out a solution on the direct-primary issue. Roosevelt said the letter was "all right, but it came a little slow."

Roosevelt carried another issue through the campaign that the regulars ridiculed. Perturbed that the courts ignored the will of the American people who were eager for reform, they were defending the privileged at the expense of people on the margins. He proposed that public referenda should be able to reverse court decisions. Taft could not have disagreed more; whereas Roosevelt thought the courts were a weak link in the American system, Taft believed they were the foundation of the system. When Roosevelt ultimately threw his hat in the ring, he said that he would run for the presidency in order to win the approval of this reform and others that conservative Republicans rejected. He promised conservation reform and pledged to support the vote for women.

To complicate matters for the Republican Party, Roosevelt was not the only challenger from within the ranks of Progressives and insurgents. Senator Robert M. La Follette of Wisconsin had served as governor prior to his election to the Senate. He was the chief engineer of the Wisconsin Idea, which included the nation's most vigorous Progressive reforms at the state level and had led to Wisconsin's reputation as the "laboratory of democracy." But Wisconsin politics seemed too radical to many voters. In 1910 the state elected Victor Berger, a Socialist, to Congress, and Milwaukee elected another Socialist, Daniel Hoan, as mayor. La Follette's campaign collapsed, however, as a result of a speech he gave in February 1912 to an audience of newspaper editors. Worried about an impending life-threatening operation on his daughter and recovering himself from illness, he gave a rambling, repetitive two-hour speech that ended after midnight, by which time most of the audience had left the hall.

The 1912 nominating process witnessed the birth of primaries, although they were much less of a factor than they would be a century later. To Progressives, who fought at the state level to win their approval, they fostered direct democracy. Few states held them, however, so even if a candidate swept all primaries it would not have been enough to guarantee the nomination. Nonetheless, the primaries were not meaningless; thirteen states held them, including some of the most populous states—New York, Illinois, Pennsylvania, and Ohio. Roosevelt played coy until late in December 1911, when he announced that he would not campaign. He would accept the nomination if offered, but he would not campaign for it. But his opponents had a head start in the early primaries. Even if La Follette's problematic speech ultimately doomed his campaign, he had been giving speeches around the nation and had many admirers. He won two of the first three primaries, in North Dakota on March 19 and in his home state of Wisconsin on April 2. No one expected him to lose Wisconsin, and North Dakota was a small prize. Between those two La Follette victories was a big win for Taft in New York, Roosevelt's home state, a testimony to the strength of Taft's organization there.

Then Roosevelt's popularity brought him a string of triumphs. He won in nine of the last ten primaries over a two-month span, beginning with Illinois on April 9 and ending with South Dakota on June 4. Along the way he captured Taft's home state of Ohio with more than 55 percent of the vote, gaining a measure of satisfaction for his loss in New York. Over that two-month span, Taft won only Massachusetts, and even that victory was tainted. The state distinguished between presidential preference and delegate selection, and while Taft won the preference vote by a narrow margin, Roosevelt won more delegates. So at the end of the primary season, Roosevelt had won 284 delegates, Taft 125, and La Follette 36. But state conventions selected most of the delegates, and there the party regulars managed the Taft campaign smoothly. Analysts gave varying estimates of the delegate count prior to the convention, but much of it was speculative—especially because the Roosevelt forces chose to challenge the counts in several states.

Many of these challenges had merit, but it was not the merit of the case that mattered; it was the power of the conservatives, who managed the appeals. These appeals were crucial to Roosevelt's chances. He had a weak case in many, and even his staunch supporters acknowledged that his protests over southern delegates were unlikely to win. In other states, however, particularly in Arizona, California, Texas, and Washington, the Roosevelt team believed he could win. But the national committee was stacked with Taft men, and they guaranteed his nomination. Taft biographer Lewis Gould suggests that the 40 Texas votes, of which 31 went to Taft and only 9 to Roosevelt, should have awarded 21 to Roosevelt and 19 to Taft, had deliberations been fair. And so it went elsewhere. Ultimately, the committee awarded 235 of the votes in play to Taft and only 19 to Roosevelt. So when the Republicans convened in Chicago, the result was virtually ensured. The question that hung in the air when the gavel fell was not who would win the nomination, but rather how Roosevelt would respond to Taft's nomination by the party regulars.

Roosevelt answered that question on the night before the convention began. He gave a speech before a crowd of devoted supporters and concluded with a memorable line that signaled his disgust with what he considered the illegal actions by the Taft regulars in depriving him of delegates and his decision to challenge Taft's inevitable convention victory. Roosevelt's campaign now began to assume the character of a crusade, saying there was a "great moral issue" at stake. He concluded his remarks by saying, "We fight in honorable fashion for the good of mankind; fearless for the future; unheeding of our individual fates; with unflinching hearts and undimmed eyes; we stand at Armageddon, and we battle for the Lord!"[2]

But Taft's forces were firmly in control of the proceedings, and everyone knew it. On the first day of the convention, they made that point by forcing approval as temporary chair of the convention Elihu

2. Cited in Edmund Morris, *Colonel Roosevelt* (New York: Random House, 2010), 198.

Root. Root had served Roosevelt as secretary of war during TR's first term but opposed Roosevelt's candidacy, and now he was firmly in Taft's retinue.

Root's situation illustrates another characteristic of the Republican split. Progressives had a tough decision to make: should they support Roosevelt or remain loyal to the Republican Party? The decision was especially difficult for those individuals who held political office. If they deserted the party, they could not expect the party to support them when they ran for reelection, and for those persons who held appointive offices, they would likely lose them unless Roosevelt won the election. Even Henry Cabot Lodge, a close personal friend of Roosevelt, could not safely bolt the party and did not attend the Progressive convention.

The balloting for the Republican nomination was a foregone conclusion. Roosevelt had lost all his challenges to the party regulars and expected Taft to win. Prior to the roll call, he asked his delegates to refrain from voting, telling them that the convention was "in no proper sense any longer a Republican convention representing the real Republican Party." Most did not vote, and the ones who did voted for Roosevelt. As everyone expected, Taft won easily on the first ballot and became the Republican nominee. With Roosevelt promising to run as a third-party candidate, however, the Republican nomination was a hollow prize. Taft thought he could win the election, but the primaries had demonstrated that Roosevelt's appeal to the voters far surpassed the nominee's. Taft was an uninspiring standard-bearer.

THE DEMOCRATS: THE EMERGENCE OF WOODROW WILSON

A week later the Democrats assembled in Baltimore. What had happened in Chicago made their decision the most meaningful one they had had in more than twenty years. They expected that they would be nominating the next president of the United States, and for the first time in a quarter century, there was firm ground for their optimism. The primaries had effectively narrowed the field to two men: Speaker of the House of Representatives James Beauchamp "Champ" Clark and New Jersey governor Woodrow Wilson. Neither man had a safe lead, so delegates expected the balloting to be close. No one could have guessed just how close it would be.

Governor Woodrow Wilson was a proud southerner despite the fact that most of his prepresidential career developed north of the Mason-Dixon line. His family was of Scotch-Irish heritage and steeped in the Presbyterian faith. Both his father and his mother's father were Presbyterian ministers. Given the birth name of Thomas Woodrow Wilson, he went by the name Tommy as a young man, but in his twenties he began using his middle name—which was his mother's family name—as his given name. He was close to both of his parents, but more so to his mother. He enjoyed physical activity, especially baseball. Ironically for a man who became a first-rate scholar, he learned to read late and was older than ten before he could read comfortably. His biographers have speculated on causes ranging from a developmental disorder to dyslexia, and Wilson himself complained that he was a slow reader in college.

Wilson began college at Davidson at the age of sixteen. He stayed for only a year and transferred to Princeton. He graduated from Princeton in 1879 and went on to law school at the University of Virginia to pursue the career that his father had envisioned for him. He practiced law in Atlanta for two years, working in an office with one of his classmates from law school. But business was slow, and by the spring of 1883 he decided to abandon law. Before he left the South, he met Ellen Axson, the daughter of a Presbyterian minister, at a service at her father's church in Rome, Georgia. Reverend Axson knew the Woodrows and Wilson's father. Wilson went on to Baltimore and to graduate work at Johns Hopkins, but the relationship with Ellen developed quickly, even at a distance for the time being. Biographers know a great deal about Wilson's developing sense of himself and his career goals during this time from his rich correspondence with Ellen.

Even before completing his doctorate, Wilson published *Congressional Government*, his most significant book, which appeared in 1885. Concerned about what he considered to be problems in the structure of American government, he elaborated by comparing it to the

British model of parliamentary government. His comparison favored the parliamentary structure because of its reliance on what he called a "Cabinet Ministry," which had responsibility to the prime minister and Parliament. He argued that the American system, in contrast, granted excessive power to Congress, with its powerful committee structure that made decisions favoring special interests behind closed doors. It lacked efficiency and needed more centralization. He faulted both the House and the Senate and their unwieldy committees, which he believed lacked accountability. The book received mixed reviews, but those individuals who praised it made the stronger case; the book has been in print ever since.

Wilson accepted a position in 1885 at Bryn Mawr, a new women's college near Philadelphia. Before the fall term began, he and Ellen were married. Beginning its first year with an enrollment of thirty-six, Bryn Mawr had a faculty of seven. Wilson taught all history and political science courses—five classes per semester in his first year. He completed his doctorate in 1886 in history and political science from Johns Hopkins. In 1888 he accepted a position at Wesleyan University in Middletown, Connecticut, where he taught for two years before finally landing his dream job on the faculty of his alma mater Princeton University.

He was an immediate success at Princeton. Publication of *The State* shortly before his arrival there ensured his academic reputation, and he became the most popular lecturer at the university, as confirmed by student votes for six years running. He had a national reputation that attracted attention. Both the University of Illinois and the University of Virginia offered him their presidencies, but he remained committed to Princeton. He developed close friendships, including a lasting one with Frederick Jackson Turner, a historian at the University of Wisconsin, one of the most prominent academics in the country after publishing his famous frontier thesis about America's westward movement. Life was good; he and Ellen had three daughters, and the family was close.

In 1902 Princeton named Wilson its president. He had ideas for reforming the school, which he believed had become too parochial, inbred, and lackadaisical to be a truly great university competitive with Harvard and Yale. He pushed for revision of its curriculum, for establishment of a graduate school located physically and intellectually in the center of the campus, and for elimination of its eating clubs (really social clubs), which he believed contributed to Princeton's lack of academic rigor. His revisions of the curriculum included establishment of a preceptorial system in which students worked directly with faculty, and the establishment of disciplinary specialization with electives. These reforms won support and approval, a significant achievement and a testimony to his leadership. But the other goals for reform ran into difficulties from the beginning. Students and alumni alike were deeply committed to the eating clubs and their traditions and resisted his interference. Princeton had barred Greek-letter fraternities, and the eating clubs had become their equivalent. The attack on the eating clubs also became entwined in Wilson's vision of a Quadrangle Plan, or Quad Plan, in which organization into colleges would replace the eating clubs.

Wilson's last years at Princeton were frustrating, with his opposition blocking the Quad Plan and succeeding in building a Graduate College off campus rather than in the heart of the campus, as Wilson preferred. Andrew West had led the campaign against Wilson's dream of a central location for the Graduate College. In the end, West won the battle, not through the power of his argument but because of a bequest to Princeton that specified West's preference. Fund-raising was perhaps Wilson's least favorite activity among his presidential responsibilities, and indeed he was not very successful at it. The bequest came from an elderly Princeton graduate named Isaac Wyman, who was near death and named West as the executor of his estate. Before the total of Wyman's gift was verified, rumors suggested it might be as much as ten million dollars. Wilson conceded that money trumped his pragmatic arguments before it became clear that the gift was eight hundred thousand dollars, enough to build the Graduate College but considerably less than had been anticipated.

By 1908 Wilson was wearing down, weary of the protracted battles inherent in campus politics. Politicians had been courting him for some time, hoping to attract him to run for political office, and these appeals seemed more attractive as his influence at Princeton declined. Wilson's biographer John Milton Cooper summarized Wilson's accomplishments as president of Princeton on two fundamental questions: How had the years there prepared him for the presidency? What had he achieved at Princeton?

On the first question, Cooper concludes that the boldness and innovation that marked his actions were also characteristic of his actions as president. He made many of his key decisions after gathering information, but then deciding on his course of action in solitary thought rather than by building a consensus. Once he made a decision he acted decisively, with insufficient preparation, convinced of the righteousness of his cause. Campus politics could be bitter, divisive, and secretive, and the battles at Princeton prepared him for the more open political disputes he faced as president. People who thought Wilson had no political experience when he entered national politics had little understanding of the nature of academic disputes—not unlike the situation forty years later when pundits criticized General Dwight Eisenhower's lack of political experience after a career in the army.

What had Wilson accomplished at Princeton? Despite the resistance by alumni and colleagues who opposed his innovative ideas about education and his defeat on the location of the Graduate College, Wilson left an indelible mark on Princeton. His vision propelled the university on a trajectory that made it competitive with Harvard and Yale. His preceptorial system invigorated academics at Princeton, and although the university retained some of its reputation for a country-club atmosphere, it would never sink back to the level of chubbiness that characterized Princeton before his presidency. He infused Princeton with an intellectual rigor that made it a great university.

Wilson's vigorous leadership at Princeton had also attracted public attention. He was a reformer in an age that valued reform, an able administrator, and a rising talent in a party that yearned for leadership. His abilities and celebrity led New Jersey's Democratic bosses to look at him as a potential gubernatorial candidate whose name recognition could help him win the election but whose lack of political experience would make him malleable. George Harvey, the editor of *Harper's Weekly*, and Jim Smith, a former senator and the political boss of the New Jersey Democrats, were the two men most responsible for Wilson's selection. Smith's second-in-command was his son-in-law James Nugent, the Newark boss. Harvey and Smith seized on the college professor as their candidate, and Nugent followed suit. Thus emerged a splendid irony: political bosses forced Wilson on the party, and the party accepted him reluctantly.

At the state Democratic convention in Trenton in September 1910, over the opposition of New Jersey Progressives, the machine controlled deliberations, handing Wilson the nomination. In his acceptance speech, the nominee told the delegates that he had made no promises and was beholden to no one. He called for three reforms: reorganizing state government, making taxes equitable, and controlling corporations. Progressives were moved by a nominee who sounded like a Wisconsin La Follette Progressive. The bosses still believed they had Wilson in their hip pocket and weren't worried. They should have been.

Wilson's political strengths emerged in the campaign. The Republicans nominated a Progressive lawyer, Vivian M. Lewis. Lewis and his supporters emphasized Wilson's ties to the bosses, but Wilson refuted the allegation in a letter that received wide circulation and said that he would dismantle the machine. Wilson was a stiff campaigner at the outset, but once in stride he began to loosen up and enjoy the process. He won by a wide margin, garnering 54 percent of the vote.

Not long after the election, Wilson had a chance to make good on his most important campaign promise. Smith decided he wanted to go back to the Senate. Wilson refused to support him. Direct election of senators had yet to be approved, so the legislature chose senators. In this case, it rejected Smith soundly, and the boss never recovered his influence in the state or his seat in the US Senate. The boss system in New Jersey was moribund.

Governor Wilson won support of his Progressive agenda, initiating election reform, regulation of utilities, and liability laws directed at employers. He did so by reaching out to Republicans, asking them for recommendations, appointing them to positions, and interacting with them in informal gatherings. Bipartisanship was more achievable, of course, when like-minded Progressives sat in the caucuses of both parties. During the first half of 1911, this Progressive coalition passed a series of reforms, including establishing a public utilities commission, mandating that state legislators vote for US Senate candidates who had won primaries, and allowing cities to create a commission form for local governments. This impressive performance lost steam after midyear, when Wilson began to take the steps that would lead to his nomination for the presidency.

Those individuals who later examined his performance as governor recognized that certain personality traits had begun to emerge that would later be characteristic of his behavior as president. His decision-making process remained much as it had been at Princeton. He would single-mindedly focus on one issue, listening to a range of arguments. Then he would retreat into isolation and think through the problem until he felt comfortable with a solution. Once he decided, he would move on and would be impatient with anyone who sought to revisit the issue. At that point, his stubborn streak and rigidity made their appearance. So by the time he made his decision, he was ready to move on. This method of governing meant that there would be little or no follow-up. Thus, during the last year and a half of his governorship, presidential politics distracted him, and the state of New Jersey had a part-time governor.

The race for the Democratic nomination proved to be one of the most dramatic contests in the history of the American presidency. As the contention between President Taft and former president Roosevelt became apparent, the Democrats believed that they had an excellent chance to win the presidency for the first time in two decades. Early in 1910, two and a half years prior to the election, there was no clear favorite. The race began to take shape in May, when Michigan's state Democratic convention nominated Ohio governor Judson Harmon. Ohio added its support to Harmon at its state convention the following month.

After the midterm elections that November, Wilson's victory in New Jersey made him a serious contender, and by early 1911 it appeared that the race might pit Wilson, the Progressive Democrat, against Harmon, a conservative. As a southerner by birth, Wilson seemed to be likely to have backing from the southern states, and indeed Harmon began to lose support there. But Wilson had spent most of his career in New Jersey, and the South was reluctant to throw its support to him. Instead, Alabama congressman Oscar Underwood entered the race and became the South's regional candidate. But a decisive shift took place early in 1912, when Congress came back into session and Champ Clark of Missouri won election as the Speaker of the House and soon emerged as a front-runner.

For the first time, many delegates to the Democratic National Convention would be chosen in state primaries—one of the Progressive reforms that brought democracy closer to the people. The primary season ran for two and a half months, from March 19 to June 4, with twenty-two states holding Democratic primaries. Underwood won all four southern primaries but did not win any states outside of the South. Clark won nine primaries, Wilson five, and Harmon two. But it was the number of delegates, not the number of states, that mattered, and the delegate count left Clark and Wilson with 185 and 184 delegates, respectively. Harmon's two states were populous prizes, New York and Ohio, which gave him 134 delegates, and Underwood trailed with 86. Wilson had also won states with a significant number of delegates, prevailing in New Jersey, Pennsylvania, Texas, Wisconsin, and Oregon. Clark's big prizes were Illinois, Massachusetts, and California, along with six smaller states.

So when the Democratic National Convention convened in Baltimore on June 25, Clark and Wilson were in the lead with no clear favorite. Convention rules stipulated that in order to win, a candidate had to tally two-thirds of the votes, with 1,088 total votes available. On the first ballot, Clark received 440.5 votes, Wilson 324, Harmon 148, and Underwood 117.5, with the rest divided among nine other candidates, none of whom were serious contenders. There was only slight movement through nine ballots, but on the tenth Tammany

Hall, the New York machine, switched its 90 votes from Harmon to Clark, giving Clark 556 votes, a majority of the votes cast, but short of the two-thirds required for the nomination. Wilson was prepared to concede, but his key strategist, William Gibbs McAdoo, talked him out of doing so. William Jennings Bryan, the party's presidential nominee in 1896, 1900, and 1908 and an influential elder statesman in 1912, contacted the Wilson team about countering the Tammany action and pledging not to accept the nomination with Tammany support. Wilson was honoring the tradition that candidates not attend the convention, but McAdoo remained in contact with him via telephone. With nothing to lose, Wilson accepted Bryan's ploy to counter Tammany, but under what terms is not clear.

Now the politicking began in earnest. After joining Bryan in condemning Tammany's bargain, Wilson's men worked feverishly to develop one of their own. They contacted state delegations that were supporting minor candidates. They offered Indiana's delegation the vice presidency for its governor, Thomas R. Marshall, in return for the state's votes. They stuck to an agreement with Underwood's supporters that neither side would withdraw in favor of Clark. Wilson edged ahead of Clark by 5 votes on the thirtieth ballot. The key breakthrough came on the forty-second ballot, when they convinced Illinois to switch some of its Clark votes to Wilson. Four ballots later, Wilson had attained the two-thirds majority, clinching the nomination.

THE PROGRESSIVE PARTY: BACK TO CHICAGO WITH TEDDY ROOSEVELT

On August 5, in the Coliseum in Chicago where the Republicans had met in June, Theodore Roosevelt and the Progressive Party assembled to launch the most effective—and the most quixotic—third-party presidential candidacy in American history. Contemporary observers and historians alike have compared the atmosphere to a religious revival. The echoes of Roosevelt's remark at the Republican convention about standing at Armageddon and doing battle for the Lord were perhaps still resounding in the rafters of the Coliseum. The New York delegation contributed to the aura, entering the convention singing "Onward, Christian Soldiers," which became something of an anthem for the convention. The meeting may have seemed unlike an ordinary political convention, too, because the "ordinary" Republican politicians had already attended their Chicago convention in June.

If the new party had their candidate, it also had formidable obstacles to confront. Theodore Roosevelt had taken an enormous gamble in splitting the Republican Party and had lost long-standing supporters in the process. Encouraging Progressives to follow him and bolt the Republican Party could damage the party for years to come. Furthermore, when the Democrats nominated Woodrow Wilson the following week, it opened an opportunity for Progressives disgusted by the Republican split to vote for a Progressive Democrat. Roosevelt knew that he was a long shot at best, and the Wilson nomination probably killed his chances. He even conceded that his career in public service would end on election day.

Progressives faced challenging questions from the outset, for they were doing more than nominating Roosevelt, which was of course their main item of business. But they were also nominally launching a new party, and they had to define what that party stood for. Roosevelt's sympathy for African Americans, and his opposition to lynching, was difficult to transfer to the platform or to policy without risking alienating the white South, and he chose not to take that risk. And how could the Progressives incorporate concern for labor without appearing to be antibusiness? The platform called for an eight-hour day; a social program to aid the elderly, disabled, and unemployed; and a minimum wage for women. Progressives also supported granting women the right to vote, a step neither of the major parties was willing to take.

Albert Beveridge nominated Roosevelt. A dynamic orator, Beveridge chaired the convention and gave the keynote address in addition to nominating Roosevelt. Beveridge had completed his second term as a senator from Indiana in 1911. Although conservative by nature, he had supported Progressive legislation during Roosevelt's presidency, and in 1912—with his Senate career behind him—he did not have to worry about punishment from the Republican Party. Jane Addams, the director of Hull House and one of the most admired women in the nation, seconded the nomination. She was concerned about the timid party stance on racial issues, but nonetheless preferred the Progressives over the alternatives.

The climax of the convention, the event that everyone had waited for, was the candidate's own speech. Roosevelt's appearance touched off an emotional demonstration, punctuated by the "Battle Hymn of the Republic" and "Onward, Christian Soldiers." The festive celebration went on for just short of an hour, and then Roosevelt took the rostrum and began a two-hour oration that he called his "Confession of Faith." The centerpiece of the speech concerned the issue that would define the campaign: the issue of the rising power of corporations. Roosevelt proposed a federal industrial commission with broad powers, including regulatory authority. As a candidate he defended the position he had taken as president: corporations generated economic progress and thus served the public good, but their excesses must be controlled. Big business was a reality, but monopolies could not be allowed. He also defended the social issues raised in the party's platform. Lewis Gould's account of the 1912 election credited Roosevelt with "the most advanced position toward a modern version of the regulatory state."[3] The next day, August 7, the Progressives nominated California governor Hiram Johnson as Roosevelt's running mate.

THE CAMPAIGN

The nature of presidential campaigns had begun to change in the previous election, and the process would continue in 1912. Campaigns as popular entertainment as they had been in the late nineteenth century, with local rallies at which political speeches gave an excuse to picnic and meet neighbors, now gave way to a more sophisticated approach.

3. Lewis L. Gould, *Four Hats in the Ring: The 1912 Election and the Birth of Modern American Politics* (Lawrence: Univ. Press of Kansas, 2008), 145.

New technology impacted elections, and as early as 1912 the automobile began to influence the ways campaigns could reach voters. Candidates on the trail could speak and interact with more voters, moving more quickly between appearances. For the first time political movies played a role, albeit a small one. Nonetheless, they gave people a chance to see the candidates and make judgments based on what they observed as well as what they heard. In the late nineteenth century, presidential candidates could lose support if it appeared that they were *too* eager to win the office. Taft, constrained more so than the others both by his natural reluctance to beg for votes and by his inclination to respect the campaign precedents of the late nineteenth century, seldom competed with the other candidates on the campaign trail.

Other factors also challenged Taft's candidacy. Despite having won the Republican nomination, in a general election he would not have the advantages that had helped win it. Conservative party regulars could not control a general election as they had managed the convention. The Republican primaries made it clear that Roosevelt was the more popular candidate of the two. The bitter nomination battle left some of the party conservatives so upset that they planned to vote for Wilson just to ensure that Roosevelt would not win the election and do further damage to the Republican Party. Then, on October 30, just days before the election, Taft's running mate, Vice President James S. Sherman, died. Taft and Sherman had never been close, but Sherman's death was a blow to a faltering campaign nonetheless.

Eugene Debs was a much more aggressive campaigner than Taft, but he harbored no unrealistic visions of staging an upset victory. There was energy nonetheless in his campaign that had long since disappeared from the Taft camp. Debs was a beloved figure, a charismatic speaker, and the bearer of a dream. His real goal was to accumulate more votes than he had won in 1908, a respectable 420,000. He also had a meager campaign chest of sixty-six thousand dollars and had to depend on donations to stay on the road. His greatest challenge was one that typically confronts all minor-party campaigns: when the major parties saw his issues gain traction, they appropriated them as their own. Debs complained in particular about Roosevelt's campaign stealing his ideas. Debs had been the first candidate to support women's suffrage, but now Roosevelt promised the same thing, and eventually Wilson did so, too.

But there was little doubt that the real campaign was between Roosevelt and Wilson. Roosevelt had sucked the air out of Taft's candidacy, and he needed to hold as many Republican votes as possible. But he could not cater to conservatives, for his battle with Wilson hinged on Progressives, and he could not allow Wilson to appear to be the more genuine Progressive. Indeed, Roosevelt had already laid out a campaign that promised support for social reform that went further than Wilson had been willing to go, going so far that it elicited criticism from Debs for stealing his issues. The only issue on which he might appeal to conservative Republicans was the tariff, an issue that he tried to duck at the Progressive Party convention.

The contest between Roosevelt and Wilson was a debate on issues between two men with reputations not only as effective politicians but also as intellectuals. Roosevelt was a historian, and in fact in 1912 he served as the president of the American Historical Association. He had written several books, including *The Naval War of 1812* (which prepared him for his tenure as assistant secretary of the navy under McKinley and in his advocacy for a stronger navy), *The Winning of the West*, and a biography of Thomas Hart Benton. Wilson's academic background and books on the structure of American government gave him authorial credentials comparable to his rival's. So this election promised a genuine debate of the sort seldom seen in American presidential politics.

The issue upon which the debate developed was the question of how to control large corporations. The former president had a record in this regard, so his task was to convince voters that his approach worked. His program, which he called the New Nationalism, accepted big government, and for that matter accepted big business as well. But he also believed that American capitalism required competition, so corporations could not be allowed to grow so large that they stifled competition. This point of view meant that he could tolerate oligopolies, which allowed competition between a few (or even only two) big companies, but not monopolies. When companies tended toward monopoly, he was willing to use government as an instrument to control them. As president he relished the nickname "Teddy the Trust Buster," and indeed he had won cases against some of the nation's largest conglomerates, including Standard Oil and the consolidated railroad giant known as the Northern Securities Company. These victories were spectacular, albeit in carefully selected cases that he had confidence he could win. And Taft's supporters liked to point out that their man had actually busted more trusts than the Trust Buster. Nonetheless, Roosevelt made a convincing case that he knew how to use the tools available to the president to get things done, which applied to more than just controlling corporations.

Wilson's task was to present a viable alternative to the New Nationalism. The challenge was that he and Roosevelt were not far apart on many of the issues of the day. Their positions on a range of Progressive topics, such as social justice and broadening citizen participation in government, for example, were only shades apart, particularly after Wilson endorsed women's suffrage. Wilson could not risk becoming a "me, too" Progressive who agreed with Roosevelt on most issues. Thus, the question of corporations became critical. Here Wilson sought the counsel of a Boston attorney, Louis Brandeis, who had criticized the legal profession for defending large corporations to the extent that they often overlooked the public interest. Brandeis urged Wilson to shift the grounds for the debate. Rather than argue about how to regulate monopolies, which in effect allowed Roosevelt to define the terms of the debate, Brandeis urged Wilson to insist that government ought to regulate *competition*, thus leveling the business playing field and allowing smaller businesses to survive. By early September Wilson began to incorporate this approach into his speeches and developed a label for his program: the New Freedom.

The campaign demonstrated other differences between the leading candidates. Roosevelt supported a protective tariff, whereas Wilson wanted lower tariff rates. Wilson advocated smaller government; Roosevelt praised the ability of a larger government to institute justice. In reality, the differences between the candidates were not extreme.

Both sought ways to limit corporate excess, and both believed the federal government offered the best chance for reform. Both endorsed a similar range of Progressive goals.

On October 14, Roosevelt appeared in Milwaukee on his midwestern swing. As he was climbing out of his car prior to the speech, an assailant shot him in the chest. The bullet struck the case for his glasses and his copy of the speech he was about to present. These obstacles may have prevented an assassination, but the injury was serious nonetheless, breaking a rib. Roosevelt insisted on proceeding with the speech against the advice of his staff, and after informing the audience what had happened, he spoke for eighty minutes. The injury took its toll, and Roosevelt took ten days to recover. Wilson suspended his campaign while Roosevelt was incapacitated.

ELECTION RETURNS

By November 5, despite the lack of polls to predict the outcome, most people expected the Republican split to lead to a Wilson victory. Although the result in this sense was not surprising, the way in which it developed gave people a lot to ponder. Wilson tallied 6,293,454 votes, or 41.9 percent of the total votes cast, winning forty states, generating 433 electoral votes. Thus, the electoral vote appeared to be a virtual landslide, while the popular vote made Wilson a minority president. Roosevelt finished second with 4,122,721 votes, six states, and 88 electoral votes. Taft had 3,486,242 votes, winning only Vermont and Utah, which yielded 8 electoral votes. Eugene Debs perhaps had the most impressive performance, since he recorded 901,551 votes, an impressive performance for a fourth-place finisher and more than doubling the number of votes he received in 1908.

The outcome offered various interpretations to those observers who chose to dissect it. For Republicans, their two candidates combined outpolled Wilson by more than 1.3 million votes. In twenty-six of the forty states that Wilson won, Taft and Roosevelt together outpolled him. Republicans thus could conclude that they were still the majority party and that if they had stayed united behind one candidate, they could have won the election. The first contention was accurate, the second questionable. If Roosevelt had not run, a Taft victory was problematic at best, for Taft had lost public support and Wilson would have drawn many Progressive Republicans. Had the Republicans nominated Roosevelt, he would have run a stronger race than Taft but would not necessarily have won the election, either. Many Republicans were adamantly opposed to a third term, and regulars would have resented his bid to destroy a sitting president of their party.

Furthermore, despite the fascinating aspects of the campaign, the turnout was disappointing, even in comparison to 1908. Wilson had fewer votes than his party's candidate in 1908, William Jennings Bryan. And the sum of Roosevelt's and Taft's votes was fewer than Taft had achieved on his own four years earlier. Republicans had virtually conceded the election and had not done much to get out the vote. Democrats, despite Wilson's minority status, had reason for hope, knowing that the Republican split would not be mended. Their hope that they had broken the Republican reign as the majority party, however, proved illusory, in spite of Wilson's reelection four years later.

SUGGESTED READINGS

In addition to the books cited for the previous chapter on Taft and Roosevelt, there are two recent biographies of Woodrow Wilson that have information pertinent to this chapter and the chapters that follow. Of the two biographies, A. Scott Berg's *Wilson* (New York: G. P. Putnam's Sons, 2013) is more sympathetic to Wilson. John Milton Cooper Jr.'s *Woodrow Wilson: A Biography* (New York: Alfred A. Knopf, 2009) is a fine biography by a noted Wilson scholar. There are also two books that deal specifically with this election: James Chace's *1912: Wilson, Roosevelt, Taft and Debs—the Election That Changed the Country* (New York: Simon and Schuster, 2005) and Lewis L. Gould's *Four Hats in the Ring: The 1912 Election and the Birth of American Politics* (Lawrence: Univ. Press of Kansas, 2008).

3

Foreign Policy before World War I

As was his fate in domestic policy, in his foreign policy President Taft had the misfortune of serving between the terms of two presidents who refashioned American foreign relations in fundamental ways. Theodore Roosevelt took action that established the United States as a world power, mediating international disputes in the Western Hemisphere, winning the Nobel Peace Prize for negotiating a settlement of the Russo-Japanese War, promulgating the corollary to the Monroe Doctrine that bears his name, building the Panama Canal, placing the relationship between Britain and the United States on firmer footing, managing protectorates in Cuba and the Philippines, and ensuring that the navy operated a world-class fleet. Taft was a fundamental figure in several of these enterprises and without question gained invaluable experience in carrying out these responsibilities. But despite Taft's instrumental role in the administration's foreign policy, these policies were Roosevelt's, not Taft's. Wilson, although he came to the presidency with little experience (or even interest) in foreign policy, left a formidable legacy, most notably leading his nation to victory in World War I; formulating his Fourteen Points, one of the most influential foreign policy documents in American history; and promoting plans for a League of Nations, which stirred enthusiastic support in some quarters and heated opposition in others, leaving an indelible legacy for the American role in international affairs.

FOREIGN RELATIONS UNDER TAFT

Taft's legacy in foreign policy pales in comparison to these two presidential giants. His biographer Lewis L. Gould suggests that Taft and his conduct of foreign policy "seem lackluster and pedestrian. No wars, no major crises, no enduring doctrines, only the deriding label of 'dollar diplomacy' remains of what he . . . tried to do."[1] The term *dollar diplomacy* underscored Taft's belief that he could find a better alternative to military intervention in Latin America, that he could rely on businessmen rather than soldiers to be the principal face of the United States in Latin America. It was a lofty goal, but as we will see what made sense as theory became difficult to implement.

Taft suffers further because of the high expectations that followed him to the White House. Few of his predecessors came close to matching his background in foreign policy at the time of his inauguration, and only one—John Quincy Adams—clearly exceeded it. The most important of his constituents—Theodore Roosevelt—certainly expected that Taft would continue along the lines of what Taft had done as Roosevelt's emissary in many matters of international relations. Under Roosevelt Taft served as secretary of war in TR's second term, supervised the building of the Panama Canal, and served as provisional governor of Cuba. He led two missions to Asia, one in 1905, the other in 1907. Ironically, the only international agreement that bears Taft's name came under Roosevelt. The Taft-Katsura Agreement with Japan gave Japan control of Korea in return for a pledge that Japan would not interfere with the American role in the Philippines.

The core of the problem once Taft became president was that he did not share Roosevelt's perspective down the line as his predecessor assumed he did. Despite his service as secretary of war, he did not rely as much on the threat or application of military force as had TR. Taft's legal background left him inclined to work out agreements rather than impose them. Taft's belief in the importance of economics in foreign policy—which of course gave rise to the term *dollar diplomacy*—meant that the navy would have a diminished role in his administration. A

1. Lewis L. Gould, *The William Howard Taft Presidency* (Lawrence: Univ. Press of Kansas, 2009), 79.

different administrative style than Roosevelt also contributed to the public perception of Taft's lack of success. Taft delegated a great deal of authority to his secretary of state, Philander Knox. So whereas no one questioned that Roosevelt was in charge of his own foreign policy, there was at least the appearance that Knox ran Taft's.

A corporate lawyer, Knox served in Roosevelt's cabinet as attorney general from 1900 to 1904 and then as a senator from Pennsylvania from 1904 until Taft nominated him as secretary of state. As the architect of Taft's dollar diplomacy, Knox concurred with the policy of economic expansion that undergirded both the Roosevelt and the Taft administrations, and indeed in that sense there was continuity between the two Republican administrations. And while critics alleged that Knox ran Taft's foreign policy, this notion was misleading in that the two men conferred frequently.

Dollar diplomacy, then, was at the center of the Taft-Knox foreign policy. Its central premise was that the United States should expand its foreign markets and increase American investment abroad. Dollars, not bullets, should be the principal instruments of American foreign policy. Investment and trade should promote stability more effectively than the military in fractious areas such as the Caribbean. Dollars rather than bullets sounded sensible, but in practice in Latin America, the region particularly targeted for dollar diplomacy, the Taft administration's tone was less sensitive than its predecessor's. Both administrations considered the United States to be dominant in Latin America, but TR's secretary of state Elihu Root had understood Latin American concerns more fully than Knox. In short, dollar diplomacy was more benign in principle than in practice. Under Taft the United States sold arms to Latin American nations, which served two purposes: it furthered the interests of the American arms industry, thus expanding trade, and it assisted Latin American nations in warding off European encroachment. But whether it assisted Latin American development or brought stability to the region was another question.

Domestic critics of dollar diplomacy accused the administration of privileging businessmen over diplomats and the military and suggested that business was the least well qualified of the three institutions to establish foreign policy. Latin American opponents resented American meddling with the internal affairs of their nations, and when Taft seized customs houses as Roosevelt had done, it became difficult for the recipients of dollar diplomacy to tell the difference between dollar diplomacy and Roosevelt's "big stick" diplomacy. Furthermore, in spite of its commitment to economic diplomacy rather than relying on force, the Taft administration did find cause for military involvement in Latin America, intervening in Nicaragua and the Dominican Republic.

Nicaragua's president José Santos Zelaya had held office since 1893 and ruled as a dictator. American interest in Central America focused on the Panama Canal, but Zelaya undercut any American role in Nicaragua. He proposed a Central American union and refinanced Nicaragua's debt through European creditors in May 1909. The agreement allowed Europeans to control Nicaragua's customs revenues. Americans involved in Nicaragua included land investors and mining interests, and they supported an insurrection by anti-Zelaya Nicaraguans led by Juan Estrada. During one confrontation between Zelaya and the American-backed rebels, Zelaya's forces seized and executed two Americans fighting with the rebels. The United States broke relations with Zelaya's government. The rebels defeated Zelaya, who went into exile in Mexico. Adolfo Díaz, who had previously worked for an American mining company, became president. Knox worked out an agreement (the Knox-Castrillo Convention) that would have allowed the United States to manage Nicaragua's customs collection and repay the European loans. The Senate rejected the treaty, but Taft and Knox continued the arrangement anyway. Nationalists in Nicaragua, including former Zelaya supporters, attacked the government. Díaz requested American assistance, and Taft sent twenty-five hundred marines and naval forces, who put down the revolt. An American military presence in Nicaragua continued until 1933, with the exception of an interlude of several months in the mid-1920s. The United States, pressured by American business interests, negotiated a new treaty in which the United States gave Nicaragua three million dollars and received naval bases, the right to build a canal across Nicaragua, and the right to intervene. The treaty was still under consideration when Woodrow Wilson became president. He supported it, and the Senate finally ratified what became known as the Bryan-Chamorro Treaty in 1916.

While he was negotiating with Nicaragua, Knox also found reason to seek similar arrangements over customs collection in other Central American countries. All of the Central American nations except El Salvador had debts to European nations that they were unable to pay, and Knox and Taft wanted to avoid European intervention to collect. Incidents of this nature had arisen during Roosevelt's presidency, and the administration worried about European intervention to collect unpaid debts. Knox negotiated with Honduras and reached an agreement with European bankers to reduce the debt. The United States agreed to make payments for Honduras in return for management of Honduran customs collection, and Knox negotiated a treaty to that effect. However, neither the Senate nor the Honduran Congress approved the treaty, the Senate because of opposition to dollar diplomacy and Honduras because it did not want the United States to control its major source of revenue. Knox tried a similar approach in Costa Rica and Guatemala, but both nations refused.

Taft approved American military intervention in the Dominican Republic and dollar diplomacy in Haiti, the two nations that occupy the island of Hispaniola. In Haiti Taft convinced the government to accept a loan in 1910, but this experiment in dollar diplomacy failed to stabilize this chronically troubled nation. The Dominican Republic had been the site of one of Roosevelt's interventions, the one in which he promulgated his corollary to the Monroe Doctrine, justifying intervention in cases in which Latin American nations failed to carry out their international debt obligations. Roosevelt had established American control of customs houses there, and Dominican president Ramón Cáceres made progress in repaying foreign loans. The assassination of Cáceres in November 1911 provoked revolutionary violence, and in 1912 the customs houses came under attack. Taft sent in a contingent of marines in September and forced a corrupt president to resign. After Wilson's election and the election of a new president in the Dominican Republic, the marines returned home in December. The Dominican Republic remained volatile, however, and ultimately the Wilson administration also intervened in another attempt to ensure stability.

WILSON AND THE MEXICAN REVOLUTION

Woodrow Wilson's first foreign policy challenge came in Mexico, and it proved a difficult one that persisted beyond his presidency. The American relationship with Mexico had been fraught with tension, misjudgment, and distrust. Mexico's wariness regarding American motives was well founded, for in the 1840s the United States had waged war and seized half of Mexico's land, territory that later became the states of Texas, New Mexico, Arizona, and California. During the 1860s, Mexican conservatives evoked American criticism but little more, as Americans confronted their own crisis, the contemporaneous American Civil War.

Ironically, by the end of the nineteenth century, the relationship between the two neighboring countries stabilized under the leadership in Mexico of dictator Porfirio Díaz. Elected to the presidency of Mexico in 1877, he ruled as dictator from 1884 until 1911. During his controversial regime, he brought material progress to Mexico, often at the expense of the lower classes. His famous slogan "Pan o palo" (Bread or the stick) threatened punishment for those individuals who did not cooperate with his regime. He encouraged foreign investment and welcomed American money and expertise, particularly in the development of the oil industry. Americans had invested more than one billion dollars in Mexico, and some forty thousand Americans lived in the country. So when Mexicans revolted against Díaz, Americans had a lot at stake.

Despite Díaz's dictatorial regime, Mexican politics were complex, and opposition mounted. Regional leaders, such as Emiliano Zapata in Morelos in the South and Francisco "Pancho" Villa in the North, had loyal followers willing to defy Díaz. In 1908 Díaz, who was nearing eighty years of age, suggested that Mexico was ready for democracy and promised elections in 1910. Francisco Madero, who hailed from a family of wealthy landowners, sought the presidency in a campaign critical of Díaz. In response, Díaz reneged on his promise, arrested Madero, and claimed an overwhelming victory in a fraudulent election. Bailed out of jail by his family, Madero fled to Texas and from there rallied his supporters (including Zapata, Villa, and Pascual Orozco, who later became president himself) and launched a revolt late in 1911 that became the trigger for the Mexican Revolution. Madero won election in his own right, but in February 1913, just days before President Wilson's inauguration, the revolution took a violent turn. Victoriano Huerta, one of Díaz's former generals, had Madero assassinated and seized power in his place. American ambassador Henry Lane Wilson (no relation to the American president-elect) said he had no alternative but to support Huerta, but in fact the ambassador had supported Huerta all along. American businessmen in Mexico, fearing anarchy, supported the ambassador's recommendation.

On March 4 Wilson took the oath of office as president and in his inaugural address called on the American people to represent a voice of morality: "Here muster, not the forces of party, but the forces of humanity," he urged, and although he mentioned neither Mexico nor Europe, he had both in mind.[2] Wilson refused to recognize the Huerta government and stuck to his decision even after the State Department advised him that recognition traditionally did not imply approval of the government in question. He would pursue the same course after the Bolshevik Revolution in Russia four and a half years later and thus set a precedent that the United States would follow after the Communist victory in China in 1949. Wilson also lifted an arms embargo, thus allowing American weapons to arm Huerta's opponent, Venustiano Carranza.

An incident on April 9, five weeks after Wilson's inauguration, inflamed relations between the two countries. Huerta's supporters

2. Lewis L. Gould, *Four Hats in the Ring: The 1912 Election and the Birth of Modern American Politics* (Lawrence: Univ. Press of Kansas, 2008), 196.

arrested a party of nine American sailors as they came ashore in Tampico. Mexican authorities released them immediately and apologized, but the American commander on the scene, Rear Admiral Henry T. Mayo, demanded a twenty-one-gun salute. The Mexican commander thought he had done enough and refused. But President Wilson, eager for a pretext to get Huerta out of office, supported Mayo.

On April 21 Wilson ratcheted up the pressure on Huerta, sending a contingent of a thousand marines and naval forces to Veracruz, the port of entry for Mexican arms. Wilson's decisions to this point demonstrated his lack of understanding of Mexican politics, and indeed a lack of knowledge of the situation in the port city. Again, advisers had urged him to reconsider; this time Secretary of State William Jennings Bryan and Secretary of the Navy Josephus Daniels wanted a peaceful resolution. Again, Wilson overruled them. He received support from Congress, but Democrats and Republicans disagreed about the rationale for intervention. Democrats supported Wilson's justification based on opposition to Huerta, while Senate Republicans, led by Henry Cabot Lodge, believed that Wilson should have ordered intervention earlier and called for intervention to protect American lives and property, a policy tantamount to a call for war.

Carranza's Constitutionalists had the most to gain from Wilson's anti-Huerta policies, but no Mexican politician could accept American support without losing his Mexican backing. Anti-American attitudes ran deep in Mexico ever since the United States had taken half of Mexico's territory after the mid-nineteenth-century war between the neighboring countries. American support for the Díaz regime also disturbed many Mexicans. So when Wilson offered assistance to Carranza, he did not realize the depth of Mexican animosity toward the United States, nor did he anticipate the antipathy he would receive from Mexico. He expected that the Mexican people would welcome his assistance in ridding the nation of a brutal dictator. Instead, he drove Carranza and Huerta together rather than advancing the one at the expense of the other.

American troops landed in Veracruz, but not without bombardment and bloodshed. They seized the customs house, preventing an incoming ship with arms for Huerta and depriving him of revenue from trade passing through Mexico's largest port. But 19 Americans and 126 Mexicans died, sparking anti-American protests throughout Mexico and in other Latin American countries. An occupation force of more than 7,000 troops took control of the city. Marines moved through its streets, suppressing sporadic gunfire.

Wilson gave strict orders for American forces to remain in Veracruz and accepted arbitration from the ABC powers (Argentina, Brazil, and Chile). During subsequent negotiations in Niagara Falls, Canada, Wilson remained adamant that Huerta had to go, but ultimately it was Carranza's Constitutionalist forces that defeated Huerta and forced him into exile in Spain.

Carranza had always been wary of American support, and after he gained control of Mexico City, he felt no need for American advice. Miffed at Carranza, Wilson turned to the northern caudillo Pancho Villa, who had quarreled with Carranza. Villa had developed a loyal following in the northern state of Chihuahua. He had a reputation as something of a Robin Hood who stole from the rich to give to the poor, but he also a long record of brutality. He had been generally supportive of American involvement in Mexico, and the Americans, who speculated that he might be malleable, considered casting their lot with Villa instead of Carranza. This relationship never went very far, and when Carranza's forces defeated Villa early in 1915, the Wilson administration decided to recognize Carranza's government.

Villa wanted revenge; in his view, he had supported the Americans, and they had betrayed him. On January 10, 1916, he stopped a train in northern Chihuahua, robbed the passengers, and killed seventeen American mining engineers. Two months later, on March 9, he led a force of some four hundred of his supporters across the border to Columbus, New Mexico. There he split his troops, sending half to the town itself and the rest to a nearby army encampment, where they attacked a stable, believing it to be barracks. Villa's men set fire to several buildings, including the town's only hotel, and killed eight civilians and seven soldiers. American soldiers, caught off guard, rallied and fired with machine guns, killing sixty-seven Mexican soldiers.

Wilson had to respond and decided to send a military force. The cabinet debated whether Wilson should inform Carranza and decided against it. Wilson sent eleven thousand soldiers under the command of General John J. "Black Jack" Pershing to pursue Villa into Mexico. There was hope that Carranza, who after all had his own differences with Villa, might assist, or at least allow the Americans to use the Mexican railroad in the region, but it was a wishful illusion. Carranza protested the violation of Mexican territory but did not follow his words with action.

Pershing's troops were unrelenting. One contingent covered more than four hundred miles in fourteen days—riding on horseback over desert terrain. But this prodigious effort yielded nothing; Villa knew the country and had the support of its people and successfully eluded the American forces. At the pursuit's greatest extent, Pershing penetrated more than five hundred miles into Mexican territory. Skirmishes and larger battles took their toll on both sides as the Americans headed north. The largest confrontation, at Carrizal, could have been avoided. A small American force with orders to avoid conflict if possible confronted a force of four hundred of Carranza's soldiers armed with rifles and a machine gun. The Mexicans killed a dozen Americans and lost thirty of their own. After three months of futility, and with protests from Carranza's government in Mexico City ringing in their ears, Pershing's men headed north empty-handed. But Pershing did not leave Mexico at once. Instead, his expeditionary force established a position some eighty-five miles south of Columbus, New Mexico, and remained there from July 1916 until January 1917. In the interim, Villa rebuilt his forces, reaching a strength of about five thousand men. His chief adversary was not Pershing but rather Carranza, whose army moved north to eliminate the threat Villa posed to his own government but without cooperating with Pershing in doing so. It was Carranza, not Pershing, who eventually put an end to Villa as a threat to Mexican stability. In comparison to Veracruz, the Pershing expedition at least had justification, even if its results were less satisfying. Ultimately, a team of mediators, three from each country,

1. General John J. "Black Jack" Pershing commanded the American punitive force that pursued Pancho Villa. During World War I, Pershing commanded American military forces in Europe. George Grantham Bain Collection, Prints and Photographs Division, Library of Congress, LC-DIG-ggbain-27971.

negotiated Pershing's withdrawal. The agreement also stipulated Wilson's recognition of the Carranza government.

Relations with Mexico evolved further in the context of the ongoing revolution in Mexico, even as the focus of American foreign policy shifted to the onset of war in Europe. Mexico played an important role, albeit a passive role, in the American entry into World War I, when in January 1917 the German foreign minister sent a telegram to Mexico offering an alliance against the United States. Known as the Zimmermann telegram (see chapter 7), the note promised in return to help Mexico win back territory it had lost to the United States in the war between the two countries in the 1840s. British intelligence intercepted the note and used it to pressure the United States to join the Allied cause. Mexico remained neutral in World War I and even tilted toward the United States in the sense that it increased trade with the nation during the conflict.

Another matter in 1917 caused further strain between the United States and Mexico. Mexico adopted a new constitution that sought to reduce the power of the church and enhance the role of labor in Mexico. One of the most disturbing provisions (in the eyes of Americans who had invested in Mexican oil) was Article 27, which decreed Mexico's ownership of its national resources, including subsoil rights to minerals and oil. Americans were heavily invested in Mexican oil, and because Mexico was one of the world's major oil-producing countries, Article 27 caused consternation among investors. It took more than twenty years to resolve this dispute; in 1938, with another European war threatening, the administration of Franklin D. Roosevelt came to an agreement with Mexico, recognizing Mexican subsoil rights and negotiating a settlement for American investors.

The administration's Latin American interventions extended beyond Mexico, in Central America (Nicaragua) and the island of Hispaniola (shared by Haiti and the Dominican Republic, both targets of intervention). These actions combined pose questions in evaluating a president who later proclaimed the virtue of self-determination. Generally, Wilson scholars explain them on the basis of Wilson's "missionary paternalism" (an effort, however misguided it may have been, to do the best for the people involved), as a continuation of the policies of his predecessors, as precautions necessary to protect the vicinity of the new Panama Canal, or as policies that Wilson approved but with which he had little to do in planning.

Nicaragua was a case of continuing a prior policy, as the Taft administration had sent in marines in order to address instability that had become a regular feature of Nicaraguan politics. Taft had authorized intervention after the end of the sixteen-year dictatorship of José Santos Zelaya, who had antagonized the United States by soliciting European investment (particularly by Germany and France) in his country. The Conservative Party sought to unseat Zelaya's successor, José Madriz, and American marines landed in 1910 to assist the rebels. Adolfo Díaz won election in 1911, but the following year the Liberal Party rebelled, and he requested American aid. Taft again authorized intervention, and Wilson and Secretary of State William Jennings Bryan determined to keep American forces in the country, thus continuing an occupation that lasted for fourteen years. One of the reasons the United States became involved in the first place was an effort by Zelaya to solicit French or German interest in a Nicaraguan canal. The Bryan-Chamorro Treaty of 1916 gave the United States exclusive rights to build such a canal.

In Haiti the Wilson administration inherited involvement initiated by President Taft but increased the American presence in ways that far exceeded what his predecessor had done. Taft's dollar diplomacy operated in Haiti in 1910, prompted by concern that poverty-induced instability might threaten the Panama Canal. Taft tied Haiti to the United States with a loan and accompanying concessions. Five years later, however, a mob attacked Haitian president Vilbrun Guillaume Sam, assassinating him. Wilson dispatched marines to Haiti to restore order, arguing that Haiti had no legitimate government in the aftermath of the violence. The marines forced Haiti to accept protectorate status, seizing the customs houses that provided a major source of revenue and taking control of Haiti's finances. The marines also organized a militia, the Gendarmerie, and marines served as its officers. The Americans used violence to quell violence, and the United States admitted to killing 3,000 Haitians over the course of the nineteen-year occupation, although more recent accountings place the figure much higher, perhaps as many as 11,500. Furthermore, the marines instituted a system of forced labor, mainly for construction projects. Ultimately, racism played a significant role in the administration of the protectorate. As Americans consistently did during this era, they justified their involvement by citing sanitation improvements, infrastructure development, and building projects. But recent historians have judged it to be an exercise in paternalism, asserting authority as a father might over his children.

The Wilson administration also ventured into the Dominican Republic. By the time Wilson became president, the United States already had a long record of relations with the Dominican Republic, focused in the late nineteenth century on American efforts to acquire or annex Samana Bay, an ideal harbor, as a coaling station for the US Navy. In the twentieth century, the primary American concern was to maintain stability in the Caribbean, particularly after the construction of the Panama Canal. Taft had sent troops but brought them home in December 1912. In 1913 the situation deteriorated. Secretary of State William Jennings Bryan agreed to supervise elections, but they produced a congress opposed to the provisional president, who refused to relinquish his office. Another rebellion ensued, and the provisional president blockaded the nation's ports to prevent supplies from reaching the rebels. Among the consequences of this action, customs revenue diminished, limiting American leverage to resolve the conflict. Eventually, the United States administered new elections, with US Navy vessels off the coast to compel compliance. In the fall of 1914, after the election, the Wilson administration proclaimed that the situation was resolved and that no more rebellions would be permitted. This announcement proved to be unfulfilled wishful thinking, and in 1916 Wilson sent troops to occupy the Dominican Republic. They remained in the country until 1922.

The Wilson administration, worried about the onset of war in Europe in August 1914, had tried to bring about peace in the Caribbean Basin, with little to show for it. The administration had the best of intentions: it was not seeking territory, and its primary objective was to bring about stable governments that would benefit the people of the region as well as American interests. Unfortunately, Wilson, his secretaries of state (Bryan and Lansing), and their staffs had little understanding of Latin American politics or Latin American distrust of American motives, particularly American paternalism. They assumed that American power, if applied for the best of intentions, would prevail in the end. Decades of American policies devised primarily in American self-interest could not be overcome by policies that Latin Americans perceived as more of the same. Historians have referred to Wilson's policies as "moral diplomacy." Latin Americans demonstrated that they did not accept Wilson's moral leadership.

SELECTED READINGS

Books dealing with the Taft and Wilson administrations cited in the first two chapters examine foreign policy issues. Robert E. Quirk's *An Affair of Honor: Woodrow Wilson and the Occupation of Veracruz* (Lexington: Univ. Press of Kentucky, 1962) remains useful for the American intervention. John S. D. Eisenhower's *Intervention! The United States and the Mexican Revolution* (New York: W. W. Norton, 1993) covers the broader range of American involvement. William Appleman Williams's *The Tragedy of American Diplomacy* (New York: W. W. Norton, 1959) is a classic study that gave rise to a revisionist view of American foreign policy. Kendrick A. Clements's *The Presidency of Woodrow Wilson* (Lawrence: Univ. Press of Kansas, 1993) pertains here as well as in the following chapters dealing with Wilson's presidency.

4

Financial Reform and Technological Progress

On the morning of March 4, 1913, Woodrow Wilson met President Taft at the White House for the ceremonial ride down Pennsylvania Avenue to the Capitol. With his hand on the same Bible he used for his inauguration as governor of New Jersey two years earlier, Wilson took the oath of office as the twenty-eighth president of the United States from Chief Justice Edward White. In his inaugural address, Wilson laid out an ambitious agenda of domestic reform. He had built a record as a reformer in his brief stint as governor of New Jersey, and he had every intention of continuing Progressive reform at the national level. During the campaign, Louis Brandeis had helped him shape a program he called the "New Freedom" that embodied these ideas. With Democrats in control of the White House and both houses of Congress, he could afford to be optimistic—and specific. He mentioned taxes and tariffs as likely targets for reform and emphasized banking reform and antitrust programs. He planned his presidency to center around these programs and had even mentioned to a colleague at Princeton before heading to Washington that it would be ironic if his administration had to deal mainly with foreign affairs.

The Wilsons were an attractive family, and the early months of the presidency included an active social life. Wilson and his wife, Ellen, brought their three daughters, all in their twenties, to Washington. Jessie, the Wilson's second daughter, had been active in the women's suffrage campaign, generating a frequent topic of conversation in the White House family quarters. The suffrage campaign was a major national issue, and Alice Paul had led a suffrage parade in Washington on the day before the inauguration, trying to influence the president-elect, who had not yet endorsed it. Jessie Wilson had been engaged to Francis Sayre, a graduate of Harvard Law School, prior to the inauguration, but the family delayed announcing the engagement until July. The couple had a White House wedding in November. The following May the youngest daughter, Eleanor (Nell), married William Gibbs McAdoo, Wilson's secretary of the treasury. (McAdoo offered to resign after the wedding, but his father-in-law wanted to keep him.) The eldest daughter, Margaret, was pursuing a singing career and often was out of Washington.

Like many of her predecessors, First Lady Ellen Axson Wilson sought to avoid the limelight but found it hard to do so. She came to recognize the influence she had and became involved in several social welfare pursuits and in particular sought to clean up some of the wretched housing in African American communities near the White House. She also became concerned about the White House itself and initiated a renovation of the third floor. She also left a lasting legacy in establishing the White House Rose Garden, which in more recent years has been a frequent site of presidential press conferences. The first lady and the president found time to enjoy each other's company, often on afternoon rides around the capital in a limousine. Wilson relied on her as a confidante and adviser, and she continued to read his speeches as she had done for many years. Wilson was one of the last presidents to write his own speeches, and because Wilson had developed a reputation for eloquence, Ellen's assistance was an important contribution.

STAFFING THE ADMINISTRATION

Three men formed Wilson's inner circle. Colonel Edward House ("Colonel" was an honorary title, as House had no military service) was a Texas political operative, influential in the election of several Texas governors. He met Wilson in 1911 and played an important role in Wilson's presidential campaign. He was central in the presidential transition, particularly in making staff and cabinet recommendations. He became an adviser on foreign policy, especially on European affairs, and often served as a personal representative of the president. Both Wilson and House said that the two of them had such rapport that House often could literally speak for the president. They corresponded regularly and conferred frequently, meeting a recorded seventeen times during Wilson's first year in office, with fifteen of those meetings in the White House. Critics would say that House learned to say what Wilson wanted to hear, but there was no question that for a time Wilson relied on him more than on any other man for counsel. Wilson's biographer John Milton Cooper considered the relationship to be "with just one exception, the most important . . . of his presidency." (The most important relationship would be with Wilson's second wife, Edith Galt Wilson.) Yet Cooper concludes that "it is not entirely clear what the relationship amounted to," because Wilson recognized some of House's shortcomings and because the two would later have a falling-out—although that came only late in Wilson's second term.[1]

Joseph Tumulty was a New Jersey native serving in the state legislature when Wilson served as president of Princeton University. Tumulty assisted Wilson's gubernatorial campaign in 1910 and then served as Governor Wilson's private secretary, and he continued in the same capacity for President Wilson. But he was more than that, and in 1916 he became chief of staff. Wilson's biographer John Milton Cooper suggests that the only reason Tumulty did not hold the title earlier was because "except for clerks, stenographers, military and naval aides, and Dr. Grayson, Tumulty was the staff."[2] From the beginning, Tumulty functioned as a chief of staff regardless of title. He handled congressional relations, managed the president's schedule, and conferred with Wilson about political issues, about which Tumulty had

1. John Milton Cooper Jr., *Woodrow Wilson: A Biography* (New York: Alfred A. Knopf, 2009), 193, 194.

2. Ibid., 200.

better instincts than Wilson. Those individuals who wanted to speak to the president had to go through Tumulty, who generally divided Wilson's morning appointments into fifteen-minute blocks and kept appointments moving efficiently. Tumulty's role benefited from his friendship with Ellen Wilson, and together they kept watch over the president's welfare.

The third man with a close relationship to Wilson was his personal physician Dr. Cary T. Grayson. Grayson was a naval aide assigned to the White House, but he became close to the president—even, according to Wilson biographer Scott Berg, "the most constant and intimate relationship the President had with a man for the rest of his life."[3] Grayson, a bachelor, moved into the White House and became a friend and companion, not an adviser in the sense that Tumulty and House were. Wilson's health needed monitoring throughout the presidency, particularly in the second term, so Grayson's proximity was invaluable. Grayson advised Wilson to play golf in order to have regular physical activity, and the two became golfing partners.

Wilson's selection process for cabinet-level appointments was almost haphazard, or at least unsystematic. Wilson did not enjoy making such selections, largely because he was uncomfortable with the pressure to consider politics in the process. He relied on House to make recommendations and to vet candidates, and Progressive Boston lawyer Louis Brandeis, who had helped Wilson formulate the themes of his campaign, also assisted. There was little question that William Jennings Bryan would be asked to join the cabinet, although in what capacity was open to question. Bryan had been the Democratic candidate for the presidency in 1896, 1900, and 1908, but in this Republican era he lost all three races. Wilson reached out to Bryan during the 1912 campaign for the Democratic nomination, and although he had not supported Wilson initially, by the time of the Democratic convention, he had come around, influenced by Wilson's flattery and the persuasion of North Carolina newspaper editor Josephus Daniels, a

3. A. Scott Berg, *Wilson* (New York: G. P. Putnam's Sons, 2013), 277.

friend of Bryan and a Wilson supporter. Wilson had a debt to pay, and he rewarded Bryan with a featured cabinet position, secretary of state.

The campaign also influenced Wilson's selection of the secretary of the treasury, a post that Wilson considered vital. He intended to seek financial reforms, including tariff and banking proposals, and needed a strong voice at the Treasury to support him. William Gibbs McAdoo, a Georgian who had been educated in the South at the University of Tennessee and made his reputation in New York, had been a key addition to the Wilson campaign team. McAdoo had organizational and political skills that the Wilson campaign lacked in the early running and as the campaign unfolded. Wilson came to respect McAdoo's skills. McAdoo became the second cabinet nominee.

From there the process became less orderly. Wilson selected Josephus Daniels, another supporter and a southerner whose judgment Wilson trusted, as secretary of the navy. Daniels selected for his assistant the young Franklin D. Roosevelt, TR's cousin and a Democrat, a choice that pleased Wilson for its likely effect on TR, who had held the same position during the McKinley administration. Wilson's choice for secretary of the army was a curious one that owed to Tumulty's influence: Lindley M. Garrison, an attorney whose New Jersey origins suggested a connection, except that Wilson and Garrison had never met before they conferred in Trenton, when Wilson offered the job and Garrison accepted.

For postmaster general, Wilson chose Albert S. Burleson, a longtime congressman from Texas who had supported Wilson during the campaign. Burleson, a party regular who knew his way around Washington politics, made a point at an early cabinet meeting that had a lasting impact. Wilson, who liked to remind people that he came to the presidency with no political debts, wanted to appoint postmasters on the basis of merit. Burleson argued that these appointments were traditionally patronage affairs cleared by congressmen from the district in which the post office resided, and if Wilson proceeded with his plan, he would be alienating the party's base, both for support in Congress and for coming elections. Wilson backed off and allowed Burleson to follow tradition.

Wilson wanted Brandeis as attorney general, but Colonel House convinced him of the political risks of appointing a Jew, especially one who had already been subject to anti-Semitism in his public life as an attorney. House argued for James C. McReynolds, a Kentuckian who had served as an assistant attorney general during the Taft presidency. McReynolds had demonstrated his support for Progressivism and had taken cases in which he had prosecuted trusts, and this background convinced Wilson.

The rest of Wilson's cabinet included David Houston, another southerner, who had served as the president of Texas A&M and the University of Texas, as secretary of agriculture. William C. Redfield, a New Yorker who had sought the vice presidency, instead became secretary of commerce. On his last day in office—Wilson's inauguration day—President Taft signed a bill creating the Department of Labor from the Department of Commerce and Labor, so Wilson had a new cabinet position to fill. It went to William B. Wilson (no relation to the president), an immigrant from Scotland who had worked in mines in Pennsylvania. He had served as a congressman and had been secretary-treasurer of the United Mine Workers of America (UMWA). During World War I, he succeeded in broadening the responsibilities of the new department. He and Josephus Daniels were the only two members of the cabinet who served throughout Wilson's two terms.

Secretary of the Interior Franklin K. Lane was a Californian who had served as a commissioner on the Interstate Commerce Commission. The Interior Department had been at the center of controversy during Taft's presidency, and it would be so again under Wilson. Lane supported the Hetch Hetchy Valley Project in California, which dammed the Tuolumne River, which had its origin in Yosemite National Park. Conservationists, including John Muir, fiercely opposed the dam, which Congress ultimately approved to provide water for San Francisco.

As was the norm in the early twentieth century, Wilson's cabinet included no women and no minorities. What provoked criticism in some quarters was the fact that more than half of its members were from the South, as were the president himself and the chairs of key committees in Congress, since chairmanships were determined by seniority and the Solid South dependably elected and reelected Democrats. Wilson's operating philosophy was to allow cabinet members a great deal of latitude in running their departments, and the combination of this freedom and the southern roots of influential cabinet members soon prompted a controversial policy on an issue that plagued the administration throughout its tenure: the question of race and of the rights of African Americans.

Just a month into the administration, Burleson and McAdoo indicated their intention to segregate their departments. Burleson in particular said that he had received complaints about Negroes and whites working together, especially about situations in which whites had black supervisors. Wilson had been raised in the segregated South and understood the basis for the complaints, allowing Burleson and McAdoo to proceed. They segregated restrooms, lunchrooms, and offices. Oswald Garrison Villard, a founder and white member of the NAACP, registered his concern, and a delegation led by William Monroe Trotter, one of the nation's leading black advocates for civil rights, visited the president to protest the policy. Wilson, just coming to terms with this delicate issue, failed to either curtail the policy or satisfy Villard or Trotter. His general approach to the issue was to continue to appoint African Americans to positions traditionally held by blacks, but he was unwilling to go much further and defended his actions to Villard by explaining that he did not consider the policy to be designed against Negroes.

THE ADMINISTRATION, BUSINESS, AND THE ECONOMY

On financial issues Wilson was more confident. He had campaigned on two matters that ranked at the top of his agenda, the tariff and banking reform. The tariff had become a fundamental issue that divided the nation, pitting the industrial Northeast against the rural South and West. After the election of 1896, when Republicans had come to dominate national politics, it placed Republicans firmly on the side of manufacturing, with Democrats defending the agrarian interests. Tariffs had originally been intended to protect American industry from foreign competition, raising the price of imports while Americans improved their products so that they could compete on their own. However, now even American manufacturers that were well established had grown accustomed to the advantages of tariffs and were not willing to relinquish them. Congress cooperated and instead of reducing tariffs pushed rates ever higher, beginning in the late nineteenth century and continuing into the twentieth. Republicans learned to brush aside any attempts to lower rates, as had been the case during Taft's presidency with the Payne-Aldrich tariff. Farmers complained that they did not have the same protection, and occasionally Congress included token protection for farmers. Consumers complained that they were paying higher prices than necessary in order to make the rich richer, but they were not organized enough to have much impact.

Wilson followed the approach he had used in New Jersey, taking on the tough issues immediately. He did so with a bold move, announcing on April 6, just a month after his inauguration, that he would address a joint session of Congress, thus breaking a tradition established more than a century earlier by Thomas Jefferson, who never appeared in person to address Congress. Wilson's critics alleged that he was violating the separation of powers, but the charge did not stick. In the House Alabama congressman Oscar Underwood, who had been a candidate for the Democratic nomination for the presidency against Wilson, was a staunch advocate of tariff reform. Because he was both the House majority leader and the chair of the powerful Ways and Means Committee, he was well positioned to do something about it. With Wilson's support, he pushed a bill through the House that contained substantial tariff revision. The Underwood bill sailed through the Democratic House with little opposition, but the Senate had traditionally been the graveyard of tariff reform. Here Wilson demonstrated that he could be an astute politician. Lobbyists fought reform, and Wilson appealed to the people, suggesting that private profit was the motive behind the opposition to reform. Republicans answered by demanding an investigation, and Wilson responded by welcoming one, urging Democrats to support it. The investigation revealed that lobbyists had spent millions of dollars to influence legislation and that members of Congress had holdings that stood to benefit from maintaining high tariffs. The outcome was still uncertain, and debate dragged on through the summer. The chair of the Senate Finance Committee, North Carolina senator Furnifold Simmons, was a conservative who had helped kill previous tariff reform, but he had promised Wilson to assist him and kept his word. In September the Senate passed the Revenue Act of 1913, popularly known as the Underwood-Simmons tariff. Tariffs would be levied on an ad valorum basis (a set percentage of the value of the commodity), and many items were added to the free list (that is, not subject to tariff).

The legislation also instituted the income tax on individuals, a reform made possible by the adoption of the Sixteenth Amendment earlier in the year. The highest rate of taxation, on incomes of more than $500,000 ($12.3 million in 2015 dollars), was 7 percent. Those individuals with an income of more than $20,000 ($494,000 in 2015 dollars) paid 2 percent.

The second issue on Wilson's agenda was even more challenging: a revision of the structure of the nation's banking system. The nation's banking system in 1913 was decentralized in the sense that there were small banks around the country that were answerable only to their investors. States also chartered banks that were responsible to state regulation. At the same time, the wealth of the nation was centralized to an extraordinary degree. A congressional committee chaired by Congressman Arsène Pujo of Louisiana, the chair of the House Banking and Currency Committee, held hearings from May 1912 until February 1913 and found that banks controlled by J. P. Morgan and the Rockefellers held 341 directorships of corporations, with a net worth of $22 billion ($543 billion in 2015 dollars). Two attempts had been made to establish a centralized banking system, the first by Alexander Hamilton, President Washington's secretary of the treasury. Opposition by the Jeffersonian Republicans, who warned against such a concentration of wealth that would protect northern industrial interests at the expense of the southern agrarian economy, killed the bank. In 1816 the nation chartered a Second Bank of the United States for a twenty-year period. President Andrew Jackson, using arguments similar to the ones that destroyed the first bank, waged a "bank war" in anticipation of the required renewal of the bank's charter and killed the bank by transferring its funds to "pet" banks. Thus, since the 1830s, the United States had not had a central banking system. The lack of such a system became apparent during occasional "panics" (recessions or depressions) that left many banks subject to fluctuations in the economy with no reserves to weather the crisis.

During the Roosevelt and Taft administrations, Congress considered banking reform and even generated a plan known as the Aldrich Plan. Named after Rhode Island's Republican senator Nelson Aldrich, who headed the commission that studied the issue, the plan advocated establishing a private National Reserve Association, dividing the nation into fifteen banking districts, each of which could make loans to troubled banks in time of emergency. The South and the West opposed the plan, arguing that a private banking organization gave too little power to the federal government and left power in the hands of bankers. So when Wilson raised the issue, he was speaking to an audience familiar with the pros and cons of centralized banking.

Wilson recognized the need for banking reform and gave it a high priority. The contours of the debate were already clear, with two issues at stake: private versus public control and centralization versus decentralization. Brandeis and McAdoo were Wilson's most reliable advisers on financial matters. McAdoo had proposed a plan of fifteen districts managed by the Treasury Department. The president conferred with Brandeis, who suggested that his plan ought to reduce the power of the "money trust," but also cautioned that when he tried to do so, the goals of the administration and the objectives of the bankers would be irreconcilable. Wilson began discussions with Congressman Carter Glass, a Democrat from Virginia and chair of the House Banking Committee. Glass's committee had already been working on a plan advancing a decentralized private system, and he had the support of big bankers. Other Democrats, including William Jennings Bryan, favored a public system under the direction and control of the federal government.

Wilson thus found himself trying to resolve the differences between Democratic proposals.

The president next met with McAdoo and the leading Democrats on banking issues in each chamber of Congress: Glass from the House and Senator Robert Owen of Oklahoma, who chaired the Senate Banking and Currency Committee. He told them that he wanted to establish a federal agency that would monitor regional banks and that those banks would distribute money to banks within their respective regions. Then, continuing his approach of direct involvement with Congress, he met with the Democrats on the House Banking Committee to elaborate his plan. Finally, on June 23, he addressed a joint session of Congress to present his goals, as he had done on the tariff bill. Two days later Glass and Owen unveiled their joint proposal for a system that they called the Federal Reserve.

Protests erupted from bankers and farmers, a good indication that the bill had succeeded in finding an effective middle ground. Money interests objected to the exclusion of bankers from the proposed Federal Reserve Board. Wilson's response was to compare the Federal Reserve to the Interstate Commerce Commission, which was meant to regulate railroads but proved to be ineffective because it was staffed with railroad men who consistently sided with the railroads. The farmers complained about the role of regional banks, which they believed could control credit. The administration made concessions to farmers, granting them access to credits against their crops. The administration and its supporters in Congress fought off major modifications, especially from bankers. The bill passed the House by a resounding margin of 285 to 85, with 23 Republicans and 10 Progressives joining with Democrats to approve. The Senate concurred by a vote of 54 to 34.

It was a triumph for the administration and the greatest legislative victory of the Wilson presidency, a judgment with which historians still agree. It succeeded by combining an element of centralization (the Federal Reserve Board) with a measure of decentralization (the twelve Federal Reserve Districts) and public supervision of a system that retained a measure of private control. Federal Reserve Notes replaced Silver Certificates as the dollars issued by the Treasury, and they were backed by the full authority of the federal government, an important step toward international recognition of the dollar as the major international instrument of exchange. It stabilized not only the dollar but the banking system itself. The legislation had flaws, and there have been many amendments over the years, but the system survives more than a century later. The most severe test came during the Great Depression of the 1930s, when hundreds of banks across the country failed or went into receivership. But state-chartered banks, which were not required to be members of the Federal Reserve, were generally the first to fail. Member banks, which had been required to place a percentage of their assets into reserve, had backing that gave them protection against the greatest financial crisis the nation had ever faced. Not all of them weathered the storm, but many more would have failed without the system. And adjustments made the system stronger; for example, state-chartered banks now had to belong. By 1913 the nation's economy was too large, and the emerging system of international trade too complex, for the old system to survive, and in the years that followed the Federal Reserve System proved its viability.

One item remained on Wilson's agenda of major issues, and it was perhaps more difficult than the other two: the problem of the trusts. As the economy had grown in the late nineteenth and early twentieth centuries, so did big business. The problem was not the existence of big business—there was agreement that big companies were necessary in a growing economy. The problem was to control businesses so they did not stifle competition. Two approaches had been tried to address this issue: antitrust legislation that allowed the government to sue big companies that were becoming monopolies (under the authority of the Sherman Antitrust Act of 1890) and regulation through regulatory agencies such as the Interstate Commerce Commission. Here the ICC stood as an example again of the problem with regulation. Commissioners had to understand the industry to regulate it effectively. But if commissioners came from the industry (and thus understood how it operated), they tended to share the point of view of the companies they were intended to regulate. They thus became "captive agencies," in effect ruling in favor of industrial leaders because they understood the problems from their perspective. This unintended consequence is what had happened with the ICC, and it had made the government wary of regulation, without having rejected it as a possible alternative. Critics concerned with this issue had suggested that there could be two kinds of regulatory agencies: one could have investigatory and advisory responsibilities, while the other could have the authority to impose rulings on the industry.

The issue of the trusts could not be ignored. Not only was this a problem that resonated with the public, but Republicans were also using it as a political issue, alleging that the president had been too lax in enforcing it. Theodore Roosevelt had nurtured his reputation as Teddy the Trust Buster, which enabled him to criticize Wilson. Union leaders also weighed in, particularly because unions had lost cases that treated the unions as trusts that operated in restraint of trade when they went on strike, and they were seeking exemption from antitrust prosecution. Wilson had sought union support and sympathized with labor's situation.

Ultimately, the administration and Congress did not choose between regulation and antitrust, but rather used both approaches. Congressman Henry D. Clayton, an Alabama Democrat, proposed legislation that would carry his name. The Clayton Antitrust Act tightened provisions of the Sherman Act, mainly by elaborating in more detail what would be considered threatening to a competitive environment such as interlocking directorates and mergers that could decrease competition. Although it did not exclude unions entirely, it did contain a clause stipulating that human labor could not be considered an article of commerce, thereby protecting unions from antitrust suits. It also restricted the use of injunctions against unions.

Furthermore, Congress established a new regulatory commission, the Federal Trade Commission, and gave it the authority to issue orders to corporations to prevent them from pursuing unfair trade practices. A coalition of conservative Republicans and Democrats sought to narrow the scope of the legislation by defining acts in restraint of trade, but the administration and its supporters in Congress held the line and established the FTC along the lines of its original intent.

TECHNOLOGY AND THE ECONOMY, PART I: TRANSPORTATION AND THE FORD MOTOR COMPANY

It's no surprise that the Wilson administration focused its attention on the economy and the banking system. The nation's economy continued to grow during the 1910s, and the financial structure supporting it became more complex. The nation experienced a transportation revolution, as new modes of travel challenged the railroad's domination of domestic travel. The rise of the automobile was the foremost of these challengers, as during the decade it went from a rich man's toy to an affordable alternative for middle-class Americans. Railroad track mileage reached its peak in the United States in 1916 at about 253,000 miles, after which the total began to decline, both because of the consolidation of railroad lines and because of the increase of automobiles and trucks and the construction of roads. The airplane remained experimental, decades from viability for commercial transportation, but its potential became more apparent, and World War I prompted innovation that eventually had commercial applications.

Transoceanic travel still required passenger ships, and early in the decade a magnificent new passenger liner came to symbolize the state of the art in luxury and safety. The British liner the *Titanic* left on its maiden voyage from Southampton, England, for New York on April 10, 1912. Launched with great fanfare, the ship carried wealthy and prominent people who could afford to pay for such luxury but also poor people traveling in cramped quarters in steerage. The ship's promotional literature advertised that the ship was virtually unsinkable. It carried enough lifeboats to accommodate only half of the 2,200 passengers and crew, since its manufacturers expected they would never be needed, except perhaps to assist another ship in trouble. Nonetheless, the ship's lifeboats did meet the legal requirement for ships of its size.

At 11:40 p.m. on the night of April 14, the *Titanic* struck an iceberg that opened five of the sixteen separate compartments, and ice-cold seawater poured in. The ship's specifications required that it must be able to withstand the rupture of four. The crew began to load lifeboats, loading women and children first as was customary, which also meant that several of the lifeboats were not at full capacity when they were launched. The *Titanic* sent out a radio distress signal and fire flares, but aboard the only ship in its proximity, the SS *Californian*, the radio operator was not at his post. Flares were visible, but the *Californian* did not respond to them. At 2:20 a.m., two hours and forty minutes after striking the iceberg, the bow of the *Titanic* began to sink. The ship split, and the stern rose in the air, with enough air in its compartments to keep it afloat for a few more minutes with people clinging to it. Then it, too, sank, plunging those passengers who were holding on into twenty-eight-degree (Fahrenheit) water, survivable for only a few minutes. Another ship, the *Carpathian*, was not close enough to render immediate assistance, but it did respond to the radio distress signal and arrived the next morning and took aboard the survivors from the *Titanic*'s lifeboats. Of the 2,224 people aboard, 710 were saved. The *Carpathian* took the passengers it had rescued to New York before continuing its voyage to the Mediterranean. The wreck of the *Titanic* rested twelve thousand feet below the surface, where a joint French-American expedition rediscovered it in 1985. The most significant of its discoveries was confirmation that the ship had split in two as it sank. Before then it was generally believed that the ship had sunk in one piece.

In the aftermath there was much angst about human hubris and about mistakes that unnecessarily cost lives that could have been saved. The United States and other nations took action to apply lessons learned from the disaster. Congress passed the Radio Act of 1912 that required that ships' radios be operated twenty-four hours a day and have backup power supplies. International agreements adopted these provisions. Another international agreement stipulated that red rockets fired at sea should be interpreted as a distress signal, and later amendments said that this requirement would be applied to all rockets.

The *Titanic* disaster did nothing to slow the advance of technology. In the United States, the preceding quarter century had already seen striking progress in the development of American industry, and technology advanced apace. At the beginning of the decade, however, manufacturing processes resembled nineteenth-century processes; this situation would change dramatically by 1920. Changes occurred for many reasons, including increased consumer demand, a general push toward efficiency, military needs during World War I, and advances in technology. Progress made in the development of the automobile became a prototype for other industries. During the 1910s, the automobile went from experimental models manufactured in small numbers—essentially a craft—to mass production, and sales numbered in the hundreds of thousands.

Nobody was more responsible for the revolution in production than Henry Ford. Ford once famously said that when he was growing up, all his toys were tools, and decades later they still were. As a young man, Ford took a series of jobs in machine shops and quickly developed a reputation for being able to solve technical problems. He worked in a shop until he believed that he had learned all he could of what that shop did, and then he would move on. He began working on a vehicle, experimenting in the kitchen and in a rented shed, and built his first vehicle in the shed. When it was ready, he realized that it was too big to fit through the door, and he used an ax to "widen" the door. The owner was enraged, but Ford had an ability to win people over. He also had the good fortune of having an understanding landlord who suggested he replace the door with a wider one, creating perhaps the first "garage" in America.

Ford was not alone in experimenting with the development of a "horseless carriage," and in the 1890s and early years of the twentieth century there were many people doing so, many working in parallel to Ford. By the late 1890s, there were several operations building and selling automobiles, although none were being produced in substantial numbers. The leading manufacturer in the United States at the turn of the century was Alexander Winton, who in 1898 sold twenty-two cars, and the following year he surpassed one hundred. Winton and other automobile builders publicized their creations with either long endurance trips or races, and Ford decided to race against Winton. The race took place in October 1901, and while there were three entrants, one dropped out, leaving only Ford and Winton. Winton's vehicle was faster and had a wider wheelbase that enabled it to handle corners on the oval track. Each driver had a mechanic, and Ford's leaned out from a narrow running board to help Ford corner. Winton for a time was far ahead but started having mechanical problems, and Ford caught him and won the race, giving him the attention he needed to gain financial support.

Ford had a firm idea of the kind of automobile he wanted to build, and it differed from the concept that dominated the emerging industry. Winton and other early automobile men wanted to make substantial vehicles that had a wide-enough wheelbase and enough weight to endure the rigors imposed by the roads of the day, some of which were no more than dirt paths rutted by wagon wheels, while others were corduroy roads that had served well in the nineteenth century but were ill-suited for automobiles. Generally, such cars sold for between three and five thousand dollars. Ford believed that this price was too high to attract the number of buyers necessary to make a company successful. He wanted to build a smaller, lighter vehicle that would sell for well less than one thousand dollars. His notion was that by selling less-expensive cars, even if the profit on each unit was small, he could market to the average person, not only the rich, and make much more than he could be restricting the market by the kinds of cars he made.

In 1903 he found enough investors to begin the Ford Motor Company. The company, however, was not under Ford's sole control, and a debate developed over what kind of a car it ought to build, so the company built prototypes for two different kinds of cars. Ford's project, which became the Model A, had a wheelbase of six feet and weighed 1,250 pounds. Ford's main rival in the company, Alexander Malcomson, wanted to build bigger, more expensive cars. While the board debated, Ford went ahead with development of the Model A and put it into production. By 1905 the company employed three hundred people and produced twenty-five Model A cars in a day. The board was nonetheless undecided, despite the profits coming in. In the meantime, Malcomson was as disenchanted as Ford in the divided-production debate and decided to form his own company while continuing to be involved at the Ford Motor Company. This decision turned the board against Malcomson, and Ford bought out Malcomson's interest in Ford.

The shakeup at the company brought about a number of changes that would affect the future of the Ford Motor Company. James Couzens, who had begun his career with Malcomson running a coal company, stayed with Ford and became the business partner. It was an ideal match. Ford knew little about administering the business side of the company, and Couzens knew even less about how cars operated, but together they were a powerful team. The departure of Malcomson left Ford as the major shareholder. The president of the company, John Gray, died of a heart attack, and Ford moved up from vice president to president. Ford was now fully in charge and would no longer have to defer to the decisions of others.

Ford was meanwhile moving ahead in the production of a new version of the car, the Model N, which had a four-cylinder engine and thus was more powerful than the two-cylinder Model A and more reliable as well. He introduced it at $500, but found it difficult to hold that price. Nonetheless, he sold more than eight thousand, so it kept a steady stream of income.

By 1907 Ford was working on the car that would vindicate his design goals and create the iconic car of the early American automobile industry, the Model T. Introduced in 1908, the Model T encompassed innovations in design, manufacturing methods, and marketing strategy that transformed the industry. The Model T had a four-cylinder engine and a chassis made of vanadium, a lightweight steel that enabled Ford to keep the weight of the vehicle down and obtain the efficiency that he sought. It had two forward gears and one reverse gear. The early models were all started by hand crank, although some later models had a battery starter. Its flywheel had a magneto attached, which provided electrical power while the car was operating, an innovation that rivals had not achieved. The entire automobile weighed only eleven hundred pounds. When the company introduced it in 1908, it sold for only $850, and remarkably, once the company refined manufacturing techniques, the price came down to as low as $300. It came in two models, one with only a front seat, the other with two seats. Later, other options became available. There was no choice of color, however. Salesmen would tell potential buyers that they could have a choice of black or black.

The Model T thus made the automobile truly affordable and attractive to middle-class Americans. The company also developed an efficient marketing plan, with dealerships and a pledge of after-the-sale service that other car companies could not begin to match. People who bought a car from Alexander Winton, for example, had to order through the factory and had no service plan. Ford quickly surpassed Winton in sales, and by 1924 Winton was out of business.

In 1906, even before building the first Model T, Ford had purchased a sixty-acre parcel of land in Highland Park, six miles north of Detroit. There he built what at the time was an enormous factory, nearly three football fields in length at 865 feet. Next to it he built a tool shop nearly as large. The assembly line that so influenced American industry in the twentieth century took shape in this factory. Ford drew on the ideas of Walter Flanders, who worked for the company for only two years but in that brief period moved Ford toward mass production. Flanders began to integrate machine tools along the line rather than maintaining an area designated for each type of machine. He also pushed Ford toward the use of interchangeable parts. Ford decided that the building would produce only one vehicle, the Model T.

The Highland Park plant opened with the new decade on January 1, 1910. Ford was attuned to the latest industrial developments and would put new machines into use if they were more efficient, even if they replaced machines that were only a few months old. A Buffalo plant was stamping out metal parts rather than casting them. Not only was the new process faster, but it also produced lighter parts that did not sacrifice performance. Ford was always looking for ways to save weight, and the new process appealed to him. When workers at the Buffalo plant went on strike, Ford had the operation moved to Highland Park. Walter Knudson, who brought this process to Ford's attention, became one of the great industrialists of the twentieth century.

Another Ford innovation was the movable assembly line, a further step toward mass production. The chassis of a new automobile would be pulled along while workers carried out their individual responsibility, whether it was attaching a part, tightening bolts, or whatever operation could be completed while the vehicle was passing in front of his workstation. Charles Sorenson, Pete Martin, and Childe Wills were the key individuals with supervisory responsibilities during this crucial period, when the concept of the assembly line became the cornerstone of Ford's success. They made constant adjustments to make the line more efficient: to speed up the operation, to minimize the time that workers had to spend walking to get parts, to eliminate bottlenecks that slowed production. Chassis and engine manufacturing were separate operations, but they had to be complementary. On Sundays, when the line was not operating, workers laid out parts at production stations so that the line was set for resumption on Monday morning. Suggestions from workers helped streamline the process. When men on one section of the line complained about backaches from bending over all day, they raised the line on their station to minimize bending.

Ford's production techniques invited discussion of the principles of scientific management, pioneered by Frederick Winslow Taylor. Indeed, Taylorism reached its peak of popularity in the 1910s, at the same time that Ford developed the assembly line at Highland Park. Taylor is best remembered for conducting time and motion studies in which he had associates break down every action taken by factory workers in order to minimize unnecessary motion and reorganize the production process in a more efficient manner. Despite the similarity of goals, Ford was not a follower of Taylor's ideas and in fact had little if any knowledge of them. Charles Sorenson, in his memoir, insisted that the Ford process developed independently and that Ford so distrusted "experts" that he would not have sought their advice. Historian Steven Watts, in his biography of Ford, explains that while Ford "certainly never read Taylor . . . much evidence suggests that the spirit of scientific management was in the air at Highland Park."[4]

4. Steven Watts, *The People's Tycoon: Henry Ford and the American Century* (New York: Alfred A. Knopf, 2005), 153.

Production went up and registered a dramatic increase in sales. In 1911, the first year of full production at Highland Park, Ford sold 34,528 Model T Ford automobiles. Model T sales and production approximately doubled as production became more efficient. In the model year 1911–12, it reached 78,440 and the following year 181,951. Ford remained committed to the principle of maximum production and small profit margins per vehicle, a formula that was increasingly effective, and at times during the next fifteen years half the vehicles on the road were Model T Fords. As sales increased, Ford cut prices, from $950 in 1909 to $780 in 1910, $600 in 1912, $550 in 1913, $490 in 1914, and, eventually, in 1924, $290, the lowest it would reach. Other dealers could not keep up, and the number of manufacturers began to drop. Alexander Winton was among the ones who folded, although he held on into the 1920s.

Efficiency had its price. A common complaint, both at Ford and at other factories that adopted the assembly line, was the tedium of doing the same process over and over. This lament was difficult to address, since efficiency depended on workers doing repetitive tasks and not leaving their positions on the line. Ford workers at the time were earning an average of about $2.43 a day, while shareholders were reaping extraordinary rewards that seemed to increase exponentially. Ultimately, the solution was not to solve the question of tedium but to address wages and to pay workers the then-incredible sum of $5.00 a day. No other automobile manufacturer came close, and in fact Ford's $2.43 was not at all out of line. Who originated the idea is not clear, but it was James Couzens who convinced Ford that the move would be great publicity for the company, and Ford decided to go along. In January 1915, at a small press conference attended by a few local reporters, the Ford Motor Company announced the new salary plan.

The announcement sent a shock through Wall Street and in the boardrooms of companies around the country. Other car companies faced a dilemma, since none of them had the operating margin that Ford did. For most of them, to double their wages meant going out of business. Some, including General Motors, increased wages without

2. Three of the great American industrialists of the early twentieth century—Henry Ford, Thomas Edison, and Harvey Firestone—meet with President Warren G. Harding in front of a cabin at Firestone's camp during Harding's presidency (1921–23). *Left to right*: Ford, Edison, Harding, and Firestone. Harris & Ewing Collection, Prints and Photographs Division, Library of Congress, LC-DIG-hec-31268.

matching Ford. Other manufacturers complained that workers were eager to share in their employers' prosperity but unwilling and unable to share in their adversity. Wall Street was aghast; some businessmen saw the Ford Five-Dollar Day as dooming the American economy.

The reaction among Progressives and factory workers was of course very different. Progressive politicians, labor leaders, and the liberal press praised the move, and Henry Ford became a hero of the common man. Samuel Gompers, founder and president of the American Federation of Labor, described Ford as bringing justice to his workers. John Reed, one of the more radical muckrakers (Progressive journalists), praised Ford as a "revolutionist . . . who translates platitudes into action." Thousands of workers from all over the country descended on the Highland Park plant seeking jobs and stood outside the gate in freezing January weather even after the company announced that there were no jobs available. The lines did not dissipate until the company announced that it would hire only workers who had been Detroit residents for at least six months. Despite the hopes of his critics that Ford would not be able to sustain the wage increase, he did so; the five-dollar-a-day decision made Ford a national icon, much more than an automobile manufacturer.

Ford had visions of an even larger operation, and in 1915, at about the same time he initiated the five-dollar day, he began to purchase land south of Detroit, near the spot where the Rouge River and the Detroit River merged. He had others buy parcels in their names so that his involvement would not be evident and prices would not shoot up prematurely, and eventually they purchased about two thousand acres. What he had in mind was an enormous enterprise in which he could build cars from raw materials to the end product in one location, a business process called vertical integration. The value of this approach would be to eliminate supply problems. Suppliers could no longer withhold materials in order to force Ford to pay higher prices. In Ford's plan, the Rouge River plant, or "the Rouge," as it became known to Ford workers, would eventually replace the Highland Park plant. The plant was not fully operational until the 1920s, but during World War I it had progressed to the point that it was used for construction of Eagle boats, which were smaller but more maneuverable than destroyers. President Wilson asked Ford to join the Shipping Board because of his expertise in mass production, and when Secretary of the Navy Josephus Daniels learned of the proposed Eagle boat, he ordered one hundred of them. Ford planned assembly-line production, but it was a more complex operation than building cars. The first Eagle came off the line in July 1918, and although Ford kept up with the initial production schedule, none of the Eagle boats saw service in the war. Ford made only a modest profit from his contract on the Eagle boats.

TECHNOLOGY AND THE ECONOMY, PART 2: AN ERA OF INNOVATION

The automobile impacted the way Americans lived for decades, but it was not the only significant technological development of the 1910s. Other inventions improved daily life or formed the basis for scientific advances. In the last years of the decade, technology changed the nature of warfare.

The Panama Canal, initiated with great fanfare during the administration of Theodore Roosevelt, was one of the major engineering feats of the twentieth century. Construction began in 1904, but it took ten years to build and opened to shipping in August 1914. George Washington Goethals had taken over direction of the canal in 1907 and remained in that position until completion. The canal followed a route across Panama initiated by a French company in the 1880s and had to overcome two major problems that had forced the French company to abandon its efforts. The first obstacle was the presence of yellow fever, a debilitating disease that had a death rate of 17.6 percent at the start of construction. William Gorgas led a team of doctors that included Walter Reed in combating the disease. They discovered that the disease was transmitted by mosquitoes, and by launching a mosquito-eradication program they were able to reduce the death rate to only 0.6 percent. The other obstacle was landslides. The canal route was short, only fifty-one miles, but stretches were bordered by mountains. One area, known as the Culebra Cut, had bedeviled the French company with persistent landslides. The Americans were finally able to conquer it with mammoth earthmoving steam shovels. The first ship passed through the canal on August 15, 1914. The first few years were disappointing, mainly because of the war in Europe, but once the war ended the canal earned its reputation alongside the Suez Canal as the world's two major international canals. The Suez Canal eliminated the need to sail around the Cape of Good Hope at the southern tip of Africa, and the Panama Canal eliminated the dangerous trip around Cape Horn at the southern tip of South America.

Improvements and inventions led to major strides in the processing and preservation of food. The tin can had been around for decades, but advances in the understanding of how bacteria endangered food made canning safer. During World War I, the government distributed food in Europe through the Food Administration, and these improvements facilitated this agency's task. It distributed millions of cans of food by the time the war ended. Pasteurization of milk, which killed bacteria often found in raw milk by heating it to 145 degrees, became commonplace quickly when its health benefits became known. More dramatic was the introduction of the first electric refrigerator, the Kelvinator, introduced by A. H. Goss in 1912. It replaced the traditional icebox, an important step in the modernization of the home kitchen.

Another breakthrough in food preservation came when Clarence Birdseye, on an extended fur-trading trip to Labrador, Canada, in 1912, observed the Eskimo practice of freezing fish in the winter. Birdseye noted that when the Eskimos froze fish immediately and quickly, it remained fresh when it was later thawed and cooked. When he returned to the States, he experimented with freezing fruits and vegetables and then introduced his Quick Freeze Machine. In 1925 he obtained financing and started the General Seafood Corporation, which was the start of the frozen-food industry and a boost to refrigeration companies.

Leo Hendrik Baekeland, an American immigrant from Belgium, made a discovery that proved to be the foundation of modern plastics. Working on developing a solvent to clean chemical residue off the experimental equipment used by chemists, he created a residue that would be especially difficult to clean in order to test his solvent. As it turned out, his "residue" was particularly difficult to clean, but it had characteristics that he thought might have other applications. It took the shape of its container as it cooled and remained hard and held that form when he tried to melt it later. He marketed it as "Bakelite" beginning in 1917.

Several European inventions of the 1910s had an impact on American industry by the end of the decade and later. A French chemist developed the first neon light, a system that had its greatest impact in the advertising industry. A German physicist, Max von Laue, discovered X-rays, for which he received the Nobel Prize in Physics in 1914 and which over the years revolutionized medical procedures. A French physicist invented sonar, which in its most immediate application was vital to the war on the North Atlantic against German submarines. After the war sonar had a wide variety of applications in oceanography.

SUGGESTED READINGS

The story of Henry Ford's contributions to the American economy and society are well documented in two recent biographies. Richard Snow's *I Invented the Modern Age: The Rise of Henry Ford* (New York: Scribner, 2013) is an engaging account; Steven Watts's *The People's Tycoon: Henry Ford and the American Century* (New York: Alfred A. Knopf, 2005) is more comprehensive.

5

Social Change in the Late Progressive Era

The decade of the 1910s witnessed social change that impacted the foundations of American politics and society in fundamental ways. The pace of change accelerated, bolstered by the maturation of organizations that had been pressing for change for years or even decades and new organizations, some formed in response to shortcomings of predecessor organizations, others by-products of an atmosphere sympathetic to change, manifested primarily under the broad banner of Progressivism. These organizations included trade unions; organizations dedicated to the rights of women, African Americans, and other disadvantaged minorities; and special interest groups, such as those organizations devoted to a decades-long temperance campaign hoping to pass an amendment devoted to Prohibition.

The most dramatic impact on American society in the 1910s resulted from demographic changes, both from the movement of people within the United States and the arrival of immigrants from Europe. Three major demographic developments had a transformative impact: an influx of people from southern and eastern Europe, a continuation of the so-called New Immigration, which had begun in the late nineteenth century and would run its course by the early 1920s; the Great Migration of African Americans from the South to northern industrial cities in particular, but to other parts of the nation as well; and the movement of people from rural areas of the United States to cities, again a continuation of a pattern of movement that had begun earlier and would culminate in a statistical milestone in the 1920 census, when for the first time the majority of Americans lived in cities. The scale of these migrations made it virtually certain that they would disrupt the status quo, and indeed many of the racial, social, and labor problems of the 1910s had their origins in the adjustment to these demographic changes.

Minorities generally did not fare well in the second decade of the twentieth century. Racism continued to plague black Americans, manifested in lynching, race riots, the reemergence of the Ku Klux Klan (KKK), and discriminatory treatment in many aspects of their lives. Because blacks were denied the vote in the South, they had little political leverage, and neither Republicans nor Democrats supported them. Black Americans could not agree on the best means to change their lot, so their leaders advocated conflicting solutions. Labor also faced challenges. With the exception of modest federal support during World War I, neither the federal government nor the state governments did much on behalf of labor. The courts remained conservative and probusiness. Congress and executive agencies usually sided with management, and in fact after the war the Wilson administration sought to crush radical unions such as the Industrial Workers of the World. Immigrants from Europe and Negroes from the South headed to the industrial cities of the Northeast and Midwest and often found themselves in competition for jobs, a circumstance that allowed employers to play them off against each other, keeping pay low and enabling them to find desperate men willing to serve as strikebreakers. Wretched working conditions and industrial accidents such as the Triangle Shirtwaist fire spawned radicalism, which in turn generated suppression rather than solutions.

THE NEW IMMIGRANTS

The New Immigration pattern, usually cited as beginning in 1890, represented a dramatic shift in the countries of origin of European immigration to the United States. From the colonial period until the late nineteenth century, most European immigrants had come from northern and western Europe—from the British Isles, the Netherlands,

Scandinavia, and Germany. They generally spoke English and were Protestant, and despite some nativist resistance they were able to assimilate into the dominant culture relatively easily. The New Immigrants came from southern and eastern Europe, from Russia, Italy, Austria-Hungary, Poland, and Greece. Few of them spoke English, and most were either Catholic or Jewish. Many came for economic reasons, attracted by stories of jobs available in burgeoning American factories or because of political problems at home. During the 1910s, more immigrants came from each of three nations (Russia, Italy, and Austria-Hungary) than from the United Kingdom, Ireland, France, Germany, Scandinavia, and the Netherlands combined. Immigration peaked in the first half of the decade, when it never fell below 800,000 and topped 1 million twice, whereas in the second half of the decade World War I slowed immigration and it never exceeded 327,000.

The New Immigrants encountered a myriad of problems when they arrived. Ellis Island in New York was the principal port of arrival, and there officials refused admission to many of them because of health issues, and they were immediately deported. When immigration officials found immigrant names difficult to pronounce, they often "Americanized" the names, shortening them to a form more easily pronounced. Once admitted, immigrants had to find housing and jobs. Those arrivals fortunate enough to have relatives meet them found the adjustment eased. In New York Tammany Hall often had agents meet arriving ships and offer assistance to new arrivals. Historians have debated the impact of this practice, for while it linked the immigrants to Tammany Hall and the corrupt boss system, it also provided real benefits to the immigrants, who otherwise would have had no connection to anyone who wielded influence. The diary of Tammany ward boss George Washington Plunkitt reveals ways in which political operatives in the boss system used their influence to curry favor with new immigrants and ensure they would vote for machine candidates but also get them jobs. But housing options for immigrants were limited, jobs were menial, and services minimal. The notorious tenements in New York were crowded environments in which diseases spread quickly, and housing was no better in other industrial cities.

The problems these new arrivals faced were not solely a result of their lack of contacts or their poor understanding of their new environment. Because they were seeking jobs and willing to accept lower wages than those people already employed, these immigrants faced opposition from workers and their unions. Because they were Catholic or Jewish, they faced religious persecution. Because they came from regions of Europe torn by political turmoil and even revolution, the immigrants were immediately suspect, even if they were apolitical. Those arrivals from Russia and Italy in particular faced charges of anarchist or socialist sympathies. Often overlooked in the examination of the rise of European immigration is the fact that it was a two-way immigration, as many immigrants returned to Europe, whether to overcome their disappointment with the opportunities in the United States, to care for their families, or, once the war began, to serve in the military of their native countries.

Despite these challenges, the New Immigrants transformed the cities in which they settled. Already at the beginning of the decade, more than three-quarters of the residents of several industrial cities—New York, Chicago, Detroit, Cleveland, and Boston—were either immigrants or the children of immigrants. Immigrants, torn between their desires to assimilate and to hold on to their native culture, influenced the culture of their new homes. They gathered in enclaves of immigrants from their native countries, forming ethnic neighborhoods in their new homeland, the Little Italies, Little Polands, and so forth that still exist a century later.

LABOR, UNIONS, AND THE GOVERNMENT

The labor movement and the New Immigration were linked in the public mind, both because most of the immigrants were looking for industrial work and thus were likely union recruits and because many Americans associated radical unions and suspect political ideologies such as socialism and anarchism with European immigrants. This association dated to the 1890s, when business leaders were successful in linking unionization with anarchism and socialism during violent strikes such as the Pullman Strike, the Haymarket Square Riot, and the Homestead Strike against Carnegie Steel in Pennsylvania.

By 1910, however, the union situation in the United States was much clearer than it had been twenty years earlier. The American Federation of Labor, founded in 1886, was well established and celebrated its first quarter century in 1911. Samuel Gompers, an immigrant himself (from Britain), was the founder and president of the AFL and remained in that office until his death in 1924. This conservative union had earned general acceptance, even among many business leaders. It organized skilled workers, who could not easily be replaced by strikebreakers, and focused on "bread-and-butter" issues (such as wages and working hours), which allowed management to make concessions without jeopardizing their control of the company. Unions such as the Knights of Labor, which had sought overthrow of the wage system, had such vague and general goals, and goals that could not have been achieved without overthrowing capitalism itself, that they had little chance of success, especially because the courts in the late nineteenth and early twentieth centuries consistently sided with management and the government and against labor and the unions.

In the 1910s, union organization focused on groups left out of the AFL, which included unskilled workers and industries on the periphery of the economy, particularly the textile, mining, and timber industries. The Industrial Workers of the World, also known as the Wobblies, had become the most reviled—or most admired—of the radical unions. It had taken on some of the most difficult unionization challenges on the fringes of the economy but became associated in the public mind with violence, sometimes unfairly. One such case was the bombing of the Los Angeles Times Building on October 1, 1910. Brothers John and James McNamara set a dynamite charge, setting it to go off during the night, when they believed no one would be working. Two things went wrong: a crew was working through the night in order to put out an early edition of the paper, and the timing of the charge misfired. The blast killed twenty-one people, and about a hundred more suffered injuries. Although the brothers were members of a local union, they had nothing to do with the IWW. The bombing seemed to bear a similarity to tactics used by Bill Haywood, an organizer for the IWW, so many believed that the IWW had been responsible, a charge that IWW opponents did not discourage. Big Bill Haywood was the most prominent of the Wobblies. An advocate of direct action—which he differentiated from violence—Haywood was at the center of many IWW activities. But neither he nor the IWW had anything to do with the bombing of the Times Building, which the McNamaras acknowledged as the case unfolded.

The textile industry was involved in two incidents in the early years of the decade, one a tragic accident, the other a major strike. Textile and garment workers were vulnerable to discriminatory acts by employers, since many of them were young women who were desperate for work and had little leverage to pressure employers. The industry also used young children and in fact became the target of Progressive reformers who protested child labor.

New York witnessed one of the most tragic events of the era, a deadly fire that exposed the dreadful nature of working conditions for women in the garment industry. The Triangle Shirtwaist Factory (shirtwaist dresses were styled similar to men's shirts above the waist, with buttons down the front) had been the target of protests in 1909, among the earliest garment-industry protests. The factory occupied the top three floors in the Asch Building, a ten-story structure near the Greenwich Village section of New York. The girls and young women, most of whom were immigrants from Italy or Russia, were mostly either Catholics or Jews. They worked in sweatshop conditions and were paid fifteen dollars for a twelve-hour day. Some of them had joined the International Ladies' Garment Workers' Union, but the factory was nonunion, so the employees were not allowed to organize.

On March 25, 1911, fire broke out in the Asch Building. The lack of safety precautions created a perfect storm, one of the worst industrial disasters in the history of the city prior to the September 11 catastrophe ninety years later. A combination of circumstances turned a fire in a rag bin into a calamitous disaster. A hose near the rag bin had rotted, so nothing stopped the fire from spreading rapidly to the upper floors. The victims were working on the ninth floor, and although

3. A crowd gathers in the aftermath of the fire at the Triangle Shirtwaist Factory in New York City on March 25, 1911. The fire killed 146 women who were trapped in the building as a result of disregard of safety regulations. George Grantham Bain Collection, Prints and Photographs Division, Library of Congress, LC-USZ62-91068.

there were two exits, fire engulfed one and the door from the other was locked from the outside because managers suspected the girls of theft and checked them daily on the way out. Some workers were able to reach a crowded fire escape, but their combined weight bent it and rendered it useless. The factory built flimsy fire escapes rather than a required third interior stairway, and when the fire began one of the fire escapes collapsed, sending about 20 women to their deaths. The fire department arrived, but the water from its hoses could not reach the ninth floor, and its ladders could reach only to the sixth floor, making them useless. Girls and women began to leap to their deaths rather than be consumed by flames. Witnesses below saw them jump and heard them hit the pavement below, and their eyewitness reports added to the sense of tragedy. A total of 146 of the workers died, either from fire or asphyxiation or from jumping. The youngest victims were only fourteen years old, and more than half of the victims (79 of 146) were twenty years old or younger.

The fire inspired another wave of protests and gave impetus to support for suffrage among women working in factory jobs. The outcry that followed led to the indictment of Max Blanck and Isaac Harris, the owners of the building. Unions assisted in rendering aid for the victims' families and in gathering testimony against the owners. Blanck and Harris claimed that their building was fireproof and that they had passed fire inspection, but they were indicted for second-degree manslaughter. A jury trial resulted in a not-guilty verdict because it could not be proved that the two had known that the doors were locked. Ultimately, families filed twenty-three civil suits against them, for which they settled, paying seventy-five dollars per death. The city held an investigation that initiated a new fire code and the passage of new state laws regarding industrial working conditions.

Less than a year after the Triangle disaster, another incident in the Northeast involving the textile industry took place in Lawrence, Massachusetts, about thirty miles north of Boston. The textile mills, particularly the American Woolen Mill, were critical to Lawrence families; it was the largest employer by far. Often husbands and wives worked there and had to put their children to work there at a young age. The average worker received less than nine dollars a week, and if they lived in company housing, as much as two-thirds of that wage had to be paid back to the company. After Massachusetts passed a law mandating a workweek of no more than fifty-four hours, employers cut wages in the textile mills in Lawrence. Workers did not learn of the pay cut until they received their pay on January 11, 1912. The next day workers went on strike. The IWW had already been involved in trying to organize in Lawrence, and national IWW organizers Joe Ettor and Arturo Giovannitti arrived there on the evening of Saturday, January 13. They spent the next day organizing the strike and made demands to the company for a fifty-four-hour workweek, a 15 percent increase in pay with double pay for overtime, and an end to bonus pay, which the company had used to manipulate workers to work extra hours. The

4. Big Bill Haywood (the tall man in the center with the black bowler hat) leads a textile strike parade in Lowell, Massachusetts, in 1912. George Grantham Bain Collection, Prints and Photographs Division, Library of Congress, LC-DIG-ggbain-10357.

workers included immigrants from Italy, eastern Europe, and Canada, and Ettor's ability to speak some of the languages of the strikers made him particularly effective.

Confrontations continued for the next two weeks, with the local police and militia assisting the company. Police turned fire hoses on the protesters in the cold January weather, and the strikers threw handfuls of ice back. On January 29 police fired into a picket line, killing a woman. Authorities blamed the strikers for inciting the violence and arrested both Ettor and Giovannitti. The IWW responded by sending some of its most well-known organizers, including Big Bill Haywood, Elizabeth Gurley Flynn, William Trautmann, and Carlo Tresca, to continue to assist the strikers. During the ten weeks of the strike, 355 strikers were arrested. The police "discovered" stashes of dynamite and blamed the IWW and the strikers, but as the story developed it came out that the local papers had printed the story before the "discovery" took place. By this time the strike was receiving national news coverage, and the company realized it was receiving bad press. Finally, the company agreed to negotiate, and on March 12 negotiators announced a settlement. Workers received pay increases ranging from 5 percent for the highest-paid workers to 20 percent for the lowest paid, and the company made concessions on overtime pay and bonus pay. It was a rare triumph for the IWW that stirred emotions early in the year of a presidential election.

The United Mine Workers of America had represented miners since 1890, but management still considered it to be a radical union. Miners in Colorado had been trying to join the UMWA, but the mining companies, particularly the Colorado Fuel and Iron Company, owned by John D. Rockefeller, had resisted recognition. In April 1914 miners in Ludlow, Colorado, went on strike. The company evicted about 1,200 miners and their families from company-owned housing, so the miners set up tents on public land. The company's security force worked with the Colorado National Guard to break the strike. On April 20 the guardsmen and the security force set up a machine gun on the outskirts of the tent compound and attacked. Miners, anticipating trouble, had dug shallow indentations under the tents so their families could avoid gunfire. The attackers used kerosene to set fires, initiating what came to be called the Ludlow Massacre. Investigators later found the bodies of 2 women and 11 children under one tent site, and in all at least 19 and perhaps as many as 26 people died. In the aftermath miners staged guerrilla attacks on mines and mining properties and had clashes with National Guardsmen that resulted in more deaths. Reports of the toll varied, with the highest estimate set at 199. A House committee investigated the massacre and its aftermath, and its report influenced child labor laws and helped establish an eight-hour day in Colorado mines.

In 1913 the Commission on Industrial Relations, a federal agency established in response to Progressive pressure in the final days of the Taft administration, began a series of hearings that continued for the next two years. It brought forth testimony that aired the grievances of workers in marginal industries, a rare occasion in a federal venue. The commission's chairman, Frank Walsh, had himself worked in a factory as a child and made sure that among the witnesses called to testify, the perspective of workers would receive its due. Witnesses included survivors of the Triangle Shirtwaist Factory calamity and the Ludlow Massacre. Big Bill Haywood was a key witness, and he described strikes in which he had participated and violence against workers by the management, often with the cooperation of the government. The commission's final report was an extraordinary document that concluded, "Violence is a natural form of protest against injustice."[1]

Child labor became a divisive issue mainly as a result of practices in the textile mills. Women especially took up the cause, and the Triangle fire and the Lawrence strike both added ammunition to their arguments. Employers fought their efforts, and families that needed even the meager wages earned by their children opposed reform, arguing that children had worked on farms for generations. Southern states, where many textile mills operated, insisted that it was a state issue, not a federal one. The National Child Labor Committee, founded in 1904 and chartered by Congress in 1907, became the strongest advocate for child labor laws at both the state and the federal levels. It pushed for the establishment of a federal agency dedicated to child labor reform, and in April 1912 this campaign paid off with the establishment of the US Children's Bureau. Julia Lathrop, who had long experience working on women's issues, including work at Hull House in Chicago with Jane Addams, headed the Children's Bureau, the first woman to preside over a federal agency.

The efforts of these organizations, aided by other Progressives, came to fruition in Congress in February 1915, with the passage of the Palmer bill in the House by a margin of 232 to 44. President Wilson

1. Cited in Beverly Gage, *The Day Wall Street Exploded: A Story of America in Its First Age of Terror* (New York: Oxford Univ. Press, 2009), 95.

was uncertain about the constitutionality of the measure, but the congressional session ended before the Senate could vote. Proponents came back the next year and passed the Keating-Owen Act in 1916. The act forbade the interstate shipment of any goods made using child labor, prevented children under age sixteen from working in dangerous locations (and under fourteen in safer situations), and made it illegal for them to work more than eight hours a day. The bill passed the House easily, but southern Democrats blocked it in the Senate, opposing it on the basis both of states' rights and the loss of cheap labor that had drawn textile mills to the South in the first place. This time President Wilson lobbied forcefully, and the southern senators did not try to filibuster. The law passed with only 12 dissenting votes. But while the states' right argument had failed in Congress, it succeeded in the Supreme Court, which declared the law unconstitutional. It took until 1941 before a national child labor law held up in Congress and the Supreme Court.

Progressive reformers were more successful in winning passage of workmen's compensation. By 1916 such measures had won approval in thirty-five states, and Congress passed the Kern-McGillicuddy Act. Reformers also fought for welfare payments for single mothers, or "mothers' pensions," as they were called at the time. The federal government failed to act in this case, but by the end of the decade thirty-nine states had approved these "pensions."

Despite modest legislative progress and the testimony before the Commission on Industrial Relations, sporadic violence continued to characterize labor-management relations in the years leading to American participation in World War I. Violence became commonplace, so much so that people spoke of an anarchist scare of 1914–15. The war itself became the focus of criticism, as protesters complained about big business profiting from the war. In July 1916 a bomb interrupted a Preparedness Parade in San Francisco, killing ten people and injuring forty others. Although the Wilson administration and police in major cities sought to control the violence, there would be more of it before the decade ended.

AFRICAN AMERICANS AND THE PERSISTENCE OF RACISM

The African American diaspora, or the Great Migration, had its roots in the post-Reconstruction problems in the American South and in the employment opportunities afforded by industrialization in the North. Beginning in 1915 African Americans began departing the segregated South in ever-increasing numbers. As soldiers left for service in World War I, job openings became plentiful. Repelled by conditions in the rural South, where agriculture had been depressed and cotton production had fallen due to boll-weevil infestation, African Americans found the opportunities in the North irresistible. Furthermore, conditions in the South for African Americans in general had eroded after the end of Reconstruction. Legal segregation impacted housing, public transportation, and public facilities.

Impediments to voting such as literacy tests, the grandfather clause, poll taxes, and the white primary rendered African Americans politically impotent. Poll taxes were usually cumulative: if an African American had the temerity to try to register to vote, he had to pay a poll tax not only for the election at hand but also for a specified number of previous elections at which he had not voted, thus requiring a fee far beyond the capacity of new voters to pay. Literacy tests, administered by segregationist registrars, required impossible demonstrations of literacy, such as reciting or interpreting a section of the state constitution to the satisfaction of the registrar, who could disqualify virtually anyone. The white primary excluded African Americans from voting in primaries run by state parties, and in the South, where victory in the Democratic Party primary ensured victory, the general election simply ratified victors in the primary. And as if these tactics were insufficient, violence, intimidation, and the threat of losing jobs or property excluded meaningful African American voting.

Lynching continued unabated: only once in the 1910s did the number of lynchings of African Americans drop below fifty, in 1917 when thirty-six lynchings occurred. Agricultural work became migratory labor, in one sense even worse than before the Civil War. Under slavery slave owners had a vested interest in maintaining the health and fitness of their workers; after Reconstruction they could tie workers to the land with a system of debt peonage, and if these laborers wore down or had health problems, farmers could fire them with no consequences and find replacements with little effort.

The Great Migration thus was a response to employment opportunities in the North and horrible conditions in the South. With no effective advocates in the South, African Americans began to take matters into their own hands. Journalist Isabel Wilkerson, whose family was part of the migration, calculates that in 1900, 90 percent of African Americans lived in the South and that between 1915 and 1970 some six million African Americans fled the region to the Northeast, the Midwest, and the West. Northern cities such as New York, Cleveland, Detroit, and Chicago experienced a 40 percent increase in their African American populations, and by 1970 half of the African Americans in the nation lived outside the South. In the South whites who had long exploited African American labor tried to prevent them from leaving.

Advocates emerged to represent African Americans, and the most prominent demonstrate the diversity in leadership and indeed among African Americans as a group. The best-known and most politically powerful of these new leaders was Booker T. Washington, whose advocacy for industrial education won support among white politicians, business leaders, and philanthropists. W. E. B. DuBois emerged as a powerful critic of Washington's approach, and as the editor of the journal of the NAACP he had a forum for developing his argument that African Americans deserved full citizenship immediately and that the "Talented Tenth" (the top 10 percent) ought to lead them in demanding these rights. Marcus Garvey, the youngest of the three, was a Jamaican-born black nationalist who sought to mobilize the African American masses through a series of enterprises in the late 1910s and early 1920s. Although ultimately Garvey failed, he inspired a generation and demonstrated the untapped potential of the African American underclass.

Foremost among African American leaders in the late nineteenth century, and at the height of his influence in the early 1910s, was Booker T. Washington. Born into slavery in 1856, Washington graduated from Hampton Institute in Virginia. In 1881 he founded Tuskegee Institute in Alabama and there developed his philosophy of industrial education (or vocational training), believing that the best route to full citizenship for African Americans was to prove their worth at manual labor. Students at Tuskegee learned to grow their own food, to make bricks, and to become self-sufficient. George Washington Carver served on the Tuskegee faculty, and his experiments with products made from peanuts and his recommendations for crop rotation to cotton farmers earned him a reputation that augmented Tuskegee's growing influence.

In 1895 Washington gave a famous address that became known as the "Atlanta Compromise," in which he urged African Americans to "cast down their buckets" where they were rather than aspiring to unrealistic goals. He urged African Americans to learn skills that were useful in the jobs that were available to them and not to worry about political equality in the short term. In turn he asked white employers to give jobs to African Americans. His appeal won the support of white elites, and when Washington approached them to ask for money to support colleges that educated African Americans who subscribed to his recipe for success, they contributed. Washington's influence grew, and soon he became the gatekeeper for white philanthropy to assist African American education—wealthy philanthropists would not contribute without Washington's approval of the applicant.

Critics soon emerged, rejecting the notion that African Americans had to accept second-class citizenship. Foremost among them was W. E. B. DuBois, who had attended Fisk University in Nashville and graduated from Harvard University, where he then pursued graduate work, earning a Phi Beta Kappa key and a PhD. DuBois was diametrically opposed to Washington's formula for African American success. DuBois argued that African Americans should not have to wait for admission to full citizenship. Hadn't they earned it through generations of enslavement? Hadn't the Fifteenth Amendment guaranteed it? In his influential book *The Souls of Black Folk* (1901), he insisted that race—the color line—was the major problem facing the nation in the dawning century. He argued that the Talented Tenth, the top

10 percent of African American students, should pursue a liberal arts education and demand full citizenship. In 1905 DuBois joined other African American intellectuals to found a new organization dedicated to achieving rights of citizenship for black Americans and an end to racial discrimination. Meeting near Niagara Falls, New York, they were unable to find lodging that would accept African Americans, so they crossed into Canada. They founded a new organization that they called the Niagara Movement. The new organization established thirty chapters but fell victim to a lack of funding and organizational problems and disbanded in 1910.

The failure of the Niagara Movement was a temporary setback and in fact provided a basis for a new national organization. In 1909 and 1910 two new national interracial organizations filled the void and became stalwarts for decades in the struggle for civil rights. The first was the National Association for the Advancement of Colored People, founded in 1909. DuBois was among the leaders of the NAACP from the beginning. Seven of the sixty founders, including DuBois and Ida B. Wells-Barnett, were African American. White founders included journalist Oswald Garrison Villard and Mary White Ovington, a social worker who had written a study of racial discrimination. The list of members included luminaries of social activism of the era, including Jane Addams, Lillian Wald, and Florence Kelley, all of whom were involved in the settlement-house movement; Clarence Darrow and brothers Joel and Arthur Spingarn, all lawyers; Mary McLeod Bethune, an African American educator who later advised President Franklin D. Roosevelt on minority affairs; John Dewey, a philosopher and educator; William Dean Howells, a prominent author, editor, and critic; and Lincoln Steffens and Ray Stannard Baker, both writers on social issues. DuBois was at the center of the enterprise and had a prominent public presence as the editor of the *Crisis*, the organization's journal.

The NAACP played a vital role in defending African Americans who were victims of discrimination. The NAACP scored some early victories. Moorfield Storey, the lead attorney in two such cases, won significant victories. In 1915 the Supreme Court invalidated

Oklahoma's grandfather clause, a law passed five years earlier that denied the vote to anyone whose grandfather had not voted before 1865, thus disqualifying African Americans from voting. Even a conservative Supreme Court had to acknowledge that the law violated the Fifteenth Amendment. Two years later, in the case *Buchanan v. Worley*, the Court struck down a Louisville law that designated blocks as white only or black only, a violation of the Fourteenth Amendment in the Court's decision.

In 1910 another organization, the Committee on Urban Conditions among Negroes, helped African Americans moving to New York find housing and jobs. It later merged with two other organizations, opened offices in other northern cities, and became known simply as the National Urban League. Another interracial group, its two founders were George Edmund Haynes, the first African American to earn a PhD at Columbia University, and white philanthropist Ruth Standish Baldwin.

The emergence of the NAACP and the Urban League gave new voice to advocates for reform of American racist policies and institutions. For the first half of the decade of the 1910s, the NAACP and the Urban League swayed the internal struggle for leadership among African Americans toward DuBois's advocacy of insistence on the rights of citizenship and away from Booker T. Washington's argument for industrial education. Supporters of DuBois and his successors never relinquished that position, and the modern civil rights movement had echoes of DuBois's victory. But historian Robert J. Norrell has argued that Washington's critics, most of whom lived, worked, and advocated change outside of the Deep South, failed to understand the limitations under which Washington had to operate. When Washington died in 1915, DuBois praised him as "the greatest Negro leader since Frederick Douglass," but summarized his criticism of Washington as bearing responsibility for "the consummation of Negro disenfranchisement, the decline of the Negro college and public school and the firmer establishment of color caste in this land."

Marcus Garvey was among those individuals inspired by Booker T. Washington's vision of Negro progress through industrial training, and he considered Washington's *Up from Slavery* (1901) an important influence. Garvey's black nationalism bore little resemblance to Washington's approach, however, and became controversial as it experienced spectacular achievements and calamitous failures. Born in Jamaica in 1887, Garvey experienced racism as a young man. Working in a printing office in Kingston, Jamaica, he gained experience in organizing workers during a strike. He also worked for the American corporation United Fruit Company in Costa Rica, where he witnessed the exploitation of black laborers. By 1914 he had established an organization he called the Universal Negro Improvement Association (UNIA), which he brought with him to the United States two years later. He had hoped to meet with Booker T. Washington, and Washington had agreed to meet with him, but the older leader died before Garvey arrived in the States in 1916.

Garvey determined to promote his vision of Negro success through the UNIA. In 1917 he crusaded in Harlem in New York City, where he established his headquarters and preached racial pride, telling his audiences that Negroes could succeed on their own, and supported a back-to-Africa movement. He began publishing a newspaper called *Negro World*, a vehicle for promoting his philosophy. Within two years Garvey claimed that it had a circulation of two hundred thousand. That number may be exaggerated, as were his estimates of the membership of the UNIA, which he claimed ran into the millions. Whatever the numbers, there is no question that he succeeded in establishing a mass membership organization of considerable influence. In 1919 he purchased Liberty Hall in Harlem, which became his headquarters and the site of UNIA conventions in the early 1920s.

Garvey's most ambitious venture, a black-owned and -managed shipping line called the Black Star Line, won support of African Americans across the country, mainly through mail and newspaper solicitations. Skeptics doubted that the effort would ever leave port, but Garvey eventually purchased three ships, and the Black Star Line became a source of intense pride among its supporters. Nonetheless, its critics had the last word, as the shipping line was a disappointing failure. Garvey overpaid for the ships, and the captain of his first ship

5. Marcus Garvey at the time of a national convention of his Universal Negro Improvement Association in New York's Madison Square Garden in August 1920. New York World-Telegram & Sun Collection, Prints and Photographs Division, Library of Congress, LC-USZ62-109627.

allegedly betrayed him, receiving a kickback for the purchase price. Garvey and his associates had little or no experience in administering or operating ships or a shipping line, and each of the voyages ended in failure owing to breakdowns or management mistakes. Ultimately, Garvey was indicted and imprisoned for mail fraud in connection with his fund-raising campaign, and after serving two years in prison he was deported to Jamaica.

The legacy of the Garvey phenomenon is as complicated as the man himself. Other black leaders castigated him after he met with the leader of the Ku Klux Klan and reached agreement on a back-to-Africa plan. Yet even his harshest critics had to acknowledge his achievements. W. E. B. DuBois called him "the most dangerous enemy of the Negro race in America and the world," but later granted his "tremendous vision" and "unselfish desire to serve." Writer Claude McKay, himself an immigrant from Jamaica, called Garvey a "West Indian charlatan," but conceded in the 1930s that he "aroused the social consciousness of the Negro masses more than any leader ever did."

The society that inspired leaders such as Washington, DuBois, and Garvey remained racist in many respects. The South after Reconstruction institutionalized segregation. Even after blacks received citizenship and the right to vote through the Fourteenth and Fifteenth Amendments, southern states found ways to deny the rights of citizens. Cities passed regulations demanding residential segregation and mandated the segregation of public facilities. States denied blacks the right to vote through devices such as poll taxes, literacy tests, and the white primary. A conservative Supreme Court routinely approved of segregation. When President Theodore Roosevelt invited Booker T. Washington to dinner at the White House, it sparked a wave of protest. President Taft had paid little attention to blacks, and in fact sought to win support from whites in the South by removing black Republicans from office in the region, although he modified this policy during his 1912 reelection campaign.

Woodrow Wilson was a southerner by birth and temperament. He never understood the depth of the racial problem, and African

Americans suffered setbacks during his presidency. William Monroe Trotter, the editor of the Boston-based African American newspaper the *Guardian*, had supported Wilson for the presidency, but on November 12, 1914, he led a delegation to meet with the president. Trotter expressed their disappointment with Wilson's performance on race issues. Wilson offered generalizations, suggesting that it takes generations to overcome prejudice. Trotter was not satisfied with palliatives and insisted that the delegation was there as "full-fledged American citizens." Wilson asked to leave politics out, but Trotter pressed on, and Wilson lost his temper. Trotter would not back off and insisted that the group was there to represent "a part of the people." Wilson retorted, "You have spoiled the whole cause for which you came." Wilson later regretted his response—but not the substance of his remarks, indicating a genuine lack of understanding of the situation African Americans faced. He told one of the southerners in his cabinet that instead of losing his temper, he should have told Trotter that of course his issue would receive attention, and "no more would be heard about the matter." Yet the issue troubled Wilson, and he tried to respond—yet seldom took action. He spoke out against lynching, for example, but did not demonstrate a commitment to end it.

The year of Washington's death also witnessed the emergence of a renewed threat to the status of African Americans. The release of the blockbuster movie *The Birth of a Nation* renewed vicious stereotypes of African Americans with a racist depiction of the Reconstruction South. Two examples suffice to demonstrate its racist content. It portrays blacks elected to the South Carolina state legislature eating fried chicken in the legislative chamber with their feet on desks. It also shows a former slave lusting after one of the white heroines and pursuing her in a chase scene that leads to rescue by the Klan, riding in on horseback in the climactic scene of the film. White audiences in the North and South cheered the Klan's rescue scene, but blacks and their supporters staged protests across the nation.

Release of *The Clansman* (the title of the film when released, although it was soon to be renamed) in January 1915 touched off protests in major cities from Los Angeles to Boston. Several obstacles made it difficult to launch a successful campaign against the film. Progressives and others who were most disturbed by the racism in the film were also likely to be opposed to government-imposed censorship. This position posed a dilemma that divided opponents of the movie: should their goal be to force censorship on the film's racist content or simply to register their opposition to its blatant racism? The NAACP was still a young organization, not yet six years old when the movie opened, and had only five thousand members. Thus, in addition to the question of whether the organization ought to take on a protest against the movie, there was the practical matter of whether local chapters could sustain a prolonged protest. Furthermore, the NAACP already had a long agenda of cases regarding discriminatory legislation.

Thomas Dixon, the author of the book upon which the movie was based, had been a classmate of President Wilson at Johns Hopkins in the 1880s, and he used that relationship to offer to show the movie to the president. Wilson accepted, and on February 18 *The Birth of a Nation* became the first movie to be shown in the White House. Dignitaries, including the chief justice of the Supreme Court, thirty-eight senators, and some fifty members of Congress, attended the showing in the East Room with Wilson and his daughters. An unproved story circulated later that upon conclusion of the showing, Wilson commented, "It is like writing history with lightning. And my only regret is that it is all so terribly true." In the 1970s the only living person to have attended the showing denied that Wilson had said anything at the end of the movie but simply left the room.

Protests in Los Angeles and New York accomplished little beyond a few minor cuts in the film. (Cuts of this sort in other cities meant that many versions of the movie circulated, making it difficult for film historians to designate an official original print.) An attempt to reverse a decision by the National Board of Censorship to allow the film resulted in an affirmation of the board's decision. In New York, where one protester claimed that opponents of the film "tried everything," these actions failed. And because the NAACP was biracial and in fact majority white, historian Melvyn Stokes concluded that the campaign failed because it was "a war fought to defend blacks but waged primarily by whites," and a small minority of whites at that.[2]

Boston, however, took a different course. The city's abolitionist tradition, Mayor James Michael Curley's reliance on black votes and formation of a minority coalition, and a press sympathetic to minority issues all contributed to a climate favorable to protest. Furthermore, the presence of one of the more radical African American leaders, William Monroe Trotter, meant that the protesters would not back down easily. Trotter had impeccable intellectual credentials. Like DuBois, he was a Harvard graduate, a Phi Beta Kappa honoree, and the editor of an influential publication that addressed the racial problem in American society—in Trotter's case an African American newspaper, the *Guardian*.

The movie also gave impetus to the revival of the Ku Klux Klan. The Klan's first incarnation occurred during Reconstruction after the Civil War, and during that era it defended the South from reforms imposed by the Radical Republicans in Congress, carpetbaggers (northerners who went South to administer Reconstruction and, in the eyes of southerners, to profit at their expense), and former slaves whom Congress sought to bring into full citizenship, including political participation (voting and running for office). Before its suppression, the KKK became a terrorist organization that targeted blacks, threatening them with violence and often carrying out those threats. The movie *The Birth of a Nation* celebrated the Klan and portrayed blacks in flagrantly racist terms.

The rebirth of the Klan was the work of William J. Simmons, a former Methodist preacher and a veteran of the war with Spain, who revived the Klan under a charter issued by the state of Georgia. On December 4, 1915, Simmons staged a ritual lighting of a cross at Stone Mountain near Atlanta. The reborn Klan was more inclusive in its victims than its earlier iteration, targeting Jews, Catholics, and

2. Melvyn Stokes, *D. W. Griffith's "Birth of a Nation"* (New York: Oxford Univ. Press, 2007), 140.

recent immigrants (and the unions that represented them) in addition to blacks. Thus, it became a national organization in comparison to the regional following of its predecessor, with genuine political power in states such as Oregon and Indiana as well as in states of the Old South. Simmons's motive in forming the Klan had more to do with moneymaking than with carrying out the Klan's ideology, and he had only modest success until 1920, when he enlisted Edward Young Clarke and Elizabeth Tyler as publicists. Clarke and Tyler received 80 percent of proceeds from the ten-dollar initiation fee and the sale of Klan regalia. They marketed the Klan as protecting America from assault by foreigners and minorities opposed to American values, projecting a "positive" message that justified the organization's underlying racism, anti-Semitism, and xenophobia. The Klan capitalized on terror and violence against its adversaries. Lynchings became common not only in the South, and the political power of southerners in Congress enabled them to forestall attempts to pass antilynching legislation by claiming it was a state issue, not federal. By 1921 the Klan exceeded one hundred thousand members, and it continued to surge into the mid-1920s, even staging a parade in 1925 of some forty thousand Klansmen down Pennsylvania Avenue in Washington, DC. Ultimately, the Klan's demise resulted from corruption, internal dissension, and newspaper exposés.

FEMINIST REFORM AND THE WOMEN'S SUFFRAGE MOVEMENT

Women had long been in the forefront of American reform movements and had often subordinated their own rights in order to press for the rights of others. During the early nineteenth century, they had championed campaigns for temperance and prison reform. Before the Civil War they had supported the abolition of slavery, and after the war they promoted citizenship rights for African Americans. By midcentury, however, women began to address issues concerning the status of women in American society and found that their concerns resonated with women across the country. They raised questions related to the rights of married women, whose property became her husband's property when they became husband and wife. This and other inequities in areas such as education, the law, the workplace, and religion became the targets of reformers. The most eloquent statement of their intentions came as a result of a conference held in Seneca Falls, New York, in 1848, where women wrote a "Declaration of Rights and Sentiments" patterned after the Declaration of Independence, insisting that married women were, "in the eye of the law, civilly dead" and that women had been deprived of their "inalienable right to the elective franchise."

Women in the early twentieth century continued to promote a variety of social causes and became involved in the Progressive movement to further reforms on issues including child labor, temperance, and civil rights. Socialist Elizabeth Gurley Flynn came to prominence as a nineteen-year-old in 1909 when she led a protest advocating free speech in Spokane, Washington, and during the 1910s she worked to organize women in the garment industry. Women became active in union activities in the 1910s, where the garment industry became a particular focus. The International Ladies' Garment Workers' Union, founded in 1900, grew to become the third-largest affiliate of the AFL in the 1910s, expanding largely as a result of textile industry strikes and industrial accidents (such as the Triangle Shirtwaist Factory disaster). Anarchist Emma Goldman, a charismatic speaker and leading feminist, published the anarchist journal *Mother Earth* from 1906 until her arrest for opposing the draft in 1917. She advocated labor reform and became one of the first reformers to advocate birth control, an issue also promoted by Margaret Sanger.

Increasingly, however, many women began to focus on winning the vote, believing that only by gaining the vote would they be able to have a lasting impact on the social issues that concerned them. In 1869 Elizabeth Cady Stanton and Susan B. Anthony formed the National Woman Suffrage Association, the first organization dedicated exclusively to women's rights. The following year Lucy Stone and Henry Blackwell, believing that the NWSA was too confrontational, founded the American Woman Suffrage Association (AWSA). The campaign for women's suffrage remained divided, with agreement that the vote for women ought to be their goal, but with disagreements over a range of questions such as whether they ought to seek a national amendment or work state by state, whether they should work with men to achieve their goal, and whether they should focus exclusively on the vote or support other social reforms as well. In 1890, however, the two major women's suffrage organizations merged, forming the National American Woman Suffrage Association (NAWSA), and the suffragettes united on the single goal of a national suffrage amendment.

By 1910 the trio of late-nineteenth-century suffrage leaders—Stanton, Anthony, and Stone—had all died, and leadership passed on to a new generation of women leaders. New leaders retained the commitment of the earlier generation, but their argument had become more pragmatic. Whereas the early leaders claimed rights based on the natural rights philosophy of the Declaration of Independence, many younger women had worked in pitiful conditions in factories in the garment industry and wanted the vote in order to pressure factory owners to respond to their grievances. This emphasis gave a new impetus to the suffrage campaign, but it also caused some fractures because women working in industrial jobs had priorities above obtaining the vote. The division between the concerns of working-class women and middle-class women festered and often undercut both the union movement and the suffrage campaign.

Other factors divided the suffrage movement. The notion of separate spheres for men and women had broad support among both genders. Women's sphere in the home, the church, and the community gave them responsibilities of crucial importance in the development of their children and society, and many people accepted this arrangement as the natural order of things. For women to enter politics, a world in which corrupting influences often emerged, would diminish their role in their natural sphere and undermine their moral leadership. Many of these women became antisuffragists and in 1911 organized the National Association Opposed to Woman Suffrage.

Women working in the garment industry began to protest working conditions, and for many women questions of economic inequality were a more urgent goal than suffrage. Women in the garment industry often had to work as many as twelve hours a day for six or seven days a week. Workers earned as little as $3.50 a week and had to provide their own needles and thread to sew on the job. Employers ignored complaints about safety violations, dim lighting, and low wages. Women mounted protests in New York, Philadelphia, Chicago, and Lowell, Massachusetts.

Horrid working conditions drove women not only to the streets for protests but to unions as well. The Women's Trade Union League (WTUL) was unusual in that it brought together working-class women and wealthier women who sympathized with their cause and who were able to persuade men in positions of influence. These middle- and upper-class women served as witnesses, raised money, and insisted that they be arrested with their striking poorer working sisters. Protest parades in New York City in 1910 and 1911 drew thousands of marchers and tens of thousands of spectators.

Another constituency among women included reformers active in Progressive campaigns in a variety of issues, many of which grew out of the concerns of women working in industry. Like those reformers inspired by the Triangle fire, they wanted laws to improve factory safety. They also sought reform in wages and working hours and regulation of child labor. They were also in the forefront of the movement in support of Prohibition.

The settlement-house movement was both an engine of reform and a training ground for leaders of the next generation of women reformers and leaders. Settlement houses were residences located in poor urban areas where women—and some men—lived in order to provide social and educational services to poor people and recent immigrants. The most prominent of the settlement houses was Hull House in Chicago, founded and run by Jane Addams. Lillian Wald, an Addams protégé, founded Henry House in New York, another prominent settlement house. Women who had been involved in the settlement-house movement were also concerned with a range of social issues. Florence Kelley, a veteran of the movement who had worked with Jane Addams at Hull House, served as vice president of the National Consumers League; she also headed the child labor committee of the General Federation of Women's Clubs and led it to endorse the suffrage campaign. Jane Addams herself was an officer in the NAWSA and a board member of the WTUL as well as an adviser to Theodore Roosevelt, and she too pressed for women's suffrage.

In spite of the merger of the AWSA and the NWSA, the suffrage movement continued to have internal disagreements. State-by-state voting had begun, with mixed results. In 1912 Arizona, Kansas, and Oregon held state referenda and passed women's suffrage, bringing the total number of states that had passed the proposal to nine. But three more populous states in the Midwest—Michigan, Ohio, and Wisconsin—all defeated women's suffrage.

In 1913 Alice Paul of the NAWSA, impatient with the pace of the campaign, formed the Congressional Union within the NAWSA with

6. Suffragettes campaign prior to President Wilson's inauguration, protesting the lack of Democratic support for women's suffrage, March 3, 1913. George Grantham Bain Collection, Prints and Photographs Division, Library of Congress, LC-DIG-ggbain-11400.

the goal of pursuing a federal amendment. She organized a protest of five thousand women to march in Washington on the day before Wilson's inauguration, demanding that the Democrats pay a price for failing to support women's suffrage. Of the three major candidates for the presidency, only Theodore Roosevelt had endorsed women's suffrage. The NAWSA was generally more conservative than Alice Paul, and the following year the Congressional Union severed its ties to the NAWSA.

Alice Paul's decision to take the Congressional Union out of the NAWSA ushered in a difficult year for the suffrage campaign. Seven states held referenda on women's suffrage, and only two of them passed it. A Senate committee published a report on suffrage, favoring its passage, but when the whole Senate voted, the amendment failed. A House committee issued a report without a recommendation, but the whole House voted it down. Paul formed a new organization, the National Women's Party, which pursued a more radical approach than the NAWSA. In 1917, in an effort to keep the focus on suffrage while people were shifting their attention to the war, the National Women's Party began picketing the White House, occasionally chaining themselves to the fence in front. Members carried placards, sometimes with quotations from the president's speeches that made it appear that he was being hypocritical in refusing to support the vote for women. Men often jeered at the picketers and reportedly beat some of them while the police looked the other way. In July several women were arrested, and although President Wilson quickly pardoned them, they received ample publicity, embarrassing the administration. Arrested again in November, they endured horrible conditions in Occoquan Workhouse. Guards beat some of the women, and all received spoiled food. Alice Paul went on a hunger strike protesting this treatment, and guards force-fed her raw eggs, which of course only put more pressure on the administration when news got out.

Former NAWSA president Carrie Chapman Catt, a protégé of Susan B. Anthony, continued her more conservative suffrage plan. In 1915 the NAWSA elected her president, and she set in motion a strategy she called a "Winning Plan." It proposed that the campaign should employ both the state-by-state approach and the quest for a national amendment. The approaches were not mutually exclusive, for when states approved women's suffrage, the movement gained elected officials who supported suffrage. And the state-by-state approach had incremental successes. Montana approved women's suffrage in 1914 and in 1916 elected Jeannette Rankin to Congress, the first woman to be so honored. In 1917 she cast a vote against American entry into World War I, and a quarter century later she also voted against entry into World War II—the only person to vote against American involvement in both world wars.

The Constitution allows two means of amendment. The only method ever used is a vote by two-thirds of both houses of Congress, followed by ratification by three-fourths of the state legislatures, which at the time meant at least thirty-six states. The other method requires a constitutional convention and has never been attempted. Catt wanted to secure the endorsement of as many states as possible prior to the votes in the House and Senate in order to demonstrate broad national interest. An important piece fell into place when President Wilson decided to endorse the amendment. Wilson had long resisted endorsing it despite being pressured by his daughters, particularly Margaret. In January 1918, Wilson came out for the amendment and urged Democrats to support it. The measure passed the House by a single vote, 274 to 136. Months later, the scene shifted to the Senate, where indications were that it was still 2 votes short. Wilson, urged by suffragists and McAdoo, decided to address the Senate prior to the vote. Speaking before Congress on September 30, 1918, he cited the support women had given to the war effort as a debt that needed to be paid. Wilson went further, proclaiming, "It is vital to the right solution of the great problems which we must settle, and settle immediately, when this war is over." His speech met with resistance from the senators, many of whom considered it a breach of the separation of powers, particularly since the president has no official role in the amendment process, and the address changed no votes. The amendment went down to defeat once again. But the president's gesture was indicative of a shifting mood in the country.

The proposal came before Congress once again in the spring of 1919. This time, momentum favored passage, and there were no cliff-hanging votes in either chamber. The House voted its approval on May 21, 1919, by a vote of 304 to 89. Two weeks later, on June 4, the Senate added its concurrence by a vote of 56 to 25. The final step was to register an affirmative vote by thirty-six of the state legislatures. The staunchest opposition came not from the antisuffragists, but rather from the liquor interests, who feared that if women got the vote, an amendment in favor of Prohibition was more likely to win approval. In states where the voting margin in the legislature was thin, liquor interests threatened to campaign against legislators who supported women's suffrage. One such story emerged in Tennessee, the thirty-sixth state to vote for ratification. On August 18, 1920, twenty-four-year-old Harry Burns, who hoped to escape voting because of such a threat, broke a 48–48 deadlock in the Tennessee Legislature after receiving an encouraging note from his mother. With his vote the Nineteenth Amendment to the Constitution was ratified, and women had the vote in time to cast ballots in the presidential election of 1920.

PROHIBITION

The temperance movement originated in the 1830s and 1840s, an earlier era of reforming zeal in which women played a prominent role. The movement took root mainly in Protestant denominations, especially the Baptist and Methodist Churches. By the 1870s, the movement had enlisted the support of many women active in the suffrage campaign, including luminaries such as Susan B. Anthony and Elizabeth Cady Stanton. The Women's Christian Temperance Union, founded in 1873, took the lead in the Prohibition crusade, especially during the tenure of its second president, Frances Willard, who presided from 1879 to 1898. The WCTU made an argument based on morality, religion, and health concerns. The formation of the Anti-Saloon League in 1893 gave the WCTU an ally, and together they worked for a constitutional amendment to prohibit alcohol in the United States. Their campaign gained allies during the Progressive Era, including Democrats and Republicans, as well as an unusual mix of other organizations such as the NAACP, the IWW, and the KKK. Politics played into the temperance movement as well. With the adoption of the income tax in 1913, the federal government was less reliant on taxes on alcohol for revenue. The beginning of World War I made it politically popular to criticize German brewers, whose beer dominated the market.

By the time proponents introduced the Eighteenth Amendment to Congress, many states had already adopted some form of Prohibition. The proposed amendment prohibited the production, transportation, and sale of alcoholic beverages. Interestingly, it did not prohibit either the possession or the consumption of alcohol by individuals. The proposal required approval by a two-thirds vote of each house of Congress and then by three-fourths of the state legislatures in order to be adopted. Introduced in the Senate on August 1, 1917, it passed easily by a margin of 65 to 20. The measure also passed with a comfortable margin in the House, 282 to 128. In December Congress turned it over to the state legislatures. Mississippi became the first state to ratify on January 7, 1918, and just over a year later, on January 16, 1919, Nebraska became the thirty-sixth state to ratify (out of the forty-eight states in the Union at the time), completing the ratification process. Ultimately, forty-six states ratified, with only Connecticut and Pennsylvania voting against ratification.

According to the Eighteenth Amendment, Prohibition was to go into effect one year after its ratification, and after Nebraska's ratification that date was set as January 17, 1920. Now Congress had to consider legislation that would specify how the amendment would be implemented. On June 27, 1919, Congressman Andrew Volstead, a Minnesota Republican, introduced a bill for that purpose. The bill passed through Congress easily. President Wilson had not spoken out for or against Prohibition, and when asked he said that he preferred a local option. When the bill came to his desk, however, he vetoed it. The House overrode his veto on the same day, and the Senate followed suit the next day, and the National Prohibition Act became law. Popularly known as the Volstead Act, the legislation spelled out in twenty-five pages what Prohibition actually meant. Individuals could keep alcohol in their homes for personal consumption, so alcohol sales increased in anticipation of the beginning of Prohibition. Consumption decreased in the years immediately after Prohibition became effective. But in the years that followed, enforcement was sporadic, organized crime flourished, and people began to feel that Prohibition was failing, making good citizens into criminals. The "Noble Experiment," as some referred to Prohibition, continued until 1933, when the Twenty-First Amendment revoked it.

SUGGESTED READINGS

On immigrants, see Alan Kraut's *The Huddled Masses: The Immigrant in American Society, 1880–1921* (Wheeling, IL: Harlan Davidson, 1982).

Melvyn Dubofsky's *Industrialism and the American Worker, 1865–1920* (Wheeling, IL: Harlan Davidson, 1996) is a classic study of this era in labor history republished in 1996. On the radical labor movement, see Beverly Gage's *The Day Wall Street Exploded: A Story of America in Its First Age of Terror* (New York: Oxford Univ. Press, 2009). Nell Irvin Painter's *Standing at Armageddon: The United States, 1817–1919* (New York: W. W. Norton, 1987) focuses particularly on labor, but also incorporates the struggles of women and minorities.

Isabel Wilkerson's *The Warmth of Other Suns: The Epic Story of America's Great Migration* (New York: Random House, 2010) tells the story of the African American diaspora in an exceptional narrative by tracing the experiences of several families beginning in the 1910s. There are several biographies of each of the major African American leaders of this decade: Booker T. Washington, W. E. B. DuBois, and Marcus Garvey.

A good overview of the women's suffrage movement with documents and essays is Marjorie Spruill Wheeler's *One Woman, One Vote: The Women's Suffrage Movement* (Troutdale, OR: NewSage Press,

1995), an edited accompaniment to the PBS series. For a biographical approach to the women's suffrage movement, see Jean H. Baker's *Sisters: The Lives of America's Suffragists* (New York: Hill and Wang, 2005). A useful introduction to women's issues in the twentieth century, with an overview of the 1910s, is Lois Banner's *Women in Modern America: A Brief History*, 4th ed. (Belmont, CA: Thompson-Wadsworth, 2005).

6

American Culture in the Teens

The self-confidence that defined Americans at the beginning of the second decade of the twentieth century, born of the emergence of the United States as a world power, an industrial dynamo, and a leading force in international trade, unleashed a period of artistic creativity so pervasive that historians referred to it as a "Little Renaissance." New trends emerged that influenced artistic development well into the twentieth century. In art, music, literature, and especially movies, the arts benefited from uniquely American themes, innovations, and creativity, exhibiting a cultural nationalism that would not have been possible just a few years earlier.

THE VISUAL ARTS

Visual artists—especially painters—remained deeply influenced by Europe, but continued to chart an increasingly independent course. New York City, the focal point of American arts, hosted a series of exhibits that signaled new trends, both European and American. If New York was the center of American art, the center of the New York scene was Alfred Stieglitz's Gallery 291, so named because of its location at 291 Fifth Avenue. Stieglitz, who made his mark as a photographer and as the owner of the most influential art gallery in the United States, introduced impressionism and other radical new forms of European art and also encouraged and supported young American artists. In shows from 1907 to 1913, he displayed European artists such as Picasso, Cézanne, and Matisse, and in 1910 he staged a show of exclusively American art. More than just a gallery director, Stieglitz introduced modern art to the United States.

In February and March 1913, one of the seminal events in twentieth-century American art occurred at the 69th Regiment Armory on Lexington Avenue in New York. Although the show later moved on to Chicago and Boston, its roots were in New York. It contributed to the city's reputation as America's cultural capital and has since been known simply as the Armory Show. Intended to offer an opportunity to young American artists and to introduce American audiences to modern art, it exhibited more than 1,250 paintings and sculptures by more than three hundred European and American artists. The most controversial painting, Marcel Duchamp's *Nude Descending a Staircase*, blended cubism (by presenting the figure in fragments) and futurism (with its dynamic sense of movement). Other prominent Europeans contributed pieces, including Vincent van Gogh, Pablo Picasso, and impressionists Edgar Degas, Claude Monet, and Pierre-Auguste Renoir. The show's impact was immediate, controversial, and transforming; it had critics, but its lasting legacy was the introduction of experimental art to an American audience. A quarter of a million people saw the show, and because two-thirds of the items displayed were by Americans, it gave them a prominent platform. Prominent American painters, and several whose careers were on the verge of renown, exhibited, including James Whistler, Mary Cassat, Albert Pinkham Ryder, Edward Hopper, Stuart Davis, and Joseph Stella.

American art had not followed the same course as European art; among the trends in American painting was the advent of the "ashcan school," a derogatory term used to describe paintings depicting the underside of urban tenement life, dealing frankly with the victims of poverty in dark tones and shadows, with street scenes providing a common theme. George Bellows's series of paintings depicting club boxers were among the more popular examples of this genre. Others adapted European styles to American themes. John Marin applied cubist techniques to New York architecture, including the Brooklyn Bridge. Georgia O'Keeffe, who in later years became famous for her paintings of the American Southwest and floral forms, in the 1910s experimented with abstract forms that demonstrated the originality of her talent and established her as the leading woman painter of her generation. If much of the art of the decade symbolized the "shock of the new," Norman Rockwell emerged as a defender of the "comfort of the familiar." The first of his many *Saturday Evening Post* covers appeared in 1916. His depictions of the rituals, celebrations, and traditions of white middle-class Americans, and especially of their rites of passage and interaction across the generations, won him immense popularity.

AMERICAN FILM: FROM NICKELODEON TO EPIC

Perhaps no popular culture medium underwent changes as dramatic as the ones experienced by the American cinema. This period was the era of silent film, and although sound was not introduced until the 1920s, changes in themes, complexity, distribution, technology, theaters, business structure, and popularity transformed the film industry in ways unimaginable at the beginning of the decade. The star system emerged and became one of the transforming agents of the industry. By mid-decade as many as twenty-five million Americans saw movies each day.

In 1910 most Americans going to the movies went to nickelodeons, usually small theaters that charged a nickel for admission, although already big cities experienced price increases to a dime. Nickelodeons showed "one-reelers" (up to 1,050 feet of 35 mm film) that ran for a maximum of seventeen minutes. These films were similar to plays, and indeed many of them were plays transferred to the screen. Producers believed that audiences had to see the entire body of the actors as they did in the live theater. Shows, especially in cities and larger venues, often included other entertainment such as music or vaudeville performances. Some showed three one-reel films, with entertainment between each film. The films celebrated action, so chase scenes were common fare. In this era of reform, movie houses were fair game for critics, who warned of poor ventilation and undue familiarity between the sexes in the darkened rooms. By mid-decade multireel feature films replaced the shorts of earlier years; some of the most popular films had as many as twelve reels and lasted more than three hours. With feature films supplanting shorts, the audience became more upscale, and picture palaces, large ornate theaters, often with decorative themes, replaced nickelodeons.

At the beginning of the decade, the Motion Pictures Patent Company, known as the Trust, tried to control production and distribution of films. Founded in 1908, the Trust included the major producers, including Edison, Vitagraph, and Biograph. But most of the major studios that came to dominate the industry already existed, and they began to challenge the Trust. While the Trust exerted control over East Coast producers, independent producers rebelled. The industry began to shift westward to California, undermining the Trust, and in 1915 the Supreme Court ruled against it, initiating a period of shifting leadership in the industry and a rise in the importance of California in film production. By 1915 California studios accounted for 75 percent of commercial film production.

While executives battled over control of the industry, the change that attracted most public attention was the emergence of the star system. At the beginning of the decade, studios featured their lead actresses, but not by name. Florence Lawrence, known simply as the Biograph Girl, became the first to challenge this tradition when she accepted an offer from Carl Laemmle, head of the Independent Moving Picture Company, for fifteen thousand dollars a year. Just a few years earlier, actors had typically received five dollars a day, so this contract was an extraordinary development that moved the industry toward recognition of stars. The first movie fan magazine appeared in 1911. The process accelerated. Some of the biggest female stars of the decade, including Mary Pickford, Lillian Gish, Florence Lawrence, and Norma Talmadge, began their careers as teenagers and soon received previously unimaginable contracts. In 1916 Paramount's Adolph Zukor paid Pickford ten thousand dollars a week plus 50 percent of the profits of her movies or five hundred thousand dollars, whichever was larger. But stars sold tickets, and as large as the contracts may have been, they paid off for the studios.

The most popular genres were comedies, dramas, and westerns. Many of the westerns sympathized with Indians, as did the Biograph film *Ramona: A Story of the White Man's Injustice to the Indian*, echoing the theme of the Helen Hunt Jackson book of the same name. All studios released comedies, but the ones by Mack Sennett were the most successful. Sennett churned out eight films a month at his peak. His slapstick Keystone Komedies, and especially the Keystone Kops, engaged in endless formulaic chase scenes. Serials became virtually a genre themselves, the most memorable of which, the *Perils of Pauline*, followed a formula that left the heroine stranded at a moment of danger, stereotypically tied to railroad tracks as a train propelled its way toward—a climactic rescue.

Directors emerged as names in the lights as prominent as stars. Thomas Ince's westerns featured cowboy and frontier heroes and starred Tom Mix and other actors who appeared regularly in these films. But without question the director who dominated the decade was D. W. Griffith, best known for dramatic epic films with elaborate staging, intricate themes, and state-of-the-art technical special effects. Many of Griffith's effects were not original, but he brought them together in creative ways that explored their potential and integrated them into a coherent narrative.

Two of his films in mid-decade, *The Birth of a Nation* in 1915 and *Intolerance* in 1916, stand out as among the decade's most controversial and spectacular achievements. *The Birth of a Nation* generated more attention than any other film, both positive (for its cinematography) and negative (for its overt racism). Based on Thomas Dixon's novel *The Clansman*, the film traces two Reconstruction-era families, one northern (the Stonemans), the other southern (the Camerons). Congressman Austin Stoneman, who represents Thaddeus Stevens, the Radical Republican who dominated congressional Reconstruction policy, emerges as a villain, while his son, Phil, and daughter, Elsie (Lillian Gish), become romantically involved with the adult offspring of the Camerons of South Carolina. The romances of Phil Stoneman and Margaret Cameron as well as Ben Cameron and Elsie Stoneman are featured in the dominant narrative thread of the film. While the romantic links and male friendships between the families create sympathy for the plight of individuals caught in the maelstrom of the Civil War, the movie's racial and sexual tension is most memorable to modern viewers.

Racist portrayals of individuals maintain stereotypes of the Reconstruction South. Of the African American characters in the film, only the loyal former slave who has remained with the Camerons after the war is treated favorably. In contrast, the Reconstruction-era South Carolina Legislature shows newly installed black legislators eating chicken in the legislative chamber with their feet on the desks. Ironically, this scene offers one of Griffith's most strident claims for the film's historical accuracy; indeed, the setting of the legislative chamber is re-created with admirable attention to detail—while the actions taking place within are fabrications and misrepresentations. Silas Lynch, a mulatto appointed by Stoneman as lieutenant governor of South Carolina, symbolizes the Radical Republican attempt to elevate ill-suited former slaves to political power over their former masters. Attempted rapes of the women of both the Stoneman and Cameron families lend drama that climaxes with Ben Cameron's heroic Ku Klux Klan riding to the rescue in the final scenes of the film. Throughout, Griffith depicts Reconstruction as a Northern attempt to subjugate the South, and despite the spurious claim to historical accuracy, the movie drew record crowds in the North and the South. It prompted vigorous protests by civil rights advocates, on the one hand, and the rebirth of the Klan, on the other (see chapter 5).

In addition to his insistence on the film's historical authenticity, Griffith made exaggerated claims for cinematic breakthroughs in the film. Close-ups, fade-outs, and the use of an iris bringing focus to a particular feature on the screen—these techniques had all appeared in other films, even some of Griffith's own earlier movies. But that does not detract from the epic achievement of *Birth*. One scene begins with a woman cradling a wounded soldier on a hilltop; the camera then pans to the valley below, showing distant troops moving across the landscape, impressive even a century later in its conception and execution and far removed from the slapstick chase scenes of contemporary one-reelers. The juxtaposition of outrageous racism with spectacular scenes, a complex narrative, and technical excellence contributed to the film's notoriety.

The onset of war in Europe in 1914 triggered a multifaceted response from American filmmakers. Certain genres faded, including prolabor movies and serials depicting damsels in distress (such as *The Perils of Pauline*). Prior to American entry in 1917, films praised neutrality or even pacifism, but once the United States entered, the movies went to war. Propaganda films whose titles reflected their content included *The Kaiser: The Beast of Berlin* and *Huns within Our Gates* (both 1918). Animated films appeared as early as 1915, but the 1918 twelve-minute short *The Sinking of the Lusitania*, a propaganda cartoon with unusually fine production values for the time, commemorated the sinking of the vessel that cost the lives of 128 Americans in 1915. D. W. Griffith headed the Motion Picture War Service Association, and stars such as Douglas Fairbanks, Charlie Chaplin, and Mary Pickford sold war bonds. Ultimately, the American movie industry benefited handsomely from the war, which devastated a vibrant European film competition. After the war, some 90 percent of films screened in Europe were American films, and nearly all films shown in Latin America came from the United States.

A major postwar change in the business side of movie production shook up the industry. The seemingly extravagant fees paid to stars obscured the fact that the studio system was entrenched and in control. But star power generated ticket sales, and the leading performers had name recognition that overshadowed the power of the studios. In 1919 four of the industry's biggest names—director D. W. Griffith and actors Douglas Fairbanks, Charlie Chaplin, and Mary Pickford—broke with the studios and established their own production company, which they named United Artists. The company struggled for several years and seemed on the verge of collapse in the mid-1920s after Griffith left and sound movies ended the careers of Fairbanks and Pickford. It survived in a much-altered form by bringing in partners and undergoing a series of structural changes.

7. In February 1919, D. W. Griffith, Mary Pickford, Charlie Chaplin (*seated*), and Douglas Fairbanks sign the contract establishing United Artists, thus challenging the power of the movie studios. New York World-Telegram & Sun Collection, Prints and Photographs Division, Library of Congress, LC-USZ62-137195.

VAUDEVILLE

In 1910 vaudeville rivaled movies in popularity, and in fact the two forms of entertainment were complementary in many ways. Both often occupied the same theaters. Comedy was an essential element of both. Many theaters interspersed movies between vaudeville acts. By 1920 movies had surged, and vaudeville had entered decline, although it still had a few years to go before it expired.

Vaudeville was a variety show that featured all manner of entertainment: musicians, dancers, comedians, jugglers, magicians, and animal acts. Film stars often got their start in vaudeville, which provided an opportunity to gain experience, much as community theater does today. Among those stars who learned their craft in vaudeville in the 1910s and later went on to movies were Fred Astaire, Charlie Chaplin, Douglas Fairbanks, George Burns, and the Marx Brothers. Vaudeville had its hierarchy, and stars emerged from within its ranks by performing on its biggest stages. New York's Strand Theater and the Palace Theater on Broadway were the big show, and performers there had contracts that required them to perform only twice a day, while in small cities performers often had to appear more regularly, as many as six performances in a day. Vaudeville had its own headliners, some of whom remained rooted in vaudeville. Harry Houdini was one of them, and in 1912 he escaped from a locked box dropped into New York Harbor. Al Jolson was perhaps vaudeville's biggest star, moving easily between vaudeville, movies, and singing. Jolson was Jewish and often performed in blackface. His 1927 movie *The Jazz Singer* was one of the movie classics of the 1920s. Bert Williams, a black performer born in the West Indies, also performed in blackface, thus leaving a complicated racial image for critics to dissect. One referred to him as "a black West Indian man impersonating a white man impersonating an ignorant black man from the American South."[1]

MUSIC: RAGTIME, THE BLUES, JAZZ, AND POPULAR MUSIC

As with movies and the visual arts, the 1910s witnessed the emergence of new forms of expression. Popular music came into its own, aided by the emergence of new technology. Recorded cylinders and discs battled for public support, just as other competing entertainment technologies would late in the twentieth century and beyond. Thomas Edison supported cylinders, and by 1913 Americans had purchased a million cylinder players. The Victor Talking Machine Company

1. Ann Douglas, cited in Mark Whalan, *American Culture in the 1910s* (Edinburgh: Edinburgh Univ. Press, 2010), 70.

marketed its disc player, using the iconic figure of a fox terrier listening to a megaphone-shaped gramophone. This new media cut into the sales of pianos and suppressed the popularity of player pianos, introduced a decade earlier in 1904.

American music—specifically African American music—made an international impact in the 1910s and 1920s matched only by movies. Two music idioms—the blues and jazz—became musical forms that captured international attention in the 1920s and beyond. A third idiom, ragtime, appeared first in the late nineteenth century and also had its roots in the African American experience. Its leading practitioner, Scott Joplin, was born in Texas in either 1867 or 1868. Ragtime was piano music that had a syncopated melody and an accented accompaniment line. Joplin's first ragtime "hit" was "Maple Leaf Rag," which he published in 1899. For the next eighteen years until his death in 1917, Joplin published and played ragtime, earning his title as the acknowledged "king of ragtime." While the blues and jazz thrived in the twenties, ragtime faded but underwent a rebirth of interest in the 1970s when Marvin Hamlisch adapted Joplin's rag "The Entertainer" as the theme music for the popular movie *The Sting*, starring Paul Newman and Robert Redford.

The blues originated in the rural South, drawing on field songs, convict-labor laments, ballads, and work songs. The blues evoked feelings of loss, suffering, and labor. Unlike the popular songs generated by Tin Pan Alley, which were sweet and sentimental, the blues dealt with the tough life of African Americans, particularly of those individuals whose suffering knew no limits. Among the best-known performers of the 1910s were Lead Belly and Blind Lemon Jefferson, both of whom hailed from East Texas. Lead Belly, a veteran of the notorious Texas prison system, played the twelve-string guitar. Jefferson's singing, which one critic described as "high voiced, lean toned," was a style exhibited in a song whose title evokes its sound, "Black Snake Moan." Blues artists, and the female singers who made the style popular, appeared as vaudeville performers and in the 1920s recorded blues ballads; among the most well known were "Ma" Rainey, Ethel Waters, and Bessie Smith. The African American diaspora took the blues north, and it became a staple of nightclubs in Memphis, St. Louis, and Chicago.

Jazz also had its roots in the African American experience in the American South but emerged in its early form in New Orleans, where it blended ragtime, the blues, and brass-band fanfares characteristic of Mardi Gras and also used in African American funeral processions. W. C. Handy, who fashioned himself as the "father of the blues," was one of the early jazzmen, and his "Memphis Blues" (1912) and "St. Louis Blues" (1914) helped to popularize the new musical form. Jelly Roll Morton, another New Orleans performer, composed in 1915 "Jelly Roll Blues," often cited as the first genuine jazz piece. Typically played in small ensembles in New Orleans, mainly by brass and woodwinds, jazz followed a path northward similar to the migration of the blues and flourished especially in Chicago but also in New York, Kansas City, and California. In the 1920s it became popular internationally, especially in Europe, where it received its first exposure during World War I.

The hits of the day were associated in the public mind with Tin Pan Alley, a street in New York City where music publishers were clustered. Between 1880 and the early 1950s, this area was the center of music publishing in the United States. George M. Cohan, whose popular patriotic songs, including "Give My Regards to Broadway" and "You're a Grand Old Flag," appeared in the first decade of the century, had the greatest song of World War I, "Over There," for which he received a Congressional Gold Medal from President Franklin D. Roosevelt. Several of the most popular composers were recent European immigrants, and Jews in particular made an impact on American popular music. Jerome Kern, the son of German Jews, wrote the scores to popular musicals.

Music also played a role in the theater, where two forms of musical entertainment became popular: the musical, in which staged songs related to a central plot, and the musical revue, in which individual performances were unified by a theme and culminated in a big production number. Foremost among the revues were productions staged by Florenz Ziegfeld, the famous Ziegfeld Follies, launched in 1907 and experiencing its peak years during the 1910s in the Amsterdam Theater in New York City. The Follies combined vaudeville with extravagant musical numbers featuring a chorus line of the Ziegfeld Girls, the main draw of the show. Several actresses had their start in the chorus line, including Marion Davies and Louise Brooks. But some of the most prominent performers of the 1910s and 1920s also appeared in the Follies, including W. C. Fields, Bert Williams, Eddie Cantor, Fanny Brice, and Will Rogers.

THE EMERGENCE OF AMERICAN FASHION

In fashion, as in the visual arts, Americans began to develop a sense of themselves, separate from Europe, if not altogether independent. Several factors influenced this trend. American business was developing an international presence that affected much of the economy, including fashion. The emergence of a strong middle class increasingly concerned with practicality made many of the turn-of-the-century fashions such as corsets and petticoats less attractive. Further bolstering this trend was an interest among women in a more active lifestyle. The popularity of the bicycle for both men and women fueled this trend, as did swimming, the popularity of the automobile, and dancing. One of the influential books of the era, Thorstein Veblen's *The Theory of the Leisure Class* (1899), bolstered this change. Veblen criticized conspicuous consumption and used fashion as a prime example, equating the following of Parisian dictates with waste and commenting on the confining nature of women's clothing. Thus, the adaptation of more comfortable, less constricting clothing became an emblem of independent thinking and the forerunner of the "flapper" style that became an iconic fashion statement of the 1920s.

Successful national magazines bolstered trends in American fashions. Some of these magazines had been published since the late nineteenth century, but now because of new methods of publication and distribution, their circulation neared or topped one million. The leading women's magazines were *Ladies' Home Journal*, *Vogue*, and *Harper's Bazar* (which later changed its spelling to *Bazaar*). These fashions could reach women who lived at some distance from large cities because of the continuing popularity of catalog sales by Sears, Roebuck as well as Montgomery Ward.

The most dramatic break with the past of high-collared dresses and corseted waists was the shirtwaist, a more informal garment with an open collar that could be worn tucked into a skirt or outside of the skirt. The shirtwaist indicated another change in women's clothing: the manufacture of simple clothing that could be produced in large quantities, bringing prices down, making them affordable to a wider market.

Americans still admired Parisian fashions but did not slavishly imitate them; when they did follow Parisian designers, it was often by purchasing inexpensive copies made of cheaper fabrics. Some unscrupulous American manufacturers sewed faux French labels into the garments they sold to American women. But Americans were also willing to buck the trend of French fashions. While Paris was selling narrow hobble skirts that made it difficult for women to walk, Americans bought skirts wider than the previous generation of dresses. Part of the reason for this change was indicative of another emerging trend: the imitation of celebrities. In this case the trendsetter was Irene Castle, a famous dancer who partnered with her husband, Vernon Castle. Irene wore loose-fitting skirts and dresses that made it easier to dance. She also bobbed her hair, establishing another trend that became popular in the 1920s.

Men's clothing also underwent dramatic changes in the 1910s. During the first decade of the twentieth century, men wore suits that had heavily padded shoulders and wide trousers pegged at the bottom. In the 1910s men's clothing also underwent a streamlining. The padding disappeared from shoulders, the rest of the suit coat was slimmer, and the trousers were slimmed down—but still roomy in order to allow more freedom of movement. Some of these new fashions imitated the slim profile of Vernon Castle, as the couple became the leading fashion trendsetters of the decade. Belts replaced suspenders, but in general men's clothing remained relatively formal. Men with office jobs wore suits to work. Hats were a regular part of men's wardrobes:

straw boaters, derbies, and Panama hats were the most popular styles. The war also influenced men's fashions by the end of the decade. Coats in particular were imitations of military coats.

AMERICAN ARCHITECTURE

American architecture had begun to emerge from the shadow of classical European architecture in the late nineteenth century, but European influence remained. The École des Beaux-Arts in Paris continued to educate many of the leading American architects, and its graduates benefited from a prestigious pedigree that led to commissions for important buildings. Stanford White of the dominant firm of McKim, Mead, and White in New York was one of its graduates and one of the most famous architects of the early twentieth century. California architect Julia Morgan, the first woman admitted to the architecture program at Beaux-Arts and the first to earn an certificate there, gained prominence after the San Francisco earthquake of 1906 because of her knowledge of earthquake-resistant reinforced-concrete construction. She is most remembered today as the architect of the Hearst Castle in San Simeon, California, begun in 1919. But she built more than seven hundred buildings, most of which were in the San Francisco Bay area.

Chicago became a center of architectural excellence in the late nineteenth century as the city rebuilt after the 1871 fire that destroyed much of it. The city's reputation grew with the Chicago World's Fair of 1893, which featured the White City, a faux-marble esplanade inspired by Beaux-Arts style. The city became an architectural showcase in the late nineteenth and early twentieth centuries, featuring early construction of steel-framed skyscrapers. Landmarks built during the 1910s include Navy Pier and the Michigan Avenue Bridge. Chicago also became known as a focal point for the architecture of Frank Lloyd Wright, whose private homes in Oak Park became known as the prairie style, after the geography of the area around Chicago. In 1913 he completed Midway Gardens in Chicago, a terraced complex that included restaurants and a concert hall. Unfortunately, the structure was demolished in the 1930s. In his long career he built houses, municipal buildings, and churches around the country. Wright became known for structures that incorporated themes from the surrounding geography and gave attention to both the exterior and the interior of his buildings, paying particular attention to interior lighting. He also designed furniture and other interior features.

SUGGESTED READINGS

Mark Whalan's *American Culture in the 1910s* (Edinburgh: Edinburgh Univ. Press, 2010) is a fine overview of the topic and part of the series Twentieth-Century American Culture, which has a volume for each decade. A similar overview of the movies of the decade is *American Cinema of the 1910s: Themes and Variations* (New Brunswick, NJ: Rutgers Univ. Press, 2009), edited by Charlie Keil and Ben Singer.

7

Wilson's Management of the Peace and Entry into World War I

World War I was a transformative event for the United States. The nation had been an emerging power since the late nineteenth century, but by the end of the war there was no question that the United States had become one of the world's great powers. Nonetheless, when the war began in Europe, the general sentiment in the United States was that it was a European matter and that the United States ought to stay out. It had been American policy for a century to stay out of European wars. That sentiment would change gradually, but as late as the presidential election of 1916, President Wilson's reelection campaign used the slogan "He Kept Us Out of War." Events early in 1917 pushed the president and the American people toward war. In April Wilson addressed Congress and asked for a declaration of war against Germany, and despite some resistance Congress concurred.

THE ORIGINS OF THE GREAT WAR IN EUROPE

War in Europe erupted in August 1914, but the forces that led to war can be traced to events that transpired four decades earlier. Prussia, the most militaristic state in central Europe, came to dominate the region through a policy that included trade and shrewd diplomacy. In the late 1860s and early 1870s, led by the kaiser's chief minister, Otto von Bismarck, Prussia provoked wars with Austria-Hungary and France in quick succession. The Franco-Prussian War in 1870–71 ensured Prussian domination of states, including the Kingdoms of

Bavaria and Saxony, and led to the establishment of the modern nation of Germany. The peace treaty that ended the war, signed in the Hall of Mirrors of the Palace of Versailles, symbolized the emergence of a new power in central Europe. Among the terms of the treaty, the most galling to France was the demand that it relinquish the province of Alsace-Lorraine to Germany. French anger and yearning for revenge over the settlement simmered, resurfaced during the war, and culminated in 1919 when it forced Germany to sign the treaty ending World War I in the same Hall of Mirrors and to return Alsace-Lorraine to France.

In the intervening years between the two conferences in the palace at Versailles, Europe underwent a period of staggering changes that reshaped its economy, social structure, politics, and diplomacy. Europe was still the center of world affairs by almost any measure. The Industrial Revolution, which had its origins in Britain, came to encompass the rest of western Europe, and by the end of the nineteenth century Germany had surpassed Britain in the production of steel, the most significant gauge of industrial development. Industrialization prompted the burgeoning of cities and their transformation from administrative and trade centers to foci of industrial production and distribution. The emergence of a substantial middle class was a consequence of this process.

Europe continued to spread its influence abroad, looking for markets for its industrial products, but also establishing colonies in Asia, penetrating markets in Latin America, and dividing the continent of Africa into colonial possessions. In the late nineteenth century, as a consequence of expansion, two geographical regions emerged as areas of potential conflict between European states. In Africa European nations embarked on what came to be called the "Scramble for Africa," establishing colonies or other arrangements of control over the entire continent with the exception of Ethiopia. Europeans used modern weapons, including the machine gun by the end of the century, so battles between Europeans and Africans often resulted in one-sided slaughter. Thus, the danger was less one of wars between Europeans and Africans than it was between European armies. Of particular danger were the conflicting goals of Britain and France, since Britain sought to establish a "Cape to Cairo" railroad and France wanted to establish control from east to west in North Africa. German chancellor Otto von Bismarck issued a call for European leaders to meet to discuss the looming crisis developing out of international competition for territory in Africa. Bismarck himself believed that colonies in Africa were an unnecessary and burdensome appendage and suggested that Germany had no aspiration to accumulate more territory in Africa—although it did intend to hold on to the land it had already colonized in East Africa. At the Congress of Berlin in 1884–85, the European powers negotiated an agreement, including ground rules for colonial competition in Africa. While some of the arrangements dealt with specific territories (such as the Congo, in which there had been competing claims), the most important agreement stipulated that for a claim to African territory to be validated, the land had to be effectively occupied. In other words, it was not sufficient to simply claim a river basin or a colony—there had to be people representing the claiming nation, be they soldiers, traders, or missionaries, "sufficient to protect existing rights." In real terms, this stipulation meant that it was the collective judgment of the European powers that African territory was not worth risking a European war over competitive claims, but it also enflamed the "Scramble," since the most aggressive colonial powers sought to establish their effective occupation in areas where they already had a presence.

The other region subject to dispute between European powers was the Balkan Peninsula, located between the Aegean and Adriatic Seas in southeastern Europe. The Ottoman Empire had occupied the peninsula since the sixteenth century. At its greatest extent, the Ottoman Empire controlled the entire coastline of the Black Sea and penetrated into Europe as far as the gates of Vienna. Greece, at the southern end of the peninsula, gained its independence in 1829, but the Ottoman Empire retained control of the Balkans to the north until the early twentieth century. At that point, the empire began to crumble, and as it lost territory, a power struggle began. Two European powers to the north, Austria-Hungary and Russia, anticipated taking territory as the

Ottoman Turks began to retreat. The Russians had already taken land along the north coast of the Black Sea and expected to continue to expand. Austria-Hungary, already a multiethnic state, had been a victim of Ottoman expansion in the past and expected to recover land it had lost before. The ethnic groups residing in the Balkans had ideas of their own, however, and saw the Ottoman withdrawal as an opportunity for autonomy and hoped to establish states of their own. They had no intention of trading one imperial master for another. The Serbs in particular, but also the Croats and Bosnians, all of whom were in closer proximity to Austria-Hungary than to Russia, worried about annexation by Austria-Hungary.

Chancellor Otto von Bismarck, the remarkable statesman who had engineered the wars of German unification (against Austria and France) and the Congress of Berlin and its agreement on Europe's African policy, was also the architect of a temporary solution to the Balkan crisis. Claiming again that Germany was a satisfied power that sought no land in the Balkans, he fashioned a series of treaties and secret agreements with Austria-Hungary and Russia to restrain them and to work out accommodations that would avoid war and allow each to acquire some of the Balkan territory. Bismarck kept his word, and until 1890 he was able to keep both Russia and Austria-Hungary satisfied. As chancellor Bismarck served at the will of the kaiser, and Germany's new kaiser, Wilhelm II, who came to power in 1888, grew impatient with Bismarck's cautious diplomacy. The kaiser dismissed Bismarck, and the seventy-five-year-old leader went into retirement. Bismarck had been given free rein since he led the German unification movement; Wilhelm bridled under Bismarck's cavalier treatment and wanted to embark on a new foreign policy. Instead of restraining Austria-Hungary and Russia, as Bismarck had done, the new kaiser cast his lot with Austria-Hungary, isolating Russia, and in the process formed an alliance that dominated central Europe. At the time, it appeared that no one could challenge this alliance, with Russia alone in the East and France just as isolated in the West. Britain and France were historical enemies, and it seemed unlikely that they could cooperate in opposing Germany.

What the kaiser had failed to anticipate was that these three nations did have in common a fear of German expansionism. In France the memory of the defeat at the hands of Germany in 1871 (one of the wars of German unification) and the loss of its territories Alsace and Lorraine to Germany was still very much alive. Bismarck had understood this fear and had pacified France by giving it favorable treatment at the Congress of Berlin, and the young kaiser had now disparaged that goodwill. Furthermore, by 1890 relations between Germany and Britain were improving, leaving France even more desperately isolated. Russia had long expected that it could depend on France in case of a crisis with Germany, but now it appeared that more formal contact would be appropriate. In 1891 a squadron of the French fleet visited the Russian port of Kronstadt. Both France and Russia feared the development of a British alliance with Germany, Austria, and Italy to preserve the status quo in the Mediterranean, which would have threatened Russia's goals in the eastern Mediterranean and France's in the western Mediterranean. All these matters pushed republican France and authoritarian Russia toward a more formal relationship, which they executed later that year.

Next, France moved to establish a better relationship with Britain. France and Britain seemed to have an irresolvable situation in Africa. Resolution of this impasse came about as a direct result of the Boer War in South Africa, which had demonstrated that Britain was truly isolated, with no allies in Europe. In 1904, at the initiative of the French foreign minister, France and Britain met to discuss colonial policy in North Africa, and they came to an accord. France acknowledged British primacy in Egypt, and in return Britain lifted its opposition to French dominance in Morocco. This rapprochement led to an agreement known as the Entente Cordiale, an initial step toward an alliance. Thus, by 1907, when Russia and England signed the Anglo-Russian Entente, ending their long rivalry in central Asia (known as the "Great Game"), the pieces were in place for the establishment of the Triple Entente, the Western alliance during the Great War.

Britain's vulnerability also presented opportunities to the United States. Through most of the nineteenth century, the two nations had an adversarial relationship, but in the 1890s Britain began to cultivate diplomatic ties. The most notable actions involved Latin America, where Britain had dominated international trade after Latin American independence from Spain and Portugal. Britain no longer opposed expansion of American trade, accepted American mediation of a dispute in Venezuela, and, most significantly, renegotiated an 1850 treaty with the United States in order to allow the Americans latitude to pursue their intentions to build a canal across the Isthmus of Panama.

The war originated in the Balkans, the region in southeastern Europe that had been under the control of the Ottoman Empire since the sixteenth century and thus had been an Islamic territory. Since the Battle of Lepanto in 1571, the Ottoman Empire had been retreating, and in the early twentieth century European powers referred to the Ottoman Empire as the "sick man of Europe." As the Turks departed from the Balkans, they left a power vacuum. Attempts to control the areas formerly under Ottoman control had been the source of strife for decades. The Crimean War of the 1850s was one consequence. Bismarck's secret treaties with Russia and Austria-Hungary were another, as he sought to monitor competition between the two powers, preventing them from provoking one another into warfare. Despite the yearning for self-rule among the Serbs, Croats, and Bosnians, Austria-Hungary and Russia considered it an issue for the major powers in the vicinity to resolve. Austria-Hungary and Russia were most directly involved; they shared borders with the Balkans and had been involved there for decades. Austria-Hungary had occupied Bosnia and neighboring Herzegovina in 1878 and annexed them in 1908–9. Russia supported the Serbs, who now feared further expansion by Austria-Hungary.

The spark that set off World War I ignited in Serbia. The Russians had fashioned themselves as protectors of the Serbs, endeavoring to keep Austria from establishing control. On June 28, 1914, Austrian archduke Franz Ferdinand, the next in line to the throne of Austria-Hungary, visited the Serbian city of Sarajevo. As his motorcade drove through the streets of Sarajevo after a reception, several possible assassins took positions along the route. They were members of the Black Hand, a secret organization dedicated to the concept of a Greater Serbia. When the driver of the archduke's car took a wrong turn, it gave Gavrilo Princip, one of the assassins, his opportunity. He fired into the car from close range, killing the archduke and his wife.

Diplomatic and military maneuvers over the course of the next six weeks led to the opening battles of the Great War, as the war became known at the time and until the beginning of World War II, when the Great War became World War I. Austria-Hungary sent an ultimatum to Serbia on July 23, intentionally making it so harsh that there was no question that Serbia would reject it, giving Austria-Hungary an excuse to intervene. Austria broke diplomatic relations with Serbia and on July 28 declared war. Russia mobilized to prevent Austria from seizing Serbia. Germany's Kaiser Wilhelm II was the cousin of Russia's Czar Nicholas II and asked him to desist from his mobilization, but Nicholas refused. Germany then took the irrevocable step of declaring war on Russia. Germany also asked France to remain neutral. France did not respond, so Germany, in the early days of August, set in motion its Schlieffen Plan, which included a wheeling motion through the Low Countries (the Netherlands, Luxembourg, and Belgium) and then a march on Paris. When the Low Countries refused to give Germany permission to march through in order to attack Paris, Germany declared war on them, too. Britain also declared war on Germany on August 4. The "guns of August" began to fire, and the Great War was under way on two fronts. Optimists predicted that it would be a short war, but British foreign minister Sir Edward Grey, who had been influential in engineering Britain's entry, made the haunting and enduring statement, "The lamps are going out all over Europe; we shall not see them lit again in our lifetime."

AMERICAN NEUTRALITY

The first official American reaction to the war in Europe came from President Wilson on August 4. He declared that the United States would be neutral. He called on the American people to be neutral "in thought as well as in deed," a statement derided by political opponents and ignored by most Americans. Wilson faced a double tragedy in the first week of August. Just two days after his call for American neutrality, his wife, Ellen, died of kidney disease.

The American situation had echoes of a century earlier, when the nation stayed out of the European wars from the wars of the French Revolution in the 1790s through the Napoleonic Wars that followed and lasted until 1814. At that time the United States was in no position to take part in European wars, but it sought to protect the same principles that remained vital to American interests in 1914. Even in the early nineteenth century, the United States considered itself a commercial nation and insisted on the rights of neutrals to trade freely with either side. Then the major adversaries were Britain and France, and neither of them put much stock in American principles.

Wilson's declaration also contained echoes of another American core belief, one that still reverberates in the twenty-first century: the notion of American exceptionalism. Americans considered their development as a nation to be unique, so much so that it could serve as an example to the world. Americans acknowledged their debt to their European origins but believed that their nation had developed in its own fashion, uncontaminated by the corrupting influences of European power politics, with the Atlantic Ocean serving as a barrier that kept the United States from being drawn into petty European rivalries.

When the war began, Wilson expected that the United States, as a nonbelligerent and a commercial nation, ought to be able to engage in trade with both sides, insisting as well that warring nations observe the same rights of neutral nations. The rights of neutral nations had come under dispute but had been codified into international law after the Crimean War in 1856. These rights, which the United States had championed since its origins, included the following principles: free ships make free goods (except for contraband, goods carried by neutral ships would be considered neutral); contraband would be narrowly defined, applying only to implements of warfare; neutrals could trade between ports of belligerent nations; and blockades were legal but had to be enforced, not simply decreed. Because these principles had been accepted into international law, the United States expected that they would be in force. Unfortunately, when the idealistic goals of the nineteenth century clashed with the realities of twentieth-century warfare, it was not the case.

Several factors entered into the impotence of neutral rights. First, Britain had accepted these principles only with reservations, and Germany agreed to abide only if Britain and its allies did so; thus, in effect, neither side agreed to comply. Second, the course of the war dictated to both Britain and Germany that it was not in their best interest to comply. By the late autumn of 1914, the land war in Europe had stabilized into a stationary front characterized by trench warfare. Thus, the war at sea became more critical to both sides, and both took liberties. New technology reinforced the tendency to ignore neutral rights. When Britain mined the North Sea, Germany's outlet to the Atlantic Ocean, it evaded both the concept of effective blockades and shut out commodities that were not considered contraband, including food. Britain unilaterally redefined contraband to include virtually every German import on the notion that all imports aided the German war effort.

SUBMARINE WARFARE

In retaliation for the British mining of the North Sea, Germany announced in February 1915 a policy of unrestricted submarine warfare. The Wilson administration responded with a sternly worded protest, pledging to hold Germany to "strict accountability" for any damage to American property or personnel. Germany justified its policy as a necessity of war and warned that passenger liners could be among its targets. While protesting the German action, Wilson ignored the British mine blockade of the North Sea, initiating what became an unstated policy of holding Germany accountable while ignoring British violations of accepted international standards.

The United States stayed on the sidelines of Europe's Great War from August 1914 until April 1917. By the time the United States entered the war, the submarine had emerged as the keystone in the German arsenal. Such a prospect seemed most unlikely when the war began. The famous German war plan, the Schlieffen Plan, was entirely a land-based enterprise.

Ironically, the Americans had been the first nation to use a submarine in naval warfare. During the Civil War, the Confederacy placed in action a primitive hand-cranked vessel called the *Hunley*, built in Mobile, Alabama. An attack on the Union's *Housatonic*, guarding Charleston Harbor in August 1863, cost the lives of its entire eight-man crew. In the aftermath of the Civil War, the United States allowed its navy to deteriorate and did nothing to pursue the development of the ill-fated submarine. In the 1880s Irish American inventor John P. Holland developed a modern version of the submarine, conducting test runs in the Hudson River. Combining the Holland boat with a torpedo tube designed by a British inventor in the 1860s brought forth the potentially lethal vessel that haunted the North Atlantic during the Great War and eventually provoked the United States to enter the war. The US Navy acquired its first Holland boat in 1901.

Germany lagged behind the other Great Powers in recognizing the potential of the submarine, and even when the country began to build a fleet of submarines, German military plans about how it could be employed lacked imagination. Naval leaders considered it a defensive weapon. The Germans did not purchase their first submarine until 1906, and then as an experimental vessel, lagging far behind other major nations, including the United States. An unlikely keystone in the German naval arsenal, the submarine became the most effective weapon in countering Britain prior to American entry.

On May 1 the British passenger liner *Lusitania* left New York, en route to Britain. Despite a warning from German authorities that the ship could be a target, British authorities believed that Germany would not attack the *Lusitania*. German submarines could manage seven knots if submerged and twelve to thirteen knots on the surface, while the *Lusitania* had a top speed of twenty-five knots. The *Lusitania* was the largest and fastest liner of the British merchant fleet, so there was reason for such confidence. Nonetheless, on May 7, as the ship approached the coast of Ireland, it slowed and stopped the recommended zigzag evasion course, leaving it vulnerable. A German submarine fired its last torpedo prior to heading home and hit the *Lusitania.* The ship went down with a loss of 1,196 lives, 128 of them Americans. In addition to its passengers, the ship carried a cargo mainly of munitions.

In the aftermath the sinking of the *Lusitania* likely did more harm than good to the German war effort. Americans and Britons were outraged at the sinking of a passenger liner, and although the Germans defended their actions on the fact that the ship was carrying contraband munitions, they did back off temporarily from their policy of unrestricted submarine warfare. There were also repercussions in the Wilson administration. Secretary of State William Jennings Bryan, a pacifist, broke with Wilson over his response to the *Lusitania.* The president considered Germany's justification for the sinking insufficient and wrote a harsh note that prompted Bryan to resign. Bryan wanted to send notes to both Germany and Britain for violations of international laws, but Wilson refused. Bryan told the cabinet that he believed he could do more from the outside to prevent war and resigned on June 9. Wilson appointed Robert Lansing, a counselor in the State Department, as Bryan's replacement. Lansing came to office believing that the *Lusitania* sinking and its aftermath demonstrated that the United States would likely have to go to war. Lansing had little latitude in any case, since increasingly Wilson took command of foreign policy. To this point Wilson reflected the mood of the American people, situated as he was between the pacifism of William Jennings Bryan and the jingoism of Theodore Roosevelt, who suggested that if he were still president, the nation would be at war.

The *Lusitania* affected Wilson's policies, particularly in his attitude toward preparedness, the term applied by persons in the military and in industry who believed that even if the United States had no intention of entering the war, it was foolhardy not to be ready if circumstances forced the nation to go to war. Several organizations began lobbying soon after the war began in Europe. The most influential was the National Security League, which included among its members former secretary of war Henry Stimson and had wealthy backers such as Cornelius Vanderbilt. The NSL and other such organizations were conservative and usually had ties to big business. Antipreparedness advocates feared the impact of preparedness on Progressive reforms and included pacifists, humanitarians, and feminists among their number. Oswald Garrison Villard, publisher and civil rights activist, was one of the most prominent antipreparedness organizers. Before the sinking of the *Lusitania*, Wilson's neutrality policy made him a favorite among such supporters, but now he came out in favor of "reasonable preparedness," and in November he announced that he would propose bills expanding the army and the navy. Antipreparedness reformers responded by creating the American Union against Militarism (AUAM), whose members included Jane Addams and other women from the settlement-house movement among other prominent reformers.

Steps to expand the military led to the Plattsburg movement, initiated in Plattsburgh, New York, in 1913 as a means to train future military officers. General Leonard Wood and former president Theodore Roosevelt were among the leading advocates of the program. Wood saw the Plattsburg camps as a means to address the paucity of trained military officers, and he directed the New York camp. By 1914 there were four such camps, and by 1916 the movement expanded to ten camps, with 10,000 volunteers attending. Those men who attended were all college graduates and had to pay their own way, a testament to the growing popularity of the preparedness movement. Among Plattsburg graduates were George C. Marshall, army chief of staff during World War II, and John J. McCloy, who directed the US occupation of Germany after World War II.

Secretary of War Lindley Garrison proposed a Continental Army Plan, with a standing army of 140,000 and reserves totaling 400,000. Although Wilson initially supported Garrison, the plan ran into opposition in Congress, where opponents feared the establishment of a permanent standing army. Garrison would not back down, and ultimately Wilson forced his resignation and brought in Newton Baker as the new secretary of war. In the summer of 1916, the administration supported the National Defense Act to expand the military by creating a National Guard and establishing a Reserve Officers' Training Corps.

Although there was a respite, the *Lusitania* was not the last U-boat attack on passenger liners. Three months after the *Lusitania*, on August 19, 1915, a German submarine sank the *Arabic*, a smaller British ship headed for the United States, with a loss of forty-four lives, including three Americans. In response, Theodore Roosevelt said that it was lamentable that the United States had not prepared for the possibility of war and that the "time for deeds has come."[1] Even within the administration, Colonel House and Secretary of State Lansing were ready to go to war. But German chancellor Theobald von Bethmann-Hollweg revealed that early in June, he had issued secret orders to submarine captains not to sink passenger ships without warning them and allowing passengers to disembark. The submarine captain excused his actions by claiming that he thought the zigzagging ship was trying to ram him. The announcement of the German secret order, which became known as the "*Arabic* pledge," averted a further diplomatic crisis for the time being.

Congress now undertook its own means of avoiding a further crisis of the sort prompted by the sinking of the *Lusitania* and the *Arabic*. Democrats (particularly Bryan supporters) who disagreed with Wilson's response to German submarine attacks introduced proposals to keep Americans out of harm's way. Jeff McLemore of Texas in the House and Thomas Gore in the Senate proposed similar resolutions: McLemore wanted to forbid American civilians from traveling on armed merchant vessels, and Gore wanted to prevent them from sailing on the ships of belligerent nations. Wilson had a contentious meeting with Democratic leaders, who despite their reservations agreed to bring Democrats in line with the president's policy. There was a strong sentiment in both chambers to support the bills, but Wilson insisted that he was doing everything possible to prevent war. He

1. Edmund Morris, *Colonel Roosevelt* (New York: Random House, 2010), 433.

lobbied aggressively and forced a risky vote in which the administration narrowly defeated the resolutions.

After the sinking of the *Arabic*, there was a lull in submarine warfare. On March 24, 1916, however, a submarine in the English Channel fired a torpedo on a passenger ship, the *Sussex*, which was steaming on a regularly scheduled route to Dieppe, France. The torpedo badly damaged the ship and caused more than fifty casualties, including injuries to American passengers. The Germans claimed they thought the ship was laying mines, but the Wilson administration considered it a violation of the *Arabic* pledge. Lansing wanted to sever relations with Germany, but Wilson directed another attempt at diplomacy.

The president drafted a memo offering to mediate between the belligerents. Colonel House forwarded the memo to Sir Edward Grey, the British foreign minister, suggesting that Wilson was concerned that if the United States entered the war, it would only prolong it. He offered that if Germany did not accept mediation, the United States would "probably" enter the war on the side of the Allies. Grey replied that he did not see how American entry would prolong the war, but rather it would likely bring it to an end. In any case, he would not enter into negotiations unless the French requested them, and they were not doing so. The British read Wilson's "probably" as a clear indication that the Americans were behind them and determined that they could continue to blockade the North Sea with impunity in spite of American protests against violations of international law by the belligerents.

Wilson then protested the *Sussex* attack, demanding that Germany end attacks on passenger and freight vessels or the United States would sever relations. Germany responded with the "*Sussex* pledge," which was a conditional promise to end unrestricted submarine warfare and not fire on armed merchant vessels without warning and allowing civilians to disembark, but only if the British would comply with international law and allow the importation of food into Germany. It was not as much as Wilson wanted, but for the rest of the year Germany honored the pledge, despite the absence of British cooperation and Britain's continued mining of the North Sea.

The lack of British response had consequences, and as diplomatic historian Robert H. Ferrell has suggested, "American relations with Britain in 1916 became almost as taut as those with Germany."[2] As the election approached, Wilson remained committed to a policy of neutrality, Britain persisted in ignoring international law in its unrepentant mining of the North Sea, and Germany agreed to restrict submarine warfare. Furthermore, British suppression of the Irish rebellion prompted protests by Irish Americans, a vocal and increasingly important voting bloc. Wilson was also perturbed when Britain announced a policy of blacklisting trade with companies in neutral countries that it suspected of trading with Germany and threatened to seize and confiscate such cargoes. The list included several American firms, and while it was accurate, Wilson considered it a deeply offensive affront to neutral rights.

THE ELECTION OF 1916

Foreign policy played a central role in the presidential election of 1916. The Great War in Europe dominated the debate over foreign policy, but the continuing revolution in Mexico also became an issue of contention. Domestic issues were also at stake, with Progressive reform still a potent force. Here Wilson had an edge, since he had carried on a vigorous Progressive agenda, while the Republicans remembered that the issue of Progressivism had split the party in 1912, and to many Republicans it had become anathema. Republicans believed they had an excellent chance to win back the White House if they could mend their wounds of the 1912 campaign, when a split in the party between the Taft and Roosevelt candidacies enabled Wilson to win in the first place. They were further heartened by their success in the off-year election of 1914.

2. Robert H. Ferrell, *American Diplomacy: A History* (New York: W. W. Norton, 1975), 466.

With no doubt that the Democrats would nominate Wilson, all the drama rested with the Republicans. Their potential candidates included prominent names such as Henry Ford and Senator Henry Cabot Lodge. By the time the Republicans held their convention in Chicago on June 7–10, however, the list of serious candidates had narrowed to four: Supreme Court justice and former New York governor Charles Evans Hughes; liberal Massachusetts senator John W. Weeks; former New York senator and secretary of state under Theodore Roosevelt Elihu Root; and Roosevelt himself. The party's platform leaned toward moderation, nodding to conservatives and Progressives alike. What emerged was a document of mixed messages, calling for reforms such as child labor laws and workmen's compensation for federal employees, but also for a protective tariff. On foreign policy, Republicans could agree in opposition to Wilson's policy in Mexico, but were more divided on the war in Europe. Some supported Roosevelt's bellicose statements, while others were more reluctant, both because of their own concerns about entering the war and because of their realization that the majority of the American people were not eager to become involved in a European war.

Charles Evans Hughes was a formidable candidate with an impressive résumé. He won election as governor of New York in 1906, defeating William Randolph Hearst, and became an anticorruption administrator who supported Progressive reforms such as regulation of business and welfare. In 1908 Taft asked him to join him on the Republican ticket as the vice presidential candidate, but Hughes chose instead to run for reelection as governor of New York. In 1910 Taft nominated him to the Supreme Court, and Hughes accepted. His service on the Court made him an attractive candidate in 1916, since it kept him out of divisive Republican politics during the contentious 1912 election and the years of Wilson's first term.

Theodore Roosevelt remained a force of nature. People were not neutral about him—they either loved him or hated him. Roosevelt himself remained at home at Sagamore Hill in Oyster Bay, New York, and admitted that he did not think the party had "any intention of nominating me." The convention listened to nominating speeches for

Hughes and Root and gave them respectful if modest demonstrations of support. After the speech placing Theodore Roosevelt's name in nomination, however, there was a boisterous demonstration that lasted thirty-six minutes, attesting to the remaining popularity among the party faithful for the former president. But Roosevelt had been right; the party bosses remembered what they considered his betrayal of the party in 1912 and rallied around Hughes. Roosevelt acknowledged privately that he considered Hughes a man of "courage and integrity," but tempered praise with his belief that Hughes was a man "of the Wilson type, but a better specimen."[3]

After the first ballot, it was clear that Hughes was the likely candidate. He received 253 votes, while Weeks and Root together in second and third places had a total of only 208. Roosevelt trailed badly in sixth place, with 81 votes. On the second ballot, Hughes picked up 73 votes, while all other candidates in the top ten lost votes. Hughes went over the top on the third ballot and became the Republican nominee.

In spite of the efforts of party regulars to achieve harmony among the Republican factions, the Progressives decided to hold their own convention. They met at the same time as the Republicans, several blocks from the Coliseum where the Republicans held their meeting. The very fact of the Progressive meeting was an affront to party unity, as was their goal, which was to have both conventions nominate Roosevelt. Doing so would have achieved unity, of course, except for the fact that the Republicans were determined to nominate anyone but Roosevelt. Shortly before the Republicans nominated Hughes, the Progressives nominated Roosevelt, overriding TR's stated intention not to seek their nomination. Roosevelt, who wanted to represent the Republican Party, recognized that the Progressive nomination would be a hollow prize and turned down the nomination "at this time," setting off another demonstration in the Progressive hall, this one of rage and regret. Delegates tore off their Roosevelt badges and ripped

3. J. Lee Thompson, *Never Call Retreat: Theodore Roosevelt and the Great War* (New York: Palgrave Macmillan, 2013), 130–31.

his posters from the wall. Later, TR's sister Corinne, who had been in Chicago, told him that the people had really wanted him. TR replied, "If they had wanted me hard enough, they could have had me."[4] Roosevelt, who had suggested Lodge to the Republicans, endorsed Hughes, but it was a painful moment for the former president. The 1916 Chicago convention was the last conclave for Roosevelt's Progressive Party, but Progressivism was not yet dead. President Wilson campaigned as a Progressive and incorporated goals that appealed to Progressives of both parties in his campaign.

The Democrats convened in St. Louis a week after the Republican convention. There was no doubt that Wilson would be nominated for a second term. There was no public debate over the vice presidency either, although there might have been. Thomas R. Marshall had served as vice president in obscurity during Wilson's first term, and Colonel House suggested to Wilson that he consider replacing him with Newton Baker, whom Wilson had named as secretary of war the previous March. But Wilson thought highly of Baker, who had engineered the selection of General Pershing for the expeditionary force that had pursued Francisco "Pancho" Villa into Mexico after his raid in Columbus, New Mexico, and chose not to "sacrifice" him to the vice presidency. Marshall would remain on the ticket. The convention nominated Wilson and Vice President Marshall by acclamation. The Democratic platform supported a child labor law and for the first time included a statement endorsing the vote for women. The Progressives had included such a statement in 1912, but this statement at least indicated support for the suffrage campaign, even if it fell short of the stronger statement for which suffrage leaders had been pressing.

Wilson's fall campaign emphasized peace, preparedness, and Progressivism. The slogan "He Kept Us Out of War" came out of the convention and proved to be effective. His opponents attacked him for doing too little, too late, to prepare the nation for war should it

4. Morris, *Colonel Roosevelt*, 460.

come, but Wilson had by fall done enough to deflect these charges, especially before an electorate that was in no mood for war. His credentials on Progressivism were impeccable, and he was the recipient of support from some of the disenchanted Republicans who had dreamed of another Roosevelt candidacy.

Charles Evans Hughes was a worthy candidate and ran a competitive race. Although less in the shadow of TR than William Howard Taft had been four years earlier, Hughes could not escape it entirely. Roosevelt called Hughes "a man of integrity and courage, with a purely lawyer's mind," not a wholehearted endorsement. TR, ever the phrasemaker, compared Hughes to Wilson and dismissed him, with his trademark mustache and beard, as "whiskered Wilson." Nor could Hughes entirely escape the Republican legacy of 1912. That legacy helped him win the nomination, but it did so not because of a stand he had taken during that previous election, but rather because as a Supreme Court justice, he had taken no stand. Thus, he was vulnerable when confronted with Republican divisions that remained unreconciled. One such case emerged on Hughes's visit to California, where conservative Republicans allowed their quarrel with Governor Hiram Johnson, the Progressive candidate for vice president in 1912, to impact the 1916 campaign. To keep out of California politics, where Johnson was now seeking a Senate seat, Hughes did not visit Johnson, even though they were staying in the same hotel.

Hughes faced the task of challenging a popular sitting president. During the campaign, with the *Sussex* pledge intact and thus the German threat to Americans tempered, Hughes realized that it would be difficult to criticize Wilson's war policy. Wilson was more vulnerable on his policies toward Mexico, but few Americans were directly impacted by developments in Mexico in the way they were by the Great War. On the domestic front, Hughes benefited in some quarters from controversial legislation such as the Revenue Act and from taxes meant to raise money to finance preparedness. His public appearances won him supporters, but he was not as gifted a speaker as his opponent and lacked Wilson's ability to leaven his speeches with humor. Nonetheless, the nation was still fundamentally Republican, and for the most part Hughes avoided the depth of Republican bitterness that existed in 1912.

Wilson won the popular vote, 9,126,868 (49.24 percent) to 8,548,728 (46.12 percent) for Hughes. The electoral vote was close: Wilson received 277 electoral votes, Hughes 254. The remaining votes went mainly to two candidates, Allan Benson, the Socialist candidate, who won just over 3 percent of the vote, and Frank Hanly, the Prohibition candidate, who won slightly more than 1 percent. Neither of them received any electoral votes. The Progressive Party, shattered by Roosevelt's refusal to accept its nomination, did not nominate another candidate and disbanded after the convention. The votes for the major-party candidates were clearly divided by region. Wilson was strong in the South and the West, Hughes in the Midwest and the Northwest. Hughes won only one state (Oregon) west of the Mississippi River, and Wilson won only one state (New Hampshire) in the Northeast. But Wilson penetrated traditional Republican territory by winning Ohio, which turned out to be the critical state in the election. Ohio had 24 electoral votes, and had Hughes won them, it would have reversed the results of the election. But Wilson won the state comfortably by 7.5 percent. California was in play the longest, and ultimately Wilson won it by fewer than 4,000 votes. As in the case of Ohio, if California had gone to Hughes, he would have won the election. The turnout exceeded that of 1916 by 3.5 million votes, indicating substantial voter interest in the critical issues of the day, and particularly in the danger of war. Wilson totaled 3 million more votes than he received in 1912, and Hughes received the highest total that any Republican candidate had received to that point.

THE ROAD TO WAR

After the election, five months remained before the United States entered the war. During that time, Wilson attended to domestic affairs and took steps to implement the Progressive reforms that had been proposed during the campaign, but his attention focused mainly on the war in Europe.

He made one last attempt at a diplomatic solution. In December he offered again to assist in bringing an end to the war, including in his appeal a proposal for a postwar league of nations. He asked both sides to submit their objectives and explained that there were common goals that might lead to a solution. He claimed that he was not seeking to mediate an end to the war, although his critics suggested that he was proposing exactly that. House predicted that the Allies would be enraged at the proposal. Furthermore, he had been conferring with German ambassador Johann von Bernstorff, who had said that Germany would be receptive to such an overture. House worried that if Germany accepted and the Allies refused, the United States would be caught in a difficult position. Lansing had the same concern and asked what would happen if Paul von Hindenburg and Erich Ludendorff urged the kaiser to resume unrestricted submarine warfare, believing that only with the submarine unleashed would they be able to defeat the Allies before the United States might enter the war. Bernstorff cautioned against the change in policy, convinced that this change would bring the United States into the war at the same time that Wilson's policies were providing an opportunity to negotiate a favorable peace while the Americans remained neutral. Bernstorff's advice did not win the argument, and on January 9 the kaiser granted permission for the submarine fleet to attack belligerent and neutral ships. For the time being, Germany did not announce the change in strategy.

On January 22, with no knowledge of the German decision, Wilson elaborated on his proposal, calling for "peace without victory," a settlement that would end the war and negotiate territorial boundaries. Rejecting the traditional European reliance on a balance of power, he called for a "community of power." He urged the European belligerents to accept the American principle of avoiding entangling alliances, making once again an argument for a settlement of the issues and terms of the current war, without American involvement in reaching such an agreement. It was idealistic and problematic—the Europeans had been fighting for two and a half years and had invested countless lives and national prestige in a favorable outcome. They were not about to abandon balance-of-power diplomacy or accept an American proposal to deviate from tradition. The American ambassador to Britain, Walter Hines Page, reported that the British believed they were fighting a war to preserve free government worldwide and that they resented Wilson's proposal, which placed Germany and Britain on the same moral ground, eliciting anger rather than hope.

The offer had little chance, as House and Lansing had anticipated. Neither side considered the offer compelling. On January 31 Bernstorff informed House of the German decision to resume unrestricted submarine warfare in February. Lansing and House urged Wilson to break relations with Germany and to dismiss Bernstorff. Wilson took the issue to his cabinet, which concurred with Lansing and House. On February 3 Wilson went before Congress and announced his decision to break diplomatic relations with Germany. He invoked the *Sussex* pledge and said that he would take no further action beyond the break in relations unless Germany acted on its threat. Three weeks later he took another defensive step, supporting a new policy: the arming of merchant ships.

At a time when dramatic developments seemed to cascade over one another, British Naval Intelligence scored a breakthrough when it intercepted a German telegram that pushed the United States closer to war. German foreign secretary Arthur Zimmermann sent a telegram to the government of Mexico, seeking to exploit the differences that had arisen between the United States and Mexico during the ongoing Mexican Revolution. In the January 17 telegram, he offered Mexico assistance in reclaiming areas in the American Southwest (in Texas, New Mexico, and Arizona) that the United States had taken in the war with Mexico in the 1840s if Mexico would declare war on the United States. The telegram also suggested that Mexico join Germany in an alliance with Japan. Britain held the intercepted telegram in order to avoid revealing their code-breaking abilities, so the Americans did not learn of the transmission until February 24, after Britain had obtained a copy from another source and did not jeopardize its code security. Thus, by the time the Americans learned about the Zimmermann telegram (as it became known), they had already broken relations with

Germany. The telegram thus further enflamed anti-German sentiment in the United States.

Almost lost in the tumultuous diplomatic developments was the sinking of another passenger liner, the RMS *Laconia* of the Cunard Line, on February 25. The ship was en route from the United States to Britain when a German submarine fired two torpedoes into its starboard side some 160 miles off the coast of Ireland. Two Americans were among the twelve victims of the attack.

March ushered in a swirl of events that ultimately propelled the United States to go to war. Wilson took the oath of office for his second term as president on March 5. In his inaugural address, Wilson hedged. He was still hoping to find a way to avoid war. Thus, he repeated some of the principles he had declared on other occasions, calling for the rights of neutrals and arms reduction, but gave no new indication of the direction in which he planned to lead the nation. He had been pressing Congress to authorize the arming of merchant vessels, but the Republicans filibustered against it. On March 11 Wilson used an antipiracy statute that dated to the late eighteenth century to authorize arming merchant vessels without congressional approval.

Then external events forced his hand. The Russian Revolution came to its first climax with the abdication of Czar Nicholas II on the Ides of March. The White House greeted the news with enthusiasm, since it brought to power a liberal democracy under the leadership of lawyer Aleksandr Kerensky. Now if the United States was to join the war, its decision would be more in line with American principles, since the alliance would include only democracies, pitted against the autocratic Central Powers. Wilson encouraged the new government to remain in the war against Germany.

On March 18 Wilson learned that German submarines had sunk three American merchant ships. Germany had activated unrestricted submarine warfare against the United States, which Bernstorff had opposed. Wilson still hoped to avoid war, but it became more difficult to do so. After Germany's announcement of the resumption of unrestricted submarine warfare, Wilson had insisted that he would not take further action if Germany did not actually carry out its threat. Now it had done so, and Wilson's advisers added their voices to those critics who had been calling for war. Lansing had favored sterner action for some time, despite Wilson's chastisement. Lansing enlisted House's support, and the colonel wrote to Wilson saying that he believed the time for war had come. On March 20 Wilson met with the cabinet, which unanimously recommended a declaration of war. German policies gave him little choice.

On the evening of April 2, 1917, President Wilson appeared in the House of Representatives chamber before a joint session of Congress, including the assembled representatives, senators, and Supreme Court justices, to request a declaration of war. It was a speech of resignation and commitment to duty, not a martial call to arms. He uttered the words that would long be linked with the moment and the war ahead: "The world must be made safe for democracy." He summoned sense of duty, of taking the nation into "the most terrible and disastrous of all wars, civilization itself seeming to be in the balance. But the right is more precious than peace, and we shall fight for the things which we have always carried nearest our hearts." Wilson's appeal to national responsibility echoed in the concluding phrase: "God helping her, she can do no other." Historians have long considered Wilson one of the greatest orators among presidents and this his greatest speech. Applause erupted in the House chamber as he stepped down from the rostrum, and people rushed forward to congratulate him. Among them was Senator Henry Cabot Lodge, who with his friend Theodore Roosevelt had been among Wilson's harshest critics, but who now praised the president for expressing "the sentiments of the American people in the loftiest possible manner."

As the Senate and the House considered the war resolution, there was no doubt that it would pass. Nonetheless, the sense of resignation that had permeated Wilson's address carried over to the debate. In the Senate Wisconsin's Progressive senator Robert La Follette, who had spoken in opposition to American involvement in a four-hour speech, and 5 other midwestern senators voted against the resolution, while

82 voted in favor. In the House the resolution passed 373 to 50. The most dramatic—and most discussed—vote was that of Representative Jeannette Rankin of Montana, the first woman elected to the House. A pacifist, but pressured by women who wanted to use her vote to demonstrate the patriotism of women, Rankin finally cast a no vote. She would do so again a quarter century later and thus was the only member of Congress to vote against American participation in both world wars.

In April 1917 the United States was not prepared to go to war. The last years of the Wilson administration, and the last years of the second decade of the twentieth century, unfolded under the shadow of war. American participation in the Great War influenced the development of American history in unanticipated ways. It shaped America's role in the world, witnessing the emergence of a great power that benefited from its geographic location to escape the ravages of war that swept across France and much of the rest of Europe. The domestic impact of the war was enormous. It engendered the growth of the American economy, but also provoked racism, labor violence, xenophobia, and disillusionment with the outcome of the war. It brought an end to Progressive reform and prompted repressive legislation to limit opposition to the war. It impacted the role of women and minorities in American society.

In a sense, Americans fought the war on two fronts: the home front and the battlefronts in Western Europe and the Atlantic Ocean. The next two chapters examine both of these fronts and the impact they had on American society, the economy, and the emergence of a new set of issues that the United States faced after the war.

SUGGESTED READINGS

The Wilson biographies mentioned earlier treat the events discussed in this chapter in some detail. The diplomatic developments that led to the American declaration of war are analyzed in Lloyd E. Ambrosius's *Wilsonian Statecraft: Theory and Practice of Liberal Internationalism during World War I* (Wilmington, DE: Scholarly Resources, 1991). Theodore Roosevelt's opposition to Wilson's diplomacy is the theme of J. Lee Thompson's *Never Call Retreat: Theodore Roosevelt and the Great War* (New York: Palgrave Macmillan, 2013). For the European background of the war, see Christopher Clark's *The Sleepwalkers: How Europe Went to War in 1914* (New York: HarperCollins, 2012).

8

The Home Front

The decision to go to war in April 1917 ended a controversy that had been a feature of American politics since shortly after the war began in Europe nearly three years earlier. Nonetheless, political divisions remained strong even as Congress debated President Wilson's request for a declaration of war. And although Congress voted overwhelmingly in support of Wilson's request, discord continued long after the debate and congressional vote. Once the nation had entered the war, questions had to be addressed by Congress and the American people. How would the war be financed? How would the war affect American civilians who did not join the military? How would divisions in American society and public life be affected by the war? How would the war impact ethnic Americans, women, and minorities? Would business and labor be able to work together during the war?

OPPOSITION TO AMERICAN ENTRY IN WORLD WAR I

Support for Wilson's campaign slogan, "He Kept Us Out of War," gave evidence of strong antiwar sentiment in the United States prior to entry. Many Americans believed that the war in Europe was more evidence of the decline of European society and that the United States ought to stay out. There were different motives for this belief. Among immigrants, even of the second or third generation in the United States, there were strong sentiments for remaining on the sidelines. German Americans had no interest in fighting against their nation of origin and became more resentful as they became targets of discrimination and sometimes of violence. Irish immigrants, whose families had been fighting for independence from Britain, were appalled at the thought of an alliance with their old adversary. Polish immigrants and Russian Jews who had come to the United States felt the same way about an alliance with Russia, which had persecuted them or their ancestors.

The Socialist Party of America opposed the war, and the day after the declaration of war it condemned the action as a crime against the American people. SPA leader Eugene Debs was imprisoned for his opposition. Another prominent Socialist, Victor Berger, who had been elected to Congress from Milwaukee and edited the Socialist newspaper the *Milwaukee Leader*, was also arrested. Among other prominent opponents were IWW leader Big Bill Haywood, Socialist Morris Hillquit, and journalist John Reed. Well-known anarchists Alexander Berkman and Emma Goldman organized rallies opposing the draft, and they, too, were arrested.

Others had moral or religious reasons for opposing American entry. Prominent reformers, including women leaders Jane Addams, Lillian Wald, and Florence Kelley, were pacifists and had been influential in forming the American Union against Militarism in 1915. Prominent industrialists Andrew Carnegie and Henry Ford participated in peace programs. Carnegie assisted in the formation of the Church Peace Union and wrote its charter. Ford commissioned a "peace ship" that sought to develop support for a peace movement among neutral countries. The ship sailed in December 1915 and made stops in Norway, Sweden, and Holland, but nothing came of it. Conscientious objectors opposed military service for religious reasons. The Fellowship of Reconciliation and the Friends Service Committee represented conscientious objectors and won an exemption for them in the draft legislation of 1917. The draft provided an option for alternative service for members of the clergy and for lay members of the historical peace churches: the Society of Friends (the Quakers), the Mennonites, and the Brethren. Also included were members of the International Bible Students Association, which later became the Jehovah's Witnesses. Not all religious leaders opposed the war, and the famous preacher Billy Sunday was an outspoken advocate for American participation.

If any doubt remained about divisions in American society, they would have been tempered by the debate in Congress over the declaration of war. While there was no question that Wilson's request would be approved, those individuals opposed to American involvement made a strong case for remaining neutral. These outspoken critics included people who had supported Wilson's campaign slogan that he had kept the nation out of war. Like many Americans, some senators and representative believed the war was a European affair and that the United States had little to gain by participating. There were isolationists and pacifists that shared this view, and their numbers included both Republicans and Democrats. Republicans such as Theodore Roosevelt and Senator Henry Cabot Lodge had been pushing Wilson to commit to aiding the Allies, but there were also Republicans who were adamantly opposed to American involvement. Senator Robert La Follette was foremost among them, and his Wisconsin constituents included many German Americans who supported that position. Senator George Norris, another Progressive Republican, argued that participation in the war would benefit only war profiteers. Reformer Jane Addams was an ardent pacifist who opposed the war. Senators defied traditions of professional courtesy in attacking La Follette, and people who had previously admired Addams now turned on her. Despite allegations of treason against them, opponents of the war claimed adherence to traditional American values, insisting they wanted to avoid commitments to entangling alliances.

ENSURING AMERICAN SUPPORT FOR THE WAR

Despite a broad base of antiwar sentiment, the majority of Americans—and the majority of senators, whose votes would determine whether the United States would enter the war—were enthusiastic supporters of Wilson's request for a declaration of war, and the proposal passed by a comfortable margin. After Congress approved the declaration of war, the Wilson administration moved to rally Americans to support the cause. The foremost instrument for doing so was the Committee on Public Information (CPI), established on April 13, less than a week after the declaration of war. Headed by George Creel, a Progressive who enlisted people such as muckrakers Ida Tarbell and Ray Stannard Baker, the organization had as its task to disseminate facts about American democracy and American ideals. Creel committed the CPI to "the facts," but in spite of Creel's insistence that the words *censorship* and *propaganda* not be used, it did both. It was not meant to be a dispassionate source of information; it was in fact a propaganda organization, untempered by critical points of view, dedicated to convincing Americans of the need to give the war effort their unconditional support. It utilized all manner of media: bulletins, posters, newspapers, and films to reach as many people as possible. Four Minute Men, a subdivision of the CPI, organized 75,000 speakers drawn from local communities to give speeches on selected topics that changed every ten days. Creel claimed that the Four Minute Men gave 7,555,190 speeches to 314,454,514 people and lauded their effort in helping to win the war. The CPI targeted specific audiences, delivering materials to teachers, editorials to newspapers, and pamphlets and documents in translation to foreign countries. The CPI established twenty foreign bureaus that distributed Wilson's speeches and other documents explaining American goals and principles. Wilson's Fourteen Points were among these documents, and they were influential in developing support for the concept of self-determination and for the League of Nations. Movies were another popular form of distributing the CPI message. Historian David Kennedy noted that these films began with positive messages in movies such as *Pershing's Crusaders*, but later in the war they had changed to overtly propagandistic presentations, including *The Prussian Cur* and *The Kaiser: The Beast of Berlin*.

Representations of German culture were subject to suppression. Under local prerogative, libraries hid (or burned) books in German, schools discontinued German-language instruction, and bands ceased the performance of German music. Movements to rename hamburgers as liberty steak seemed absurd, but nonetheless created twenty-first-century echoes when France disagreed with American policy in the

Middle East, and Americans took their revenge by (briefly and rarely) renaming french fries "freedom fries." Mark Sullivan, in his detailed report on American society published in the mid-1920s, reported that in places in the West, German measles became liberty measles and dachshunds became liberty pups. The town of East Germantown, Indiana, took the name Pershing after the general leading the American Expeditionary Force (AEF) in France. Citizens of Berlin, New Hampshire, however, voted to retain the name of their town.

More serious were actions directed against individuals with German surnames. A mob in Collinsville, Illinois, lynched a man named Robert Prager under suspicion of spying. The Justice Department compiled a list of some 480,000 German aliens in the United States and imprisoned about 4,000 of them. Author John Steinbeck later recalled incidents of anti-German discrimination as a young man in Salinas, California. In Tulsa a mob attacked members of the Industrial Workers of the World, a radical labor union, whipping them and pouring tar on their wounds.

FINANCING THE WAR AND ORGANIZING FOR WARTIME PRODUCTION

The declaration of war quickly exposed the fact that there had been little planning for the eventuality that the United States might enter the war. Such was the cost of an administration—and a public that supported it—committed to keeping the nation out of war. Despite the lag, it took months to coordinate a wartime economy and compel it to function in a fashion that at least approached efficiency. There were many reasons for this delay. In April 1917 it was not even clear how the United States would contribute to the Allied cause, and it took until the fall before events in Europe made it imperative that the nation contribute a large army to help the Allies win the war. Before decisions could be made about how to organize the economy, Congress and the president had to resolve who had the authority to do so. The questions they had to resolve were thorny, and the answers threatened to alienate the very people and organizations that were essential to the task at hand. How could business be convinced to support the war, to convert from consumer production to wartime production? And how could their efforts be coordinated to minimize duplication and waste? How could the War Department and the army and navy work with the private sector to ensure that their needs would be met? How could labor be convinced to cooperate, and what would business be willing to do to ensure labor's cooperation?

Ultimately, the outcome of wartime industrial production was in increased centralization of the economy, characterized by increased cooperation between the federal government and big business. The process led to other developments that set a pattern for the remaining decades of the twentieth century: an increase in the size and authority of the federal government, a growth of the power of the president at the expense of Congress, enhanced independence (with limits on regulation) of the private sector, and a growth in the capacity of the American economy. War thus transformed the economy in ways that gave American business a competitive advantage in the years following the war. At the same time, there were costs to these developments. Giving business more power meant giving labor less. Wartime developments sowed the seeds of postwar disputes, many of which emerged in the immediate aftermath of the war, some of which festered for years and became apparent only with the onset of the Great Depression, a decade after the end of the war.

What planning had been done prior to the declaration of war was *not* centralized. A group of engineers contributed significantly to this process. Howard E. Coffin, who had been vice president of the Hudson Motor Car Company, learned in the automobile industry the need for standardization and brought this guidance to the government. With the concurrence of President Wilson, Coffin instituted a national industrial inventory. Meanwhile, Hollis Godfrey, another engineer and the president of the Drexel Institute in Philadelphia, had begun his own study in 1916 to make an estimate of possible war needs if the United States were to enter the war. Their work, and pressure from the preparedness movement, led the administration to establish the National Council of Defense. Its membership included Coffin and

Godfrey, along with financier Bernard Baruch, labor leader Samuel Gompers, other business leaders, and the secretaries of war, the navy, agriculture, commerce, labor, and the interior. The council acted with a rather indefinite set of guidelines and set about conceiving of a plan centered in the states, with each state having a council. Once the United States entered the war, this system proved impractical, and an alternative proposal led to a series of administrative units defined by function. This division led to the implementation of a set of "superagencies": the Food Administration, Fuel Administration, Railroad Administration, and War Industries Board (WIB).

Before establishing superagencies, a basic question had to be addressed. How would the war be financed? Wilson gave the task to his son-in-law, husband of his daughter Eleanor, Secretary of the Treasury William Gibbs McAdoo. McAdoo held high office not because he was married to the president's daughter, but because of his undoubted competence. He had built a subway line beneath the Hudson River in New York City, defying critics who believed it could not be done. He built a personal fortune in the stock market. Financing the war, however, was an extraordinary challenge. First, no one knew how much money would be needed, but it was clear that it would be an astronomical figure. One credible estimate was that the first year of the war would cost about $10 billion, an astonishing figure given that the entire cost of the federal government since its establishment in 1789 had been $24 billion. Complicating the issue further was the fact that the government's principal means of raising money had been the tariff, and tariff money was plunging because the war had diminished international trade to a trickle. The Sixteenth Amendment to the Constitution, passed by Congress in 1909 and ratified by three-quarters of the states in 1913, established the income tax. But to attempt to use the income tax solely to pay for the war ran the risk of alienating the American people even as the tax was gaining confidence among them at a top rate of 2 percent. Some suggested that it was manifestly unfair to send soldiers to fight in France and then expect them to pay off war debts through taxes when they returned home. McAdoo chose to supplement taxes with war bonds that paid an interest rate of between 3.5

and 4.5 percent. His initial goal was to have a fifty-fifty split between war bonds and taxes, but he ultimately decided to maintain as closely as possible a two-to-one ratio of bonds to taxes. The Treasury was able to come very close to the target ratio. In the fiscal years 1918 and 1919, the government raised $15.5 billion in bonds and $8.8 billion in taxes. The bond campaign succeeded largely because the government employed emerging advertising methods, calling the bonds "Liberty Loans" and playing on patriotism by asking people to put their money on the line while soldiers in Europe were putting their lives on the line. Prominent Hollywood actors including Douglas Fairbanks, Mary Pickford, and Al Jolson lent their names and energy to the campaign. War bonds were so popular that in many communities, people harassed neighbors who did not participate in the campaigns and ridiculed them as "slackers."

But taxes were essential, especially because early estimates of the cost of the war quickly proved to be insufficient. The president appeared before Congress on May 27 and asked for taxes on incomes, war profits, and luxury purchases. He made a plea, controversial then and later, that "politics is adjourned." That request sounded patriotic at the time, but it would be thrown back at Wilson in the fall when he asked the American people to elect a Democratic Congress. In the War Revenue Act passed in October 1917, Congress raised individual and corporate tax rates. The rate for a comfortable middle-class income of $10,000 rose from 1.2 percent to 7.8 percent. The rate for the very wealthy earning $1 million rose from 10.3 percent to 70.3 percent. By the end of 1917, it was clear that more revenue would be needed, and by spring deficits rose to unprecedented levels of $1 billion per month—essentially the annual budget prior to the war. McAdoo turned once again to taxes, especially corporate taxes, the preferred approach of Progressives. He not only believed he could not avoid taxes, but also believed that new taxes would strengthen the sale of Liberty Bonds because they were exempt from taxes. Congress was torn by the issue, fearing heading home for the coming election campaign after a session of tax increases. Ultimately, as economist Hugh Rockoff summarized, the new taxes "raised revenues from $930 million in 1916 to

$4,388 million in 1918. Federal expenditures, however, increased from $1,333 million in 1916 to $15,585 million in 1918."[1]

The Food Administration became the first of the superagencies to organize. For administrator, President Wilson selected Herbert Hoover, who was at the time head of the Commission for the Relief of Belgium, ideal preparation for the work at hand. Hoover came to Washington with a sterling reputation. Trained as an engineer at Stanford University, he had been a successful mining engineer, which had made him a rich man. Like McAdoo, Hoover had succeeded at everything he tried. Like McAdoo, he realized that Americans would respond better to voluntary programs rather than to coercive ones.

As food administrator, Hoover faced a considerable challenge. He was of course familiar with the pressing need for food among America's European allies, but he also faced problems at home, where the grain harvests of 1916 and 1917 had been disappointing, and food prices in the United States had been increasing. Hoover's task was to increase production and develop a system of distribution that incorporated American farmers, distributors from the field to the market, and consumers and also provided for the pressing needs of Europe. He determined to avoid rationing and instead pursued a course of voluntary cooperation, and in doing so he inspired a sense that everyone could have a role in winning the war. His office pitched appeals to housewives to have "meatless" days and "wheatless" days, and they responded. The Food Administration realized the importance of reaching women, who after all prepared most of the food consumed in America. The Food Administration sent representatives into communities to teach food conservation and nutrition. It produced posters with pithy messages:

- Sow the seeds of Victory! Plant and raise your own vegetables.
- Every garden a munitions plant.

1. Hugh Rockoff, "U.S. Economy in World War I," http://eh.net/encyclopedia/u-s-economy-in-world-war-i/.

- Food will win the war.
- Wheatless days in America make sleepless nights in Germany.

Other posters were educational:

- Eat more corn, oats and rye products—Fish and poultry—Fruits, vegetables, and potatoes—Baked, boiled and broiled foods. Eat less wheat, meat, sugar, and fats to save for the army and our allies.

Hoover used a similar approach—encouragement rather than coercion—to convince farmers to increase production; rather than establish production quotas, he established higher prices for agricultural commodities and convinced distributors to agree. Farmers who had been suffering from a seemingly endless debt cycle responded, and the war years proved to be so successful for American farmers that wartime prices became a standard for leaner years that followed. Wheat was in demand in European countries as well as in the United States, and Hoover encouraged farmers to increase the acreage in production. Even so, shortages occurred, and speculators bought wheat and sold it for inflated prices. The Food Administration formed a Grain Corporation to buy all wheat and force the speculators out of business. As the war progressed, Europe could absorb virtually all the surplus American farmers could produce. Before the war, the United States had exported 7 million tons of food to Europe. In 1919 that number had risen to 19 million tons. In both 1917 and 1918, the United States and Canada together shipped more than 235 million bushels of wheat to Britain, France, and Italy. Farm income increased from $7.6 billion in 1914 to $17.7 billion in 1919.

Not all government programs achieved the level of success that marked the Treasury program or the Food Administration. The Fuel Administration failed for several reasons, not the least of which was an attempt to use coercion rather than voluntary cooperation as a means to compel citizen compliance. Hampered by a shortage of fuel in general and coal in particular, the Fuel Administration had to confront the coldest winter in a half century in 1917–18. The context in which the Fuel Administration organized made its work more difficult. The Committee on Coal Production, controlled by the industry, had come to an agreement on pricing and production levels, and to the Fuel Administration these agreements were suspect, raising the specter of a coal trust. In an attempt to bring relief to people suffering from the frigid temperatures, the Fuel Administration overrode the committee's decision and mandated the price of coal at $2 a ton. While well intentioned, this decision had the opposite effect. Unlike the approach of the Food Administration, which set prices high to encourage production, the Fuel Administration had to deal with prices so low that they discouraged production. Shortages of coal ran in the range of 6 million tons a month.

The fuel administrator was part of the problem. Harry Garfield, the son of President James Garfield, was an acquaintance of Wilson's from his time at Princeton, but proved not to have the ability to handle the admittedly complex problems he faced. It was more than a matter of pricing. Transportation was equally vexing, and the attempt to get war supplies to East Coast ports created a bottleneck that made distribution of coal and other consumer goods nearly impossible. Civil order was breaking down as people stole coal, and local officials along transportation routes seized train cars of coal for their citizens. Garfield responded by closing all factories east of the Mississippi River for four days to clear the logjam, to little effect. He mandated "heatless Mondays" but failed to convince the public as Hoover had done with his meatless and wheatless days. Garfield survived the war as fuel administrator, but his legacy was not a proud one.

Given the magnitude of issues involved in moving from a peacetime economy to a wartime one, it was not surprising that the new agencies had a mixed record. But by early 1918 it was apparent that one of the problems was that there was no overall coordination. Much of the blame initially fell on Secretary of War Newton Baker, whose critics blamed him for failing to coordinate wartime production. Among those critics was Colonel House, who had the president's ear and began to use that access to try to get rid of Baker. Congressional hearings exposed supply problems, and Baker was at the center of the storm. The secretary finally offered his resignation, but Wilson refused to accept it. It turned out to be a good decision, as Baker went on to prove his competence in managing the War Department.

But that did not solve the problem, and ultimately Wilson addressed it not by firing anyone but instead by bringing in an administrator to have the overall authority needed to bring order out of chaos. The man who energized the process, Bernard Baruch, was a wealthy financier and philanthropist, one of the richest men in the country. He was vain, egotistical, and a relentless self-promoter, but he had ideas and knew how to get things done. He served on several wartime boards, including the General Munitions Board and the Advisory Commission to the Council of National Defense. He functioned on these panels mainly as an adviser, but he came into contact with key people involved in organizing the war effort. He and McAdoo became friends, and he worked with Secretary of War Baker and Secretary of the Navy Josephus Daniels. His imagination, creativity, and business acumen got the attention of these key figures in the administration and of the president. Wilson found a place for him, heading an advisory group called the War Industries Board. Under Baruch's leadership, it became much more, ultimately serving as what historian John Milton Cooper called "the spark plug of industrial mobilization."[2] The War Industries Board had the task of coordinating between war needs and consumer needs, or, as he explained it, to distinguish "civilian *needs* [from] civilian *wants*." It also meant reforming military procurement, which was fragmented between bureaus with little coordination, meaning that the military lost out on price cuts it could have obtained with bulk purchases. Standardization was another way to consolidate purchases, and the War Industries Board convinced business to assist, sometimes with great advances in efficiency. It slashed the number of colors of typewriter ribbons, for example, from 150 to 5.

2. John Milton Cooper Jr., *Woodrow Wilson: A Biography* (New York: Alfred A. Knopf, 2009), 392.

The legislation that enabled the president to create wartime agencies came about only after a protracted debate between the administration and Congress over the war powers of the executive. The consequence of this debate for Wilson was that it led to a more antagonistic relationship with Congress. For Baruch, the consequence was that it limited his authority. He could not dictate policy to business, could not set prices, and had to function with a limited staff that thus could not effectively monitor business conduct across the board. The positive side of this arrangement was that it virtually forced Baruch to follow the approach that had worked well for McAdoo and Hoover before him: to work through voluntary cooperation rather than coercion.

Baruch found ways to work around these limitations and to make cooperation a virtue. If he could not set prices, he could establish priorities, which often resulted in the same thing. He established twenty-one production zones around the country and found businessmen to head advisory committees in each zone, and they became his agents of cooperation. While the army refused to give up its authority over procurement, its representative to the War Industries Board found that it worked to the benefit of the army to cooperate with the board. In all of these arrangements, Baruch's reputation—self-created though it may have been—served him well. Cooper describes him as a "benevolent czar," so both parties benefited from a cooperative relationship.[3] Congress was reluctant to criticize Baruch, whose popularity rivaled Herbert Hoover's.

MOBILIZATION OF THE ECONOMY

When the United States declared war in April 1917, it was not prepared to participate in a meaningful way, nor was it certain of how it could contribute. For the remainder of 1917 and well into 1918, Americans in various ways confronted the realities of modern warfare. The

3. Ibid., 427.

nation had last fought a war in 1898, and it had been a brief affair in Cuba and the Philippines in which the United States faced a weak, declining power in Spain that had to fight far from its homeland. Now, a generation later, the very nature of warfare had transformed. It was an industrial age, and the technology of warfare had brought about a revolution in weapons. The advent of submarine warfare at sea and the use of the machine gun and poison gas on land meant that the tactics employed in 1898 were entirely outmoded. The airplane was another innovation, but its value in warfare had not yet matured, and its use in the war was far less effective than the submarine or the machine gun. Before the war with Spain, the United States had engaged in an unprecedented shipbuilding program that by the turn of the century had made the nation a world-class naval power, but in the intervening years the great European powers had surpassed it. In 1917 the United States did not have the surface ships to match Britain or Germany and certainly not a submarine fleet to compete with the German navy.

The United States had also made a decision after the war with Spain not to have a large standing army. The decision of the Wilson administration to stay out of the war through the election of 1916 and into early 1917 meant that it had done little to prepare for the eventuality that the United States might be forced to enter the conflict. So in April 1917, the United States was a member of the group of Allies opposing Germany, but it had yet to raise an army that could contribute to winning the war.

But the problem was not merely one of weapons or manpower. It was also a conceptual issue, a matter of how to confront what was now a national emergency that required raising an army, organizing a consumer economy into one that could equip that army, and convincing an independent-minded citizenry to make the sacrifices necessary to make it all possible.

Ultimately, the performance of the American economy was mixed. It faced extraordinary problems, and it took months to solve many of them. Because the United States was involved in the war for only nineteen months, there was not sufficient time for industry to produce armaments needed for twentieth-century warfare. Shipbuilding, for example, was a complicated process that could not be organized quickly. The cargo ships needed in World War I each required some 250,000 parts and about 500,000 rivets. These parts had to be requisitioned from factories that were converting from other kinds of construction. Once they went into full production, shipyards could turn out a ship every other day. It was an extraordinary achievement, but it came too late to have a major impact on the outcome of the war. As it was, the United States had to rely on British ships or captured German ships to transport troops and war supplies to France. As historian Robert H. Ferrell summarized the performance of the economy, if the war had lasted into 1919 or 1920, this level of construction would have contributed mightily to the Allied cause and to victory.

Mobilization of the economy got off to a rocky start. In addition to the human conflicts and lack of planning, the weather had an enormous impact on production. The winter of 1917–18 was one of the worst on record. Subzero temperatures influenced manufacturing processes and transportation of materials needed for production. For two months a succession of gales swept across the country east of the Rockies. Snowdrifts impeded railroads, and engineers had a hard time keeping up steam in their locomotives. In a system that was already overburdened with freight and revised schedules to satisfy wartime demands, this winter weather was the tipping point. Some companies had to suspend operations at times; others had to shut down completely. It was the kind of winter that is disastrous in normal times. In wartime, it was catastrophic.

American leaders, of course, had been following events in Europe, but until the United States actually entered the war, they had done little planning. Once the nation committed to war, it took time to gear up production. Several factors interfered with the transition to wartime production and made this process less effective than it might have been. Administrative inefficiency was an overriding issue, and at the outset decision makers truly did not understand its complexities. Problems emerged from the top down. The only experience that the nation had that offered precedents was the Civil War, and its lessons were limited because of the change in weaponry, the distances involved, the coordination required for participation in an alliance, and the changes in industrial production. There was far too little coordination within the military and between military leaders and civilians in industry. There was a lack of trust between the military and civilians. The military did not run its operation effectively, allowing bureaus to place their orders without coordination within and without consultation with civilians. Within the War Industries Board, Baruch gave principal authority to the military. As a result, military leaders issued requisitions without understanding the problems facing industry, and when industry did not respond, the little trust that existed evaporated.

A crucial step in breaking the logjam came in April 1918 when Army Chief of Staff General Peyton March appointed General Hugh S. Johnson as director of the Purchase and Supply Branch of the General Staff. Neither March nor Johnson thought much of the civilians with whom they had to work, but Johnson took the position in good faith. As he worked with Baruch, the two men came to respect one another and appreciate the problems each side faced. By setting up procurement with counterparts on both the army and the civilian sides, the system improved. The time involved in developing these relationships illustrates one of the reasons for the disappointing performance of American industry during the war. Johnson's appointment came a year after the United States entered the war and only seven months before it ended. The lack of preparation for war prior to American entry had costs, and there are countless other examples of how the delay impacted American participation in the war.

One way to analyze the performance of the wartime economy is to look at specific weapons systems. In some cases, Americans had to decide whether to use designs supplied by their allies or develop their own design. Production of artillery pieces proved to be a disappointment. When the United States entered the war, the army hoped to use an American-designed gun, but delays forced the army to rely on the French 75 mm gun, which had stood the test of wartime performance. Plans to manufacture this model in the United States ran into problems; the French were reluctant to share their plans for the gun with foreigners, and the manufacture of the gun in France relied on artisans and thus was difficult to translate into assembly-line mass production. (This period was an era of transition in the manufacturing process, and Americans ran into similar problems with their own rifle production.) Ultimately, France provided artillery guns, the French 75, for American artillery batteries to use in France. What added to the American disappointment was that later tests showed that an American artillery gun developed in 1902, which the army had not considered for use in World War I, actually had advantages over the French 75. It was sturdier, easier to maneuver, and as accurate as the French 75.

American manufacturing fared better in the production of rifles and machine guns. When the United States entered the war, its army used Model 1903 Springfield rifles, which were accurate but still relied on artisan production. At the time, American companies were manufacturing another rifle, the Enfield, for Britain. The army decided to modify the Enfield so that it could use Springfield cartridges, and the modified rifle became the Lee-Enfield. The US Army thus used both the Springfield and the Lee-Enfield, and American manufacturers produced 2.5 million rifles by war's end, the majority of which were Lee-Enfields, which could be produced on the assembly line.

Machine-gun production was another success story. Machine guns had proved to be essential weapons in the first battles of the war in 1914, which was no less the case in 1917. At the beginning, the AEF used British and French machine guns, but by February 1918 the American Browning machine gun was in production, and it proved to be superior to any other machine gun.

So although there were notable failures in American manufacturing, there were also demonstrable successes. Given the limited time involved—nineteen months from the declaration of war to the Armistice—it was a respectable record. Given the time involved in making decisions, coordinating procurement needs, enlisting manufacturers in production contracts, and cooperating with European allies, some of the achievements were remarkable and the setbacks are at least understandable.

BUSINESS, LABOR, AND GOVERNMENT DURING WORLD WAR I

Business had plenty of reasons to cooperate with the federal government during the war, and they went far beyond the charms of Bernard Baruch and Herbert Hoover. There was money to be made in federal contracts, after all. But beyond that incentive, the government needed industry to cooperate and was willing to make concessions to businessmen to get them on board. It was expensive to convert to wartime production, to shift from automobiles to tanks or from passenger ships to warships. So the government offered incentives such as the cost-plus contract. This arrangement meant that manufacturers covered their costs and also received a certain figure or percentage above costs; thus, the contract guaranteed that they would receive a profit.

The government cooperated especially with big businesses. These companies were of course in the best position to convert to wartime production, and in most cases the government already had experience working with them, so both sides knew how to work with one another. The government also agreed to suspend antitrust laws for the duration of the war. Another advantage for big corporations was the creation of positions for "dollar-a-year" men. Corporations "loaned" employees with needed skills to the government for a token payment of a dollar per year. On the surface it seemed like an act of corporate generosity and patriotism, but it also brought great advantages to the corporations who gained prior knowledge of forthcoming government decisions and could also help to direct government contracts to their employers, who were after all still paying salaries to these employees. The biggest companies were the major beneficiaries; J. P. Morgan's firm, for example, had several dollar-a-year men working in government positions. The government also formed industrial committees to give advice on prices and purchases, which created a situation not unlike the dollar-a-year men, since their advice predictably favored their own companies. The chairman of the aluminum advisory committee, for instance, was the president of the nation's largest aluminum company. The War Industries Board's mission included addressing some of these inequities, but this task was subordinate to creating policies to increase efficiency and to increase production—both of which were more effective in dealing with big companies.

The government-business partnership formed during the war reversed many of the economic reforms of the Progressive movement. With antitrust suspended and regulatory commissions such as the Interstate Commerce Commission staffed by railroad men, there was no effective check on the growth of business. Progressivism, and reform of any sort, took a backseat to winning the war.

When the United States entered the war, labor was fragmented. The American Federation of Labor, under the leadership of Samuel Gompers since its establishment in 1886, represented skilled workers and as such was essentially a conservative union that represented mainly white men. It did not encourage minorities or women to join. As a union of skilled workers, it had clout that many other unions lacked, as its workers were not easily replaced, and thus management was more likely to negotiate with its leaders to avoid or end a strike. Gompers supported the president's policy, believing that the war offered labor an opportunity to gain influence that would survive after the war. Wilson rewarded his loyalty and appointed Gompers to the Advisory Commission of the Council of National Defense. Hugh Frayne, another official in the AFL, won an Army Distinguished Service Medal for work he did for the labor division of the War Industries Board.

Not surprisingly, support for the war was thinner in other unions. When the federal government had taken a position on strikes in the previous decades, it generally sided with management. The federal government had helped to break strikes in the previous quarter century and especially in the 1890s had been willing to use violence to do so. By the time the war began, unions had begun to see the Republican Party as the party of business, but the Democratic Party had not always demonstrated that it supported labor, although Wilson supported the eight-hour workday. In 1917 there was broad labor unrest; there were 4,450 strikes, the most there had been in any one year in American history. Railroad unions were threatening a strike when the war began over lack of enforcement of the eight-hour day. Miners in the United Mine Workers were generally opposed to the war. The Industrial Workers of the World was organizing workers in the timber industry in the Northwest, copper mining in Arizona and Montana, and shipyards on the West Coast. The president sent Felix Frankfurter, then a young attorney and later a justice on the Supreme Court, to investigate the situation. He found that where unions had tried to organize, employers suppressed them. In one such case in a Bisbee, Arizona, copper mine in June 1917, the county sheriff called for federal help in breaking a strike, but when a government representative found nothing illegal about the strike, the sheriff sent a force of two thousand deputized enforcers to round up twelve hundred strikers and ship them on railroad boxcars to a siding in New Mexico, abandoned until rescuers found them two days later. Bisbee became an armed camp and hired replacements. The IWW had its greatest success in industries that were notoriously hard to organize, such as mining and timber. But these industries flourished in remote areas, where there was little supervision by the government and where employers had the isolation to operate against workers with impunity. Furthermore, the federal government considered the IWW to be subversive and later did what it could to destroy it, beginning with raids against its offices in the Pacific Northwest in the fall.

Nonetheless, the Wilson administration sought to form a partnership with labor as it had with business. Although there were some positive results, labor was much less a beneficiary of government policy than business, and the venture failed to live up to Gompers's expectation of a better relationship between labor and government after the war. Moderate labor unions cooperated with the Wilson administration, however, so the president got much of what he wanted. The government formed the National War Labor Board (NWLB), which governed relations between labor and management. Although it had no real enforcement authority, its rulings were evenhanded and generally respected by both sides, and Wilson put the authority of his office behind their recommendations. The twelve-member board had representatives of labor and management, cochaired by former president William Howard Taft. Taft was astonished at the low wages received by workers, wondering how they could live on such paltry earnings. He pushed for higher wages, and businesses were doing so well that they generally accepted wage increases that doubled and even tripled. However, many companies rolled them back after the war. The NWLB ruled against both strikes and lockouts, but it did push for collective bargaining, the first time that the federal government did so. It supported the eight-hour day for workers and equal pay for women workers. Union membership increased from 2.6 million in 1914 to 5 million by 1920.

WOMEN AND THE IMPACT OF WORLD WAR I

The war opened opportunities for women in the workforce. As some two million men departed for service in France, women and minorities, especially African Americans, were able to move into jobs they left behind and to gain employment in newly created jobs as companies converted to wartime production. The coalescence of the suffrage movement and the war gave impetus to increasing opportunities for women in the workplace, and the fact that women performed well on the job in turn forced the government to take the feminist cause more seriously. The question the nation faced was whether women's employment would lead to permanent changes in American society or it would be a short-term change for the duration of the war. For women who were already working, the war gave them a chance to move up into better jobs that paid more than the traditional women's jobs of nursing, teaching, and secretarial work. Women who had never worked before also entered the labor market, but their numbers were relatively small—only about 5 percent of women workers.

When the census of 1920 recorded the jobs that women held, it found that more than eight million women held jobs in 437 distinctly classified jobs. New positions for women opened in munitions factories, which employed about a hundred thousand women. Women became telegraph messengers, elevator operators, preachers, office managers, bookkeepers, cashiers, plasterers, police officers, and lawyers. One female lawyer defended a man who had been accused of murder.

This infusion of women in the workplace ushered in debates over their roles, some of which remain issues today. One such issue was the question of whether women ought to receive the same pay as men if they performed the same job. The War Labor Board insisted that women performing identical jobs should receive the same pay, although it was difficult to enforce what amounted to a recommendation rather than a mandate. In New York only 9 percent of women doing identical work actually received equal pay. At the time this discrepancy did not develop into a broad demand, and in fact many employers liked to hire women because they could pay them less than they paid men. Another such issue was the debate over protective legislation, laws that provided conditions on the job that recognized their differences from men, such as regulations that they would not be required to lift items over a specified weight or that they be given longer or more frequent rest breaks. Women differed on this question: Some believed that it was desirable to provide such protection, since employers would not necessarily provide it. Other women argued that if women were going to compete with men for jobs, they should not expect to require any difference in their job description.

The employment of women during the war did not lead to major changes in American society. Male veterans returning after the war expected to get their jobs back, and employers expected to give them back. Some employers in fact considered it the culmination of the patriotic duty of women to relinquish their jobs, and in many cases men protested if the women did not do so willingly. While some analysts later made the case that women's experiences during the war led to changes in the role of women in the 1920s, there is little evidence to support this notion.

Women also served the war effort, both in the United States and in Europe, some with the military, others in support organizations. Many women in the States served as volunteers, raising money through bond drives and supporting private and public organizations in many capacities. The navy was the first service to admit women and issued a call for volunteers shortly after the United States declared war in April 1917. Women enlisted as yeomen, officially Yeomen (F), or more popularly yeomenettes. Many of them served in clerical or secretarial positions, although the Naval Reserve also enlisted women as electricians, chemists, pharmacists, and accountants. At a peak in 1918, 11,000 women served in the navy. The US Marines also welcomed women, although not until August 1918, just four months before the end of the war. Applicants had to fill out an application and submit to rigorous entrance standards, including an interview and a requirement for character references; by war's end, only 305 women had been admitted. They became known as "marinettes."

Nurses served in both the army and the navy in France. The Red Cross supplied the army with most of its nurses, who remained under Red Cross authority at base hospitals until receiving an assignment to go forward with military units. Whether at base hospitals or forward positions, the nurses encountered harsh conditions, often treating soldiers who had received serious wounds and arrived in large numbers at field hospitals. The demands on nurses exceeded their civilian experience and forced them to adjust quickly. In one case after a major battle, a base hospital staffed with two doctors, twenty Red Cross nurses, and a few civilians from a nearby French village received some 2,000 seriously wounded soldiers over a four-day period. No army nurses died from combat wounds, although some received serious injuries, and a few received military decorations for courageous service.

Other service organizations contributed support. The Salvation Army, led by Commander Evangeline Booth, began organizing long before the United States entered the war, enlisting women in the spirit of "service to humanity." In France the Salvation Army's "doughnut girls" became a hallmark of the organization, providing baked goods for soldiers. The Salvation Army became a social service agency, providing services from mending uniforms to caring for wounded soldiers. Women working for the YMCA provided similar services, operating canteens that provided lemonade, chocolate, and even tobacco to the soldiers. Both organizations generally worked with the Service of

Supply (SOS), which operated in secure areas some distance from the front. Responding to a request from General Pershing, the Army Signal Corps recruited bilingual women who could speak French as well as English to serve as telephone operators and work as both operators and translators behind the front in France. These young women, who became known as the "Hello Girls," provided vital communication skills in support of the army.

AFRICAN AMERICANS AND THE GREAT WAR

For African Americans, the first challenge offered by the war was whether they ought to support it. For some, it made little sense to fight for democracy in France when they were not allowed to participate freely in democracy at home. President Wilson had not used his office to open more opportunities for African Americans, and in fact civil rights had taken a backward step during his presidency. He had not objected to Postmaster General Burleson and Treasury Secretary McAdoo segregating their departments early in his first term, and he had abruptly dismissed a delegation of African Americans led by William Monroe Trotter. His understanding of race relations in the South was formed by his own experiences there as a young man, which meant that he was comfortable with segregation. Protesters in a parade down Fifth Avenue in New York carried a placard that read, "Mr. President, why not make AMERICA safe for democracy?"

African American leaders were divided. A. Philip Randolph, later a prominent labor organizer who led protests during World War II, argued that African Americans should not support the war. W. E. B. DuBois, however, presented the most persuasive argument in the *Crisis*, the official journal of the NAACP that he edited: "Let us, while this war lasts, forget our special grievances and close our ranks shoulder to shoulder with our own white fellow citizens." African Americans supported the war, trusting that their loyalty would be rewarded with greater access to the rights of citizenship after the war ended.

African Americans who served in the army encountered prejudice and discrimination from training camp through active duty and after their release. Black troops training in the South were particular targets, both within the camps and when they visited nearby towns. Even African American soldiers in uniform became targets of harassment by civilians and prejudicial treatment by white soldiers and officers. The YMCA in the South often refused to serve them. The government provided property for Hostess Houses for training white soldiers to socialize with female visitors, but did not do so in segregated facilities for African American soldiers until April 1918. Such thoughtless discrimination was commonplace.

African Americans were also targets of violence, and authorities invariably blamed them for initiating trouble. The most flagrant case occurred at a camp near Houston in August 1917. Most of the soldiers were from the North, and they resented the restrictions placed on them in the southern city. Various reports surfaced regarding the start of trouble, but all confirmed a tense relationship between the soldiers and the white community. A fight broke out, and black soldiers sought revenge for what they considered to be unjust treatment. It soon got out of hand, and in the ensuing riot fifteen whites and three African Americans died. The army hanged thirteen black soldiers and sentenced forty-one others to life in prison. Later the army court-martialed other black soldiers and sentenced another sixteen to execution, although this sentence was not carried out.

In the aftermath, Secretary Baker met with black leaders, including Robert Russa Moton, the president of Tuskegee Institute, the Alabama college founded by Booker T. Washington. The African American leaders said that any plan for using African American soldiers had to include a combat role. Baker agreed and carried out a plan to train black officers, establishing a camp to do so near Des Moines, Iowa. But Baker was an exception to the usual white insistence on segregation and the common belief among white soldiers that blacks were not reliable soldiers. Baker was also an exception within the Wilson administration, which showed little sympathy for African Americans in any circumstance. When Wilson received a letter from a white soldier who complained that he could not work under black officers, he expressed sympathy for the insubordinate soldier's point of view and passed the complaint on to Baker, who handled the matter without sanctioning the complaining soldier.

The commanding officer of the Des Moines camp, General Charles C. Ballou, was a white officer who demonstrated sympathy for the African Americans under his command that was unusual for the era—and especially for the army. But Ballou had to follow army directives that themselves were discriminatory. And Ballou, despite his sympathies, made decisions that created distance between him and the officer trainees. The potential officers who reported to the camp in Des Moines encountered discrimination in the city's stores and movie houses. Iowa had a policy of nondiscrimination, but when one of the African Americans tried to buy a ticket at a local movie theater, the owner refused to admit him. General Ballou criticized the soldier for provoking the dispute.

Black officers received orders to units for which they had no training—infantry officers to artillery regiments, for example. African American soldiers complained that the best black officers were sent to noncombatant units, the worst to France. In response to such discrimination, W. E. B. DuBois in the *Crisis* questioned whether the army wanted black units to fail. In response to the controversy, Baker's camp closed after the initial class graduated, and black soldiers in Europe served under white officers.

Army policies did nothing to dispel DuBois's criticism, and even if the army did not want African American soldiers to fail, it did little to ensure their success. Often training for African American soldiers was cut short in comparison to white soldiers. When there was conflict with the local community near the training camps, the army often sought to avoid further confrontations by sending the soldiers to France quickly, even if they had not completed training. The army also anticipated using most of the black soldiers in labor units rather than on the front lines, distrusting them in combat and believing that they were best suited for labor assignments. Then, in France, some were sent to combat units, and because they had little proper training they performed poorly, in what amounted to a self-fulfilling prophecy.

Of the 367,000 African Americans who served in the army during the war, about a fourth of them served in Europe. The 92nd Division was an all-black division, commanded by white officers at the higher ranks, although some of the junior officers were African Americans. The 93rd Division, also a black division, and some of its regiments fought under French command and performed well. The presumption of black inferiority carried over into all army activities in the army, however, and eventually the 92nd Division received harsh criticism (as elaborated in chapter 9).

The war also gave further impetus to the African American diaspora already under way. By 1910 the boll weevil was spreading across the cotton fields of the South, and agricultural work for African Americans was declining. Jobs in northern industrial factories opened as factory workers left to join the military. For many years, factory owners had looked to European immigrants as a source of new workers, but when the war began in Europe, it shut down that source of labor. So now employers were willing to consider hiring applicants they had not earlier accepted, including women and African Americans. As early as 1916, agents representing northern factories began recruiting workers in the South, promising free transportation and attractive salaries. By 1915 trains and steamships were carrying potential factory workers northward. Suddenly, the South realized it could lose its supply of cheap labor and reacted either by seeking better relations with the African Americans it had been exploiting or by trying to hold them by placing restrictions on recruiting agents or on African Americans themselves. But the word spread rapidly among African Americans, and their flight from the South accelerated, and as individuals and families moved north, they encouraged relatives to follow.

When African Americans arrived in the North, they found not the promised land but rather a hostile reception. Industrial cities such as St. Louis, Chicago, Milwaukee, Detroit, and Cleveland were popular destinations. The *Chicago Defender*, one of the nation's preeminent African American newspapers, had promoted the city as a prime destination, and by the end of the war some sixty thousand African Americans had come to the city. Most of the migrants were from rural areas in the South, and the adjustment to life in northern industrial cities was difficult in any case. But they also experienced racism and resistance, not the welcome they had been led to expect. The wave of strikes that plagued factories in 1916 and early 1917 caused eruptions of violence when African American workers arrived, crossing picket lines set up by striking workers. Often, however, breaking strikes was the only way they could get jobs, and employers knew it and exploited them.

The Aluminum Ore Company in East St. Louis experienced a strike beginning late in 1916. The company and others in the vicinity had recruited black workers, and the unions representing workers in these companies refused to extend membership to them. Black workers were willing to accept lower wages and to cross picket lines since the unions were not willing to let them join anyway. Thus, striking workers treated them as strikebreakers, and incidents of violence became common. The Wilson administration refused to take any action and without substantiating evidence blamed the violence on Republicans for bringing African Americans into the area in order to increase their base of voters. Then, on July 2, violence escalated into what historian David Kennedy described as "a full-scale race war."[4] Whites entered the area where black workers and their families lived and began setting fires that left nine whites dead. According to the attorney general's report, more than 250 buildings were burned and more than a hundred African Americans were shot, beaten, or both. Lynching, which had declined in the years leading up to the war, increased once again in each of the years of the war. The NAACP carried on a vigorous campaign seeking to end lynching, but the South's control of key committees in Congress was able to resist attempts to pass antilynching legislation.

Despite the violence and racism that occurred in these northern industrial cities, the movement of African Americans to the North

4. David M. Kennedy, *Over Here: The First World War and American Society* (New York: Oxford Univ. Press, 1980), 282.

continued unabated. African Americans had experienced similar treatment in the South, of course, and in the North at least there were opportunities for jobs. The discouraging circumstances that African Americans confronted when they arrived in northern cities led some of them to return to the South. Most, however, had no intention of returning, and despite the difficulties with which they had to contend, they did not consider going back to life in the South, which had fewer possibilities even than the meager ones they found in northern cities. Most migrants thus remained in the North, contributing to the multiracial, multiethnic composition of these industrial cities from that point forward.

THE WAR AND CIVIL LIBERTIES

If the planning for raising an army and producing ships and weapons to support American forces in Europe took time, the implementation of a broad program of suppressing dissent went forward with stunning speed, executing a series of actions over the course of three weeks. On April 6, 1917, Wilson issued a proclamation addressing possible activities by enemy aliens, prohibiting criticism of the US government and its policies and the US Army. His justification was the Alien Enemies Act of 1798, which gave the president the authority to imprison or deport citizens of enemy nations, one of the harshly criticized Alien and Sedition Acts of the administration of John Adams. The next day, Wilson initiated a secret loyalty program that allowed department heads the right to dismiss any employees they believed acted in a suspicious manner. A week later, Wilson created the Committee on Public Information and directed that it should have a censorship function. Its director, George Creel, carried out this responsibility by encouraging self-censorship of the press; the press went along reluctantly, but did cooperate. The passage of the Espionage Act later removed this responsibility from the CPI, and the CPI avoided involvement with censorship thenceforth. Wilson issued an executive order on April 28, expanding the censorship authority of the Navy and War Departments over messages sent out of the United States on telegraph lines, meaning that these departments could control news sent to foreign newspapers.

Even earlier, Wilson had submitted to Congress a broader bill intended to give him much more authority over dissent. The Espionage Act, the administration explained, was to combat spies and subversive activities by enemy agents. But it authorized much more. By combining seventeen bills, it gave the administration carte blanche for unprecedented tools to suppress criticism of its policies. It allowed the president to censor the press and included a number of clauses that permitted the president to stifle critics of the war. Several Republicans, especially Senator William Borah of Idaho, spoke out against these provisions. Newspapers complained that in spite of their loyalty, they were being lumped with foreign publications that criticized the administration, placing them in the same category as Socialist papers that had always criticized the administration's policies. Borah spoke out against prior restraint, which would place critics on guard even before they did anything that the administration might decide was illegal under the legislation. Borah warned that once established, there was no guarantee that these limitations would not continue after the war ended. Ultimately, the House voted at the end of May and defeated the provisions related to censorship of the press by a vote of 184 to 144. The Senate chose not to consider the action of the House, in effect accepting the defeat of press censorship.

The administration fought back but was unable to restore press censorship to the bill. Nevertheless, when the amended bill passed in June, it still had plenty of authority over dissent in several provisions, and the administration used them with impunity. The law allowed the government to prosecute those individuals who made false statements against the military, attempted to cause insubordination or disloyalty in the military, or sought to obstruct recruitment. The administration used these provisions to obtain convictions against more than a thousand people, including leaders of the IWW and Eugene Debs, who had been a presidential candidate as a Socialist in four previous elections. Debs was imprisoned and ran again for the presidency while in prison in 1920. The act forbade the mailing of material advocating treasonous actions or insurrections. Wilson gave the postmaster general the authority to carry out these actions. Postmaster General Burleson interpreted his authority broadly and was relentless in pursuing alleged violators.

Three additional bills passed Congress in 1918, completing what constitutional scholar Paul Murphy called "an airtight national repression network."[5] The first of these acts, the Sedition Act, was technically an amendment to the Espionage Act. It elaborated in more detail the prohibitions suggested in the Espionage Act, outlawing "uttering, printing, writing, or publishing any disloyal, profane, scurrilous, or abusive language intended to cause contempt, scorn, contumely or disrepute as regards the form of government of the United States, or the Constitution, or the flag, or the uniform of the Army or Navy, or any language intended to incite resistance to the United States or to promote the cause of its enemies." Violations would be punished by a fine of ten thousand dollars or not more than twenty years in prison or a combination of both.

There were several provisions in the bill that raised objections. Even Attorney General Thomas Watt Gregory regretted that the bill gave more authority to Postmaster General Burleson, who Gregory among others believed had been too zealous in enforcing the original Espionage Act. Former president Teddy Roosevelt rose in opposition, charging that Burleson had been political in executing his duties under the Espionage Act, allowing the actions of the Hearst newspapers, which defended the administration's management of the war despite its inefficiencies, and prosecuting critics of these policies. Even newspapers that generally supported the administration came out against Burleson's conduct. The *New York World* accused Burleson's bureaucrats of trying to set up "an intellectual reign of terror." Particularly offensive to many Republicans, including Roosevelt, was a provision in the bill that would have made it seditious to criticize the president. TR

5. Paul Murphy, *World War I and the Origin of Civil Liberties in the United States* (New York: W. W. Norton, 1979), 81.

attacked this provision as misguided; sedition, he said, was against the country, not the president. Congress withdrew this provision prior to voting on the bill, so the issue became moot.

Again, although many Senate Republicans rose in opposition to the bill, the administration was able to muster enough votes to ensure passage, in part by suggesting that the government needed this authority in order to quell vigilantism against German Americans and other minorities, arguing that if the government could prosecute those persons guilty of these offenses, private citizens would be less likely to take matters into their own hands.

Finally, the Alien Act, passed on October 16, 1918, less than a month before the Armistice, expanded earlier legislation that sought to root out anarchism. It gave the secretary of labor the authority to deport any alien who had at any point become a member of an anarchist organization.

This collection of laws, as historian Paul Murphy suggested, not only created a climate at the national level of the suppression of civil liberties, but also encouraged the states to join in the crusade of suppression. Many of the states did so, increasing pressure on immigrants from the Axis countries. The resulting hostility to debate, to immigrants, and to the free exchange of ideas had a daunting impact on the nation in the years that followed the war. Provisions regarding deportation of immigrants persisted into the postwar years, and other laws created the excuse for the suppression after the war of alleged radicals and their organizations. This sweeping repression in turn led to the undermining of many of the reforms of the Progressive Era and facilitated the rise of racism, labor violence, and a superficial prosperity that benefited mainly the wealthy.

In spite of the strictures enumerated in these repressive laws, many Americans spoke out against them, and the government prosecuted the most prominent among them. Roger Baldwin, a member of the American Union against Militarism, in opposition to conscription and the restrictions on civil liberties, formed the Civil Liberties Bureau, a division of the AUAM. It later became independent of the

AUAM, taking the title American Civil Liberties Union, still headed by Baldwin.

Ultimately, the Espionage Act went before the Supreme Court in a case promoted by Charles T. Schenck, who was the general secretary of the Socialist Party. Associate Justice Oliver Wendell Holmes wrote the Court's opinion in *Schenck v. United States*. Holmes granted that in ordinary times, the First Amendment would have protected the kinds of acts prohibited under the Espionage Act, but because of the national emergency, it was acceptable for the government to place limitations on free speech. The question, he argued, was whether the opposition posed a "clear and present danger" to the nation—words that have been central in other similar cases during other wars over the course of the past century.

The government employed its new powers with impunity. In June 1917 police in New York arrested Emma Goldman and Alexander Berkman for violation of the Selective Service Act for conspiring to convince people not to register for the draft. Their sentence stipulated two years in jail, a fine of ten thousand dollars, and deportation to Russia. On September 5 federal officials staged a raid on offices of the Industrial Workers of the World, arresting 166 Wobblies in cities across the country in the largest such federal raid in American history. Most prominent of those individuals arrested was Big Bill Haywood, taken at IWW headquarters in Chicago. Of more than seventeen thousand charges against the IWW, most dealt with publications, and not one charge alleged an act of violence. The action against the IWW removed most of its leaders, virtually destroying the organization, although it emerged in a weaker form during the Great Depression of the 1930s.

THE 1918 INFLUENZA EPIDEMIC

In August 1918, as World War I entered its final stages, the world experienced another catastrophe that rivaled the war in terms of deaths and that at its peak was even more frightening because it knew no boundaries. Occurring at the end of a century of progress in health care, in which scientists had developed inoculations for terrifying diseases such as smallpox and isolated the causes of others such as cholera, the sudden outbreak of influenza seemed as mystifying as the Black Death had been in the fourteenth century and seemed to be as deadly. People were of course familiar with the flu, but this variety was puzzling both because it caused so many deaths and because it was most devastating to people between ages twenty and forty, whereas flu usually impacted the elderly and young people disproportionately. Thus, the wartime situation helped it to spread rapidly, as soldiers, particularly those aboard troopships crossing the Atlantic, were living in crowded conditions.

At the time, speculation about the origin of the influenza outbreak led Americans to refer to it as the Spanish flu. Later speculation held that its origin may have been in China. But it truly was not understood, and only in the late twentieth century were scientists able to isolate the virus that caused the epidemic. They found that it was a particularly virulent strain of an avian flu and that it probably originated in North America. There was an outbreak of flu in the spring of 1918 at Fort Riley in Kansas, where soldiers were training before being deployed in France. On March 11 the flu struck at the fort, with 107 cases reported. By the end of the week, there were 522 cases, and over the course of the next month more than 1,000 soldiers had the flu. Forty-eight of them died. The virus mutated and became more virulent in August, probably in Brest, France, and then spread across Europe, into Africa, and back to the United States in its more potent form.

When people caught the flu, their lungs filled with liquid. They coughed and choked on the bloody fluid. People reported that the faces of victims turned gray, then purple, then brown. Their blood thickened, and people likened it to tar. Victims felt pain behind their eyes, which then spread to their ears, neck, spine, and legs. They experienced fever and chills and became delirious. If they survived, the flu would subside after three or four days, but some developed pneumonia, which could also be fatal. The flu spread through coughing and sneezing, which propelled bacterial and viral particles in the surrounding area. One sneeze could scatter forty-six hundred viral particles for a distance of up to twelve feet, and the particles would remain in the air for a half hour.

In August the new strain appeared at port cities: Brest in France; Freetown, Sierra Leone, in West Africa; and Boston in the United States. Public officials generally minimized its likely impact until it became clear that this virus was no ordinary flu. Twelve thousand Americans died in September and 195,000 in October. Anecdotes reported how quickly the flu could take its victims. In one such report, four women played bridge one night, and the next morning the only survivor learned that all three of her friends had died that night. Young girls who could not understand what was happening sang a song as they skipped rope:

> I had a little bird,
> Its name was Enza,
> I opened the window,
> And in-flu-enza.

The epidemic influenced the course of the war. Influenza swept through crowded camps on both sides. Germany's General Erich von Ludendorff's soldiers experienced an outbreak during his spring and summer offensives that impacted their performance during the Second Battle of the Marne. The Allies battled the flu in September, briefly giving the Germans hope that the flu might enable them to hold on. Soldiers on both sides were exhausted as the war reached its final offensives in September, and neither side was prepared to deal effectively with the emergency. There were too few doctors and medics, and facilities were overcrowded. There were too few coffins to bury the dead. Ships transporting soldiers began burying men at sea rather than carrying their bodies into port.

In the fall, with the flu making its second onslaught, President Wilson faced two decisions in which the flu and the course of the war were intertwined. On October 6 he received a request from Prince

Maximilian of Baden, the imperial chancellor, to begin negotiations that could lead to peace. Wilson was torn, because there was no certainty that the chancellor could ensure that such negotiations would be respected by the German military or the public. Still, both nations were ravaged by the flu. Wilson concluded that only a military victory would guarantee a peace settlement and chose not to pursue this option.

Influenza posed another military dilemma. Did it make sense to continue sending fresh American soldiers to Europe when many of them would die before reaching the battlefields in France? The crowded conditions in Stateside training facilities and then on transport ships virtually guaranteed that many would succumb to the flu before reaching Europe. Training camps were already reporting high rates of influenza and mounting death tolls, and most of them were under quarantine. However, General Pershing, leading the American Expeditionary Force in France, desperately needed more because he was in the middle of an offensive that he hoped would end the war, and the AEF, too, was decimated by the influenza. In one week, sixteen thousand soldiers came down with the flu, bringing the total to eighty-six thousand. Pershing pleaded that he not only needed more soldiers, but also needed more nurses to treat the sick. Wilson conferred with the army chief of staff, General Peyton March, who suggested that even those soldiers who died en route to France would have died for a good cause. Wilson decided to continue sending soldiers to Pershing. The war ended thirty-three days later, just as the influenza seemed to be tapering off.

In the United States, public health officials were ill-equipped to deal with a crisis of this magnitude. Nearly two hundred thousand people died during October. Surgeon General Rupert Blue had helped efforts countering yellow fever and the bubonic plague, but the influenza epidemic outstripped anything in his experience. The Public Health Service, which he administered, had too small a staff to be of any assistance to cities that requested aid. Other than the actions of the surgeon general, the Wilson administration did nothing about the epidemic, although in reality there was little it could have done. Doctors were on their own, and their remedies were insufficient to blunt the assault. Public officials responded in a sensible way, ordering facilities where crowds gathered to close. Churches closed, but parishioners complained that now was the time when they most needed to meet to pray together. Otherwise, there was little opposition to the policy.

When the flu reached its peak, the impact was beyond anyone's experience. There was a shortage of coffins, and when they were available people often stole them. In many places, victims had to be buried in mass graves. Public officials called for volunteers to help confront the flu, and many women in particular risked their own lives to help people who were ill. It was not uncommon for people to check on neighbors and find that entire families had died.

The continuing problem was that no one understood the cause of the influenza. Medical science had progressed a good deal in the previous century, and doctors followed their experience in seeking a cure. Vaccines against bacterial agents had been used for more than a century; the vaccines used a small sample of the disease in an inoculation, and the patient would develop immunity. Several doctors and scientists thought they had isolated the bacterial cause and inoculated patients. However, although it was not known at the time, the cause of the flu was a virus, not bacteria, so none of the inoculations did any good. Furthermore, the gauze masks distributed by the Red Cross and many other agencies and cities provided at best minimal protection, because the viral particles were small enough to penetrate the gauze. Other attempts to ward off the flu were worse than useless. Doctors in England suggested that tobacco smoke was a germicide and allowed smoking in factories. A doctor in Virginia had patients with the flu soak their feet in scalding water. Doctors debated the use of alcohol; some prescribed it, while others forbade it. Various concoctions and folk cures gained regional support. But it was all guesswork. Some people stayed indoors, believing that the flu would be present in the outside air. Fresh air would have been beneficial, however, and in cases where patients did get fresh air, their survival rate was higher than people who did not. Many cities took flu victims to hospitals, as much to isolate them from people who had not contracted the disease as to try to cure them. Death rates in hospitals were generally high, because they provided no respite from the disease.

In the absence of a cure, or even an effective deterrent, a sense of denial was common in many cities. Doctors urged that the flu not be mentioned in obituaries. The war was front-page news, while the flu, which was more deadly, received less attention. In cities where prohibitions against public gatherings were especially rigid, people began to ignore them. People stopped wearing masks, even if public officials still insisted on compliance.

The flu finally ran its course. September and October were the worst months, not only in the United States but worldwide. Strictly by coincidence, the flu began to subside around the time of the Armistice on November 11, as people around the world who survived began to develop immunity. Celebrations for the end of the war brought people into the streets in large crowds, which brought on a brief resurgence of the flu. There were local variations, but in general the flu tapered off in November but surged again in late December and January 1919, although never again reaching the high death rates of September and October. Then it tapered off again but spiked once more in March. Then it truly did subside and did not return.

The influenza of 1918–19 was truly a worldwide pandemic. Several other countries suffered more desperately than the United States. India endured the greatest toll, with 12 to 20 million people succumbing to the flu. Deaths among Americans were much below the rates of India but were nonetheless staggering. Ten times as many Americans died of the flu as died from German arms. The 675,000 American deaths were more than the number of soldiers and sailors who died in all American wars of the twentieth century. The Civil War is rightly remembered for its carnage, yet the 498,000 soldiers lost in that war is 177,000 fewer than the number who died from the pandemic of 1918–19. The United States entered the Great War two and a half years after it began in August 1914, and early tactics (mass charges across no-man's-land into machine-gun fire) were particularly deadly. Yet the total of 10 million combat deaths paled in comparison to the 21 to 40 million flu-related deaths worldwide.

Despite the enormous impact of the influenza pandemic, people have largely forgotten it. Americans remembered World War I with Armistice Day in commemoration of the end of hostilities on November 11, 1918—the eleventh hour of the eleventh day of the eleventh month. (In 1954 President Eisenhower signed legislation renaming Armistice Day as Veterans Day to honor World War II and Korean War veterans, and it now honors veterans of all wars.) But even in 1918, there was a strange silence regarding the flu. At the peak of the flu's impact in September and October 1918, President Wilson talked about the vote for women and his campaign for a league of nations but not about the flu. Public officials in cities across the country said little about the flu, perhaps because there was little they could do about it. In recent years, several books have appeared about the 1918 outbreak, stimulated by concern about another possible pandemic after scares such as the bird flu, Asian flu, H1N1, and Ebola.

SUGGESTED READINGS

Two excellent books that deal with the home front during World War I are Robert H. Ferrell's *Woodrow Wilson and World War I, 1917–1921* (New York: Harper and Row, 1985) and the twenty-fifth anniversary edition of David M. Kennedy's *Over Here: The First World War and American Society* (New York: Oxford Univ. Press, 2004).

Lettie Gavin's *American Women in World War I: They Also Served* (Niwot: Univ. Press of Colorado, 1997) examines women's service during the war in both civilian and military positions. The military service of African Americans is examined in Arthur E. Barbeau and Florette Henri's *The Unknown Soldiers: African-American Troops in World War I* (Philadelphia: Temple Univ. Press, 1974, reprinted in paperback by Da Capo Press in 1996) and more recently in Chad L. Williams's *Torchbearers of Democracy: African American Soldiers in the World War I Era* (Chapel Hill: Univ. of North Carolina Press, 2010).

On civil liberties, see Paul L. Murphy's *World War I and the Origin of Civil Liberties in the United States* (New York: W. W. Norton, 1979).

With the concern recently about worldwide epidemics, there are several fine recent books on the influenza outbreak of 1918. One very accessible book accompanied the *American Experience* television presentation on the epidemic: Lynette Iezzoni's *Influenza, 1918: The Worst Epidemic in American History* (New York: TV Books, 1999).

9

The American Expeditionary Force in Europe

When the United States declared war against the Axis powers in April 1917, the war in Europe had settled into an uneasy and brutal stalemate. Early land battles on the western front such as the Battle of the Marne in September 1914, the Battle of Ypres in October, and the Battle of the Somme in July 1916 had been battles of attrition, with high casualty rates, often as a result of attacks on trench lines in which new weapons, especially the machine gun, demonstrated the futility of such tactics. Both sides dug elaborate trenches, establishing a stable front. The nobility of warfare of earlier centuries had given way to a demoralizing war of rain, mud, poison gas, and artillery, with no resolution in sight. German strategy had dictated that the best hope for victory was to rely on the submarine to disrupt North Atlantic shipping. The decision to resume unrestricted submarine warfare, of course, was the decision that brought the United States into the war.

The United States, however, was ill prepared to enter the war. The challenge that the nation now faced was to raise an army, train it, outfit it, transport it to France, and make an impact in the European war. When the United States entered the war, it had an active-duty force of about 100,000 men, with an additional 115,000 in the National Guard. By the end of the war, 4 million men had served in the military. Secretary of War Newton D. Baker bore much of the responsibility for executing this task. He had been a student of Wilson's at Johns Hopkins, and he resisted when Wilson asked him to take the position in 1916, but Wilson insisted. Baker, a pacifist and a reformer who had served as mayor of Cleveland, seemed an unlikely candidate. At just over five feet tall and with a boyish appearance, Baker usually seemed physically overmatched, and some have suggested that it left him at a psychological disadvantage when talking to military men. Yet despite criticism from some quarters that he moved too slowly, he got things done.

When Baker took up his duties, he had the assistance of two major generals, Chief of Staff Hugh Scott and his assistant Tasker Bliss, both of whom were sixty-three years old and near retirement. Scott was a veteran of Indian wars of the late nineteenth century and of the suppression of the Moros in the Philippines during Roosevelt's presidency. Bliss had taught at West Point and the Naval War College and had been among a group of officers who had gone to Europe to observe the war in progress. They tutored Baker in the intricacies of dealing with the army, but neither was up to date with the kind of fighting going on in Europe, and historian Robert H. Ferrell considers both to have been incompetent. Baker's decision not to interfere with military leaders on military matters made things worse.

Fortunately, prior to American entry, the General Staff had developed a plan to raise an army. It originally involved measures such as universal military training, but ultimately it boiled down to a draft. The draft riots of the Civil War era plagued planners, who feared that the individualism of Americans might lead them to oppose conscription. Unlike the Civil War draft, civilians at the local level administered the 1917 draft, ensuring that the process would have more community support. Another lesson from the disastrous Civil War draft eliminated provisions that allowed wealthy citizens to hire substitutes, but the 1917 act did allow for exemptions for men in jobs vital to the war effort. Opponents of the draft argued that men drafted would be less effective than those men who volunteered, but they volunteered at a rate too slow to be effective. Baker stood by his plan, and Wilson concurred. Congress approved the draft, and on July 20 a blindfolded Baker drew draft numbers from a fish bowl—the numbers assigned by the local draft boards. General Enoch Crowder commanded the national headquarters of the Selective Service System, and by the end of the war 4,648 draft boards around the country registered 24 million men, 2.76 million of whom served in the armed forces. The system became a model for draft boards during subsequent wars until the establishment of an all-volunteer army in the 1970s.

In spite of generally broad support, the draft did encounter opposition. Critics of the draft filed a suit against the law, arguing that it deprived Americans of their individual freedoms. The Supreme Court heard arguments and ruled against the draft opponents 9–0 early in 1918, in the process validating not only the 1917 law itself but the concept of conscription. Another challenge to the draft and the efforts of the army to become more professional came from an unexpected quarter. Theodore Roosevelt offered his service to lead a volunteer force as he had done with his famous Rough Riders in Cuba during the war with Spain. Ironically, the professionalization of the army reflected the influence of the Progressive movement, so Roosevelt's offer stood to undermine his own support for professionalization. Furthermore, the administration realized that it would be detrimental to have two separate policies for assembling an army and that Roosevelt's reputation would distract from the draft and lure recruits into a unit that would be difficult to control. The Rough Riders were of a different era; a lot had changed in the previous two decades, and the army and the Wilson administration concurred in rejecting Roosevelt's offer.

Drafting men was but the first step in raising an army. As hundreds of thousands of men began to report for duty, they had to be clothed, housed, and provisioned. These functions were the responsibility of the Quartermaster Corps, but the dimensions of its duties quickly overwhelmed its insufficient staff. By the end of the year, its staffing (officers and enlisted men) increased from 8,100 to 139,000. To supply this army in the making was complex because of its magnitude and the limited time available and because the supply system had limits on how fast it could respond. Congress had to pass appropriations bills before the Quartermaster Corps could contract for purchase, and in some cases small companies that had contracted with the government were unable to fulfill their contracts because of competition for raw materials. There were few reserves of material since Congress had not authorized such purchases prior to the war in an effort to hold the line on defense expenditures.

Another formidable problem was camp housing for the new army during an interval of training prior to joining the war in France. Historian Edward Coffman put the problem in perspective, saying that in the summer of 1917, construction crews totaling 200,000 workers had to build thirty-two cities, each for 40,000 residents. These cantonments were only two-thirds complete by fall, and it took until December to complete some of them. This issue is one of many reasons that the schedule for raising an army fell behind and one of the reasons that many soldiers arrived in France with insufficient training.

Training was not the only challenge, as planners began to come to terms with twentieth-century warfare. It was a time of transition for the army, and experiences in France hastened and complicated that transition. Attempts to overrun enemy positions, which had been effective in the nineteenth century, did not reckon with the impact of the machine gun and led to astronomically high casualty rates in early battles. The United States was still in the planning stages but encountered mixed-era procurement long before joining the fight. The Americans began to build tanks but also purchased three hundred thousand horses and mules; the army would continue to use horses and mules through the 1920s, not only for transportation but also to haul artillery pieces, caissons, and mobile kitchens.

The command structure of the army was also changing. Most of the senior American commanders had been to the Leavenworth Staff College and understood the importance of staff for the performance of the army in the field. Not all of the Staff College graduates were West Point graduates, and the tension between line officers and staff officers added to the ongoing rivalry between the regular army and the National Guard.

When the army began to plan for war in February 1917, planners expected that ordnance would need a longer lead time for production than other supplies. Producing machine guns to supply the army would take eighteen months, and some ordnance items could take two years, since manufacturers would need to retool and gear up production. This conundrum proved prophetic. Congressional action slowed procurement even more, since Congress often reduced funding below the army's requests. American industrial capacity had extraordinary potential, but the United States was getting a late start, and it showed. The Americans were developing a three-inch artillery piece, but as it turned out it was too complex and thus too difficult to keep in operation. In contrast, the French had developed a 75 mm artillery gun that was less complicated but more dependable—and it was already in use, while the American three-inch gun was still in development. Ultimately, American artillerymen used the French gun.

From weapons to the ships required to transport soldiers to France, the story was the same: too little, too late. President Wilson's decision to keep the country out of war had repercussions, and not the least of them was that the United States had done little to prepare if the country were to be drawn in. The United States built Liberty aircraft engines, and shipped 4,435 overseas, but few planes. For a time, the United States built British De Havilland aircraft in the States and delivered 1,213 to American forces in Germany. But this number was far short of the 20,000 Baker had promised, and the De Havilland had a fatal flaw—its fuel tank often exploded when it landed, and so soldiers began to refer to it as the "Flying Coffin."

Shipbuilding illustrates how poor planning had a potentially calamitous result. General George W. Goethals had demonstrated his abilities in the construction of the Panama Canal, but after the president appointed him to head the shipping board, clashes with civilians on the board led to irreconcilable conflicts, wasting valuable time and forcing Wilson to fire both Goethals and his civilian counterpart and appoint two civilians to coordinate the enterprise. A herculean effort after the United States entered the war demonstrated the enormous potential of American industrial production, and by mid-1918 the largest shipyard, Hogs Island in Philadelphia, could produce a new ship every other day. But before production got to that point, through 1917, German submarines were sinking more tonnage of shipping capacity than the Allies were able to produce. The United States had to rely on captured German vessels and British ships to get American soldiers to France.

The man chosen to lead American forces into battle was General John J. Pershing, who had led the last major American military command, the punitive expedition into Mexico in pursuit of Pancho Villa. Pershing, an 1886 graduate of West Point, had been a junior officer in some of the last engagements against the Indians, and at age fifty-six he was no longer a young man. He fought in Cuba and led troops in the Philippines in 1902 and 1903, where he distinguished himself and marked the beginning of the rise of his career. His service in Mexico, while unsuccessful in apprehending Villa, did break up Villa's supporters and rendered effective service over difficult terrain. His recent experience thus made him the best-qualified candidate to lead American forces in France. His main rival, General Leonard Wood, had similar experience in the Philippines, but since then had held administrative positions and also had been an outspoken critic of Wilson's policies. Secretary Baker considered that it was his job to give Pershing whatever he needed to win the war, so the relationship between the staff in Washington and the leadership in the field was cooperative.

Prior to departing for Europe, Pershing met with officials in the War Department and saw firsthand the chaotic organization that existed early in the war as the army sought to respond to the emergency. He met with the president, who promised his backing, and received instructions to keep his forces together and independent. These instructions were the crux of debates with the Europeans in discussions about the role of American forces. The Europeans wanted the Americans to fill in their depleted ranks, whereas the Americans refused to place their soldiers under the command of foreign commanders. Ultimately, the Americans won the argument. The American Expeditionary Force would have its own sector on the front.

The system of training, outfitting, and transporting the US Army to Europe took many months, and it was not until the summer of 1918 that American forces in substantial numbers began to take part in the war. When Congress declared war, the army had only eighteen thousand officers, including both regular army and National Guard, many of whom were near retirement and whose experiences were outdated. By the time the army reached full strength, it needed two hundred thousand officers.

Training officers and enlisted men for modern combat took months. Captain Harry S. Truman, the future president, was a National Guard officer whose unit was federalized and sent to France in time to participate in the big drive in September and October 1918 that forced Germany to surrender. As such, this artillery regiment offers a fairly typical preparation that illustrates some of the problems inherent in raising an army and integrating it along the front.

Truman's National Guard artillery regiment operated in Kansas City and Independence, Missouri. It took fifteen months to train the regiment and transport it to Europe and another two months before it took part in significant action, a typical schedule. In the summer of 1917, the regiment began drilling in parks in Kansas City, using broomsticks to drill since rifles were not available. The government federalized the unit as the 129th Field Artillery Regiment, part of the 35th Division, and ordered it to report to Fort Sill, Oklahoma, in September. In Oklahoma they received classroom and field instruction in artillery, learning how to operate the field pieces efficiently, how to bracket barrages, and how to compute range and elevation. This training continued through the winter months.

In the spring the regiment's commanding officer selected Truman as one of a group of junior officers to travel to France in advance of the rest of the regiment to receive training at Chaumont, Pershing's headquarters. In March the advance detail embarked for France and for Chaumont, where they trained until July. In July the rest of the regiment crossed the Atlantic, and the advance detail reunited with them. Truman took command of a battery of nearly two hundred soldiers, charged with operating French 75 mm artillery pieces. Assigned to a "quiet sector" along the front, where action was sparse and battle-weary soldiers on both sides had a respite, they stirred up some minor action with the German forces aligned against them. In September

8. An artillery battery firing a French 75 artillery piece commonly used by American forces during World War I. Popular Graphic Arts Collection, Prints and Photographs Division, Library of Congress, LC-DIG-pga-03876. Copyright by Wendell Westover.

they were in position to participate in the Meuse-Argonne offensive and in the major Allied drive beginning later in the month.

One of Baker's most significant contributions was to elevate Major General Peyton C. March to the key position of army chief of staff. March had a distinguished career. A West Point graduate as an artillery officer, he had served in the Philippines between 1898 and 1902 and there developed a reputation as an able administrator. He served on the General Staff and in the adjutant general's office prior to World War I and gained experience commanding an artillery regiment as well. Once the war began, he commanded an artillery brigade and in August 1917 became commander of all AEF artillery. In March 1918 Baker summoned him to Washington to serve as chief of staff.

March made an immediate impact, elevating the importance of his office and increasing his staff, dismissing deadwood and bringing in talented officers to replace them, and making decisions that impacted the way Americans fought. He and General Pershing, commander of the American Expeditionary Force, often clashed, and did so especially over March's decision that reserve and National Guard officers would be treated the same as regular army officers during the war. But March's impact was enormous. Historian Robert H. Ferrell concluded that what he accomplished was "to deliver the department from its past."[1] March streamlined the chain of command, centralizing authority and creating new functions (such as the air service, tank corps, and chemical warfare service) to meet the demands of modern warfare. He expanded military intelligence from 4 men when the United States joined the war to 282 officers, 29 noncommissioned officers, and 948 civilians.

SUBMARINE WARFARE AND THE BATTLE FOR THE NORTH ATLANTIC

The first American encounter with the enemy was not on the fields of France but on the high seas of the North Atlantic. Prior to the war, the state of the art in naval warfare dictated that battleships would be the essential vessels in modern warfare. Battleships had been growing in size (displacement) and in the power of their guns since the United States had begun to modernize its navy a quarter century before World War I began. Britain had set the standard with the launching of the Royal Navy's *Dreadnought* in 1906, and thenceforth the new class of battleships became known as dreadnoughts and then even larger ships as superdreadnoughts. Even before the United States entered the war, it had begun to build battleships of a subdreadnought class at a rate of about two a year, a pace that continued through the end of the

1. Robert H. Ferrell, *Woodrow Wilson and World War I, 1917–1921* (New York: Harper and Row, 1985), 30.

war, and as late as November 1915 American planners considered the battleship to be the measure of naval strength. Two developments dramatically altered that thinking. First, the Battle of Jutland in May and June 1916 between Britain and Germany in which both sides claimed victory demonstrated the futility of traditional battleship warfare and led Germany to resume unrestricted submarine warfare. Second, the submarine proved to be so effective that ships had to be built that could counter it, and battleships were too cumbersome and expensive to carry out that mission.

The command structure in the navy was more complicated than it was in the army. Secretary Josephus Daniels selected Rear Admiral William S. Sims to meet with the British Admiralty to determine how the United States could best work with the British. Sims had previously worked with the Admiralty, and its leadership welcomed his appointment. Sims did not have the latitude that Pershing had under Secretary Baker. There were several reasons. Sims was a junior admiral and received a promotion that had lifted him above many senior officers, and as such he was vulnerable to criticism from senior officers. Because Sims had worked closely with the British before, there was some concern that he might be overly willing to support the British point of view. The responsibilities of the navy differed from the requirements of the army. It was very clear what Pershing's mission was, and he had been given instructions to keep his forces together and under his command. The navy's task was quite different. First, Sims's orders specified that he was to cooperate with the British, whereas Pershing's orders stipulated that he should keep American forces under American command. The navy had a more complicated mission, too. Its responsibilities stretched beyond the North Atlantic and included protecting the American Atlantic Coast and the Caribbean, which were beyond Sims's authority. Sims's orders to cooperate with the Admiralty worked well nonetheless. Sheer numbers dictated that the US Navy would be subordinate to the British fleet, which numbered some 5,000 vessels compared to 373 American ships at the peak. Sims's relationship with his counterparts, however, was such that he had more influence than these numbers might suggest. He was influential in persuading Admiral John Jellicoe, the commander of the British fleet, to accept the convoy system that proved critical in countering the German submarine threat.

The German decision to resume unrestricted submarine warfare was the principal issue that brought the United States into the war, and countering it was the first test the Americans faced. The German subs, or U-boats, were a serious threat to the Allied war effort, because everyone and everything needed to fight in France had to be transported by ship. The submarine was an exceedingly effective weapon, and often ships would nearly reach their destination in Britain, only to be picked off by German submarines lurking off the British coast and targeting ships silhouetted against a background of harbor lights. Over the course of the war, German submarines sank nearly 13 million tons of Allied shipping. The worst month for the Allies was April 1917, the month in which the United States entered the war, when the Germans sank 881,000 tons of shipping. In all, nearly 5,000 ships fell victim to submarines, and some 15,000 Allied sailors lost their lives in these attacks.

The United States took steps to counter the threat even before joining the war, when the Wilson administration authorized the arming of merchant vessels. This decision was only minimally effective, and in fact made merchant ships more likely to be targeted. The US Navy and its British counterpart focused on the submarine menace and found the answer in convoys. Ships traveling in formation, escorted by surface warships, were much less vulnerable. Shippers had tried convoys earlier in the war, but they had been unpopular with ship captains, who argued that convoys slowed ships down, because they could go only as fast as the slowest ship; they made it more difficult to maneuver because of the large concentration of ships; and they made them vulnerable as they traveled in packs. The British also resisted implementation of convoys, but under American pressure they agreed.

Convoys were dramatically successful from their first use. The first convoy sailed from the United States to Britain on May 24, 1917, and the only ship lost was a straggling merchant vessel. Remarkably, not a single convoyed ship fell victim to submarines in June. Systematic convoys began operating in the summer, and monthly losses began to drop. October losses were 459,000 tons, nearly half what they had been in April. After October losses never again topped 400,000 tons. Depth charges became more effective and made submarine captains less likely to take risks. The speed of convoys varied, allowing faster ships to travel together. By the end of the war, the Allies were using aircraft to locate submarines and notify surface ships of where they were. The United States also established the Shipping Board, tasked with accelerating the production of merchant vessels, and activated captured German ships, both of which helped to counter losses to German submarines. August 1918, the month before the final land-based offenses of the war began, was the last month in which losses to submarines topped 200,000 tons. The war in the North Atlantic ended with an Allied victory before the land war did.

TRAINING IN FRANCE

As Americans began to arrive in France, cultural differences among the Allies strained relations, and the problems transcended the expected ones related to language. The French and the British had been fighting a common enemy since 1914 but still had trouble working together. American soldiers complained about the manure piles in front of French houses in the countryside. They also believed that the people they had come to save were taking advantage of them by raising prices. A rumor circulated (falsely, it turned out) that the French even charged rent for the use of trenches. General Pershing and his staff were particularly concerned about the spread of venereal disease and kept track of VD rates in each unit, asking for an explanation when a substantial increase occurred. French president Georges Clemenceau scandalized the Americans by offering to help establish licensed brothels.

Pershing's training schedule was rigorous and even included a fabricated trench to replicate the problems that might be encountered at the front. When French observers critiqued the performance of their newly arrived American allies, they were unsparing, and many Americans thought them unfair. The Americans complained that the French were too accustomed to fighting a defensive war from trenches and that only an offensive strategy could win the war. The British, too, seemed defense oriented. Pershing spoke of open warfare, as opposed to the defensive approach that defined trench warfare. The Americans canceled inspections, rejected what they considered failed doctrine, and announced that the standards for training would thenceforth be the same as West Point's. Training for officers included tactics, maneuvers, communications, and logistics.

The rate at which American forces arrived in Europe affected strategy on both sides. For the Allies, it made sense to delay major offensive action until the influx of American soldiers gave then a numerical advantage. For the Germans, the opposite was true: if they intended to launch an attack, they ought to do so before American forces arrived in large numbers. Other factors reinforced this approach. The Bolshevik Revolution in Russia in November 1917 forced Russia out of the war and allowed the Germans to transfer as many as forty divisions to the western front. So the Germans could achieve numerical superiority in the short run.

As more Americans landed in France, the Allies debated how these new troops could best be employed along the front. The French and British wanted to incorporate American soldiers into their positions, an approach that became known as amalgamation. Americans thus could fill in for losses and make it possible to fend off attacks and hold the line, or the war might be lost before the Americans could make a contribution. Pershing steadfastly held that American forces would fight under American leadership. Holding the line was precisely the strategy that had stalemated the war and led to prolonged trench warfare, Pershing believed. The Wilson administration inadvertently made Pershing's position difficult to defend. British and French leaders tried to circumvent Pershing and go directly to Washington. While insisting that the decision about how to employ American troops was in Pershing's hands, the administration also let it be known that it would not oppose amalgamation. Secretary Baker's consistent support for Pershing made it possible for Pershing to insist on continuing to keep his army together under his command.

The next issue on Pershing's agenda was to determine where the Americans would take their position on the long front that stretched from Belgium diagonally across northern France. He requested a sector between the Argonne Forest and the Vosges Mountains in the province of Lorraine. Allied authorities approved the request, and Pershing moved his headquarters from Paris to Chaumont, nearer the American sector and close to railroads essential for troop transport and provisioning. He established schools and a regimen that prepared the green American soldiers for their move to the front. Inadequate training would be one of the shortcomings of the preparation of the AEF. In the last months of the war, as pressure mounted on the Americans to contribute tens of thousands of troops, soldiers often had abbreviated training schedules in the States and in Pershing's schools in France.

By the time the Americans entered the war, aviation had become a fixture in Europe. The United States had begun preparation for participation in an air war, and a joint army-navy committee met to discuss coordination. The National Advisory Committee for Aeronautics already had the task of coordinating production with private industry. Early in the war, both sides considered the primary value of planes and balloons to be reconnaissance and with this notion in mind the army assigned aviation to the Signal Corps.

But the French, British, and Germans were far ahead of the Americans in production and had gained experience in the air over France. Americans realized just how far behind they were when in May 1917 France requested American production of 4,500 planes, 5,000 trained pilots, and 50,000 mechanics by 1918. These objectives were nearly inconceivable, but the United States began to plan and decided to produce the French Spad and the British Bristol (both fighters), the British De Havilland (DH-4) for daytime bombing and the Italian Caproni as a night bomber. These plans were ambitious, and actually only the DH-4 went into mass production in the States. Americans did develop an aircraft engine called the Liberty engine and produced some 15,000 units. Although it had a reputation for reliability, it was too heavy for fighters. Lieutenant Colonel William (Billy) Mitchell commanded the American air operations and had to rely on Allied planes. In the St. Mihiel offensive in September 1918 he had 1,481 planes at his disposal. Mitchell was on the verge of having a major impact when the war ended.

THE GERMAN OFFENSIVE OF 1918

The German high command, Field Marshal Paul von Hindenburg and General Erich Ludendorff, began preparation for an offensive that they hoped might end the war. They launched a series of five assaults, beginning on March 21 and stretching over the next four months. The first attack came in the Somme Valley and penetrated some sixty miles into Allied territory. Heavy losses on both sides did not obscure a significant German advance to the city of Amiens in the Somme Valley, from which they could reach Paris with long-range guns. The Germans launched another offensive on April 9 and a third on May 27, when it appeared that the road to Paris was opening to the Germans, and the exhausted French had no answer.

The Allies responded with a shuffling of command at the highest levels. They had been plagued by lack of unity of command, with each nation's military devising its own tactics. Now they came together and agreed to appoint France's General Ferdinand Foch as the supreme commander of Allied forces. Americans, including General Pershing, concurred. Field Marshal Douglas Haig (the supreme commander of British forces) requested that Pershing transfer American forces to assist British and French forces. This petition opened the old argument about whether American forces would serve only under American command, but this time Pershing responded generously. Haig wanted three regiments of engineers; Pershing sent them and promised two regiments of heavy artillery.

The first American action occurred early in the morning of May 28 in the French sector at a small village called Cantigny, southeast of Amiens on the way to Paris. The town was situated at a salient in the

German lines, a point at which the French and Germans had battled since the German spring offensives began. The French had promised heavy artillery support, but the beginning of the third major German thrust on the day before forced France to move all of its artillery to defend against a possible assault on Paris. With General Pershing watching, the attack on Cantigny went on as planned and proceeded on schedule, taking the town by midafternoon with light casualties and capturing 240 German prisoners. Then the Germans counterattacked, and for three days the Americans were under fire. They held, but 200 officers and enlisted men were killed and another 669 wounded. Later reflection questioned whether the objective justified such losses. Nonetheless, the battle demonstrated to doubting Europeans that Americans could fight. It was a small operation, but it gave the Americans confidence and strengthened Pershing's hand in Allied conferences.

Americans played a larger—and more devastating—role a week later at Château-Thierry and nearby Belleau Wood, forty miles northeast of Paris. With French forces being driven back, the American Second Division's Marine Brigade and its Army Brigade arrived and plunged into battle. For the first time, the influx of fresh American troops made an impact. The battle featured intense fighting at close quarters, particularly in Belleau Wood, where the dense woods made it difficult to gauge the course of the battle. Communications were interrupted frequently, and many of the soldiers and Marines were ill with diarrhea and fever. The battle raged for nearly three weeks, with illness among the troops on both sides, the Germans suffering from diarrhea and influenza. This battle was one of many in the Great War that provoked questions later. The Marines lost 5,183 of the 8,000 who entered the two square miles of Belleau Wood, and critics asked why they did not wait for artillery and whether the objective was important enough to risk such high casualties. The Marines received most of the praise, although the US Army performed valiantly as well. And a month later, in early July, the Army Brigade performed a well-executed attack on the nearby village of Vaux, demonstrating the value of planning to a military operation.

These early conflicts renewed the question of when contingents of Americans would arrive in substantial numbers. By the end of June, there were 800,000 American troops in France, but they were fighting under French or British command, not yet achieving Pershing's goal of taking an army under American command into battle. General Foch had said that he needed a hundred American divisions by June 1919 to win the war, an incredible figure that would have required 5 million soldiers to fulfill. Secretary of War Baker studied the request and concluded that it was counterproductive because it caused consternation and confusion while under evaluation. Chief of Staff Peyton March sensibly argued that while the Americans needed to do everything they could to contribute to winning the war, a hundred divisions was beyond the nation's capacity. Eventually, about 2 million Americans fought in France, so the one-hundred-division figure was indeed staggering.

Troops began to arrive in large numbers in late June—not large enough to satisfy Foch, but the beginning of an influx of shiploads of soldiers that continued into the fall. Fourteen thousand men landed in France at the end of June. These men would not make an immediate impact on the course of the war, however. In order to provide support as quickly as possible, Stateside training had been reduced, so the new arrivals would still need training before they could engage the enemy. It would be September before the American Expeditionary Force would take the field as an independent army. Nonetheless, in a gathering of grateful Parisians on the Fourth of July, an American officer, Colonel Charles Stanton, proclaimed, "Lafayette, we are here!"

On July 15 Ludendorff launched another attack in the vicinity of the Marne River, north of Château-Thierry and about thirty miles west of Reims. The French called the ensuing battle the Second Battle of the Marne, and the Americans called it the Battle of Soissons, after a city north of the battlefield on the Aisne River. The American 1st and 2nd Divisions participated in the battle and fared well in the early going, but the "fog of battle" interrupted their progress. Artillery barrages were not far enough to offer protection, communications broke down, and so did organization, as soldiers moved through the heavily forested terrain. The two divisions together suffered more than 10,000 casualties. But a combined force of French and American forces launched a counterattack on July 18, and the fortunes of war began to turn. The Allies forced the Germans to retreat north of the Aisne River and back to the famous Hindenburg line (Kriemhilde Stellung) of well-established defenses. This spot was the area from which Ludendorff had launched his series of attacks in March, so the German series of offensive action, so promising for the first three months, now had lost all it had gained.

Shortly afterward came one of the decisive battles of the war near Amiens, where British forces drove the Germans back with an attack of tanks, so devastating that Ludendorff referred to August 8 as a "black day." With American troops landing at a rate of 250,000 a month, Ludendorff's series of attacks amounted to a last chance, and he knew it. He offered his resignation, but the kaiser refused to accept it. His subordinate officers began to question his judgment. He lost the confidence he had exhibited during the spring campaigns and never recovered it.

THE ST. MIHIEL OFFENSIVE, SEPTEMBER 12–15, 1918

On July 10, 1918, General Foch, the commanding general of Allied forces in France, informed General Pershing that because there were 1 million Americans now fighting in France, an American army must become a reality. Pershing's insistence on maintaining the integrity of an American army would finally be realized. By early August, they agreed that the American army would have its debut at the St. Mihiel salient, a German-held penetration into French lines that separated Nancy from Verdun. The base of the salient was the town of St. Mihiel, forty miles southwest of Metz and twenty-two miles south of Verdun. German forces had held St. Mihiel since the opening offensives in 1914. The area had seen heavy fighting. Verdun had endured several bombardments throughout the war, and few structures remained standing. The goal of the American offensive would be to take St. Mihiel, reduce the salient, and advance toward Metz.

American forces benefited from two developments prior to the attack on September 12. They created a deception that the American attack would take place farther east, near Mulhouse in the Alsace, where France shared a border with Germany and Switzerland. The idea for the deception came from French general Henri-Philippe Pétain, and was indicative of increased cooperation between the French and the Americans. Pershing needed French equipment, troops, and assistance in transportation and worked with Pétain and General Foch to coordinate the American contribution to the offensive.

Even without the deception, the Americans had an additional advantage. General Ludendorff had ordered withdrawal from the salient on September 8, and his forces were carrying out that order when the Americans attacked. In fact, the Germans began removing their heavy artillery just hours before the American artillery barrage began. This turn of events was fortunate, because the Germans had held the salient long enough to have established strong defensive positions, using the terrain to their advantage. The salient occupied the heights above the Meuse River, and the slope to the east was heavily forested.

Not everything broke well for the AEF. The movement into position for the offensive was chaotic, nearly a logistical disaster. With two hundred thousand American troops and forty-eight thousand French troops moving into position, and an equal number in reserve and in support roles, communication confusion was perhaps inevitable, but it was further complicated by a drenching rain during the operation and the requirement to travel only at night in order to maintain secrecy. Narrow roads turned to mud, and crossroads quickly clogged, with horse-drawn wagons and caissons mixing with trucks and soldiers on foot, while strident claims of right-of-way added to the confusion. French premier Clemenceau was visiting the front, and he experienced a delay of several hours, leaving him with an impression of American mismanagement at the front.

Allied artillery fire began at 1:00 a.m. on September 12, with both forces firing French artillery pieces—the Americans had none of their own in this battle. The attack began with a heavy bombardment, followed by a rolling barrage when the infantry went "over the top" at 5:00 a.m. The attack exceeded expectations, and by the end of the first day most of the Allied units had achieved their objectives for the second day. The Germans had been caught retreating, and as military historian S. L. A. Marshall explained, "An army in retreat cannot about face and fight doggedly."[2]

It was an auspicious debut for the US Army. The Americans fired phosgene gas shells, disabling many German soldiers. Scores of German soldiers who had not yet retreated surrendered, and ultimately the Allies took at least thirteen thousand German prisoners. Colonel Douglas MacArthur, looking at Metz through his binoculars, concluded that the city was lightly defended and that the Americans could take it if they carried the attack forward. General Foch's orders prohibited advancing that far because it might expose the army's flanks to attack, so the attack halted before reaching Metz.

Despite the undeniable success, there were detractors. The German retreat weighed heavily in critical comments, and some referred to the battle as one in which the Americans relieved the Germans, suggesting that it was not much of a victory. French commanders were more generous. On September 13 French soldiers entered the town of St. Mihiel, accompanied by Generals Pétain and Pershing. When the residents came out to thank their liberators, Pétain gave credit to the Americans.

THE BEGINNING OF THE END: THE MEUSE-ARGONNE OFFENSIVE

The St. Mihiel offensive was a significant achievement, but it was only a prelude to the great offensive action that began two weeks after the beginning of the St. Mihiel operation. Americans remember this battle as the Meuse-Argonne offensive, the label given to the sector assigned to General Pershing's First Army. But it was a coordinated

2. S. L. A. Marshall, *World War I* (New York: American Heritage, 1985), 428.

attack by French, British, and American armies that stretched across northern France.

The decision to stage the late-September attack in the Meuse-Argonne was Pershing's call. The alternative would have been to attack Metz, which was within range of St. Mihiel, and in fact many of those men present at the time believed that they could have taken Metz during St. Mihiel if they had received permission to do so. An attack on Metz would have avoided many of the problems that emerged in the Meuse-Argonne campaign, both in preparation and in execution. But Pershing believed that the Germans would expect an attack on Metz, as it presented a logical advance from the territory gained in the St. Mihiel offensive. The Meuse-Argonne attack thus offered a chance to surprise the Germans, and intelligence reports indicated that defenses would be lighter for at least the first three days of the campaign, after which the Germans would be able to move more divisions into the area.

The terrain Pershing and his staff selected would be difficult to manage, even if the Germans were surprised. The American sector was bounded on the east by the Meuse River and on the west by the Argonne Forest, a corridor nearly twenty miles wide. In the center were a series of hills, the dominant one of which was Montfaucon (Mount Falcon), an early target in the battle plan. Then the plan directed a two-pronged attack around either side of the hill. This push would then coalesce into a single assault on the Kriemhilde Stellung, also known as the Hindenburg line. The Germans considered the line to be impregnable; it included concrete bunkers, gun emplacements, coils of barbed wire, and deep trenches.

To achieve surprise, the Meuse-Argonne attack required night marches, relocation of divisions, complicated communications, and the employment of inexperienced troops and leaders. Most roads between St. Mihiel and the Meuse-Argonne ran north–south, which required longer marches to reach the battlefield. Colonel George C. Marshall, who in World War II would serve as the army chief of staff, organized the advance. He directed motor vehicles to take one road and soldiers on foot to take another, even though it meant temporarily breaking up units. Further complicating the operation was the fact that French soldiers would have to use some of the same roads. The roads were muddy, and in places where it was unavoidable to have vehicles and foot soldiers use the same road, the trucks often splashed more mud on the walkers. As it turned out, the Germans were aware that a major movement was under way, but they did not know its destination.

By the night of September 25, the American First Army was arrayed in three corps, with each corps composed of three divisions. I Corps on the west included the 77th (soldiers from New York), the 28th (from Pennsylvania, which Pershing called the Iron Division but was more commonly known as the Keystone Division), and the 35th (the Santa Fe Division, a National Guard division from Kansas and Missouri). The 77th had to attack directly into the Argonne Forest, the toughest assignment of all nine divisions. The 28th and 35th had some tanks operating with them, but they had little impact on the outcome of the battle. The 28th, attacking on the eastern edge of the Argonne Forest, would come under heavy fire from the heights of the forest.

V Corps, in the center of the American line, included the 91st (the Pine Tree, or Wild West, Division from Fort Lewis, Washington), the 37th (the Buckeye Division, a National Guard division from Ohio), and the 79th (a regular army division that earned the title Cross of Lorraine Division for its defense of France).

On the right flank of the American line, III Corps included the 4th (the Ivey Division, a play on the roman numeral IV, was a regular division from North Carolina), the 80th (the Blue Ridge Division, made up of draftees from Virginia, West Virginia, Maryland, and Pennsylvania), and the 33rd (the Illinois Division, a National Guard division).

Each division, each battalion, and each regiment had its orders and went over them the night before the battle. The attack was to commence at 5:30 a.m. on the morning of September 26, so heavy artillery began to fire barrages at 11:30 p.m. the night before. At 2:30 a.m., all artillery along the entire front, virtually all of northern France, began to fire. In the American sector alone there were twenty-seven hundred guns, and they created a cacophony of deafening sound and a light show of blasts that soldiers remembered for the rest of their lives.

Morning fog and smoke from the artillery concealed the advancing troops but also made communication between units difficult, and some units had trouble navigating with reduced visibility. As the infantry advanced, artillery began a sequence of rolling barrages meant to land just in advance of the infantry. The fog and smoke also made the task of the artillery more difficult because it was hard to tell if the line was advancing in accordance with the schedule. Communications during a battle were always difficult, and this assault was no exception. Nonetheless, the attack started out much according to plan, as the infantry moved forward. In most areas along the front, defenses were light.

There were few landmarks on the battlefield of the first day, except for Montfaucon in the middle of the American sector, about four miles behind German lines at the beginning of the day. The 79th Division had responsibility to take the hill, but here problems developed. Germans fell back and added to the defenses of the hill. After trying one assault with the assistance of French tanks, the American regiment organized for a second attempt. The French commander refused to provide tanks, and neighboring divisions were occupied with their own responsibilities and were reluctant to cross sector lines in any case. At the end of the day, Montfaucon remained in German hands.

The 91st and 37th Divisions would later receive criticism for poor leadership that affected their performance. The 91st, for example, had one of its regiments attack in column rather than side by side, thus having actually only one regiment engaged at the outset, while its neighboring regiment had all six regiments flanking one another and engaged in the battle. The soldiers in these divisions were green, being exposed to fire for the first time, and the fire was especially heavy in the center of the line. The 79th Division, on the right of V Corps, also disappointed because it failed to take Montfaucon until the second day of the battle, even though it was a first-day objective. III Corps had stronger leadership than the other two and performed better as a result. The 33rd, even though it was a National Guard division, performed at a higher level than the others. Both the 4th and the 33rd Divisions reached their first-day objectives. I Corps and III Corps both performed well in the early going.

ASSESSING FAILURE: THE 35TH DIVISION AND THE AFRICAN AMERICAN 92ND DIVISION

Of the nine divisions involved in the offensive, the most disappointing performance was that of the 35th Division, and its problems illustrate both the internal and the external challenges that the American sector faced. The 35th Division suffered the most casualties of any of the divisions, reportedly between 6,000 and 8,000, but reports varied. In mid-September the army assigned replacements for several of the key officers in the division, including the commanders of both infantry brigades, three infantry regiments, and one of the artillery regiments as well as the division's chief of staff. There was too little time for the new officers and the men they commanded to get to know and trust one another. The division included soldiers from Kansas and Missouri (including Captain Harry S. Truman, commander of the 129th Field Artillery Regiment) and a mix of National Guardsmen and regular soldiers, and there was friction between the two that persisted after the war during investigations of their performance. The division did well during the first day, reaching its objective. But on the second day it encountered Germany's First Guard Division, reputedly the best German unit in the American sector. It offered stiff resistance and attacked the 35th Division five times in four days. This pressure led to what historian Edward M. Coffman described as the disintegration of the division. Communications broke down, and casualties mounted. On October 1 the division was relieved and played no part in the fighting that remained. After the war, the army investigated the collapse of the division in a rancorous inquiry.

African American soldiers also came under scrutiny for their performance during the early days of the Meuse-Argonne offensive. Two divisions, the 92nd and 93rd, were African American divisions, with African American enlisted men and junior officers (first and second lieutenants), but with white officers in command and administrative positions. The 93rd Division performed well, but the 92nd performed poorly, and its record overshadowed the 93rd's. For the next thirty years, the army used the failure of the 92nd Division to demonstrate that African American troops were substandard and could not be trusted to carry out their military responsibilities.

Because of the importance attributed to the failure of the 92nd Division, this case needs further investigation, both because of what happened in the Argonne and because of issues related to the training of African American soldiers. Even before the division saw action, contention emerged between General Charles Ballou and his superior, Lieutenant General Robert Bullard, the commander of the 2nd Army, which included the 92nd Division. Bullard was a racist, convinced that African Americans could not be trusted in battle. Senior leadership reminded African Americans of their second-class status at every opportunity. Black officers, who were to be equal to white officers of the same rank, found it not to be the case. Aboard ship en route to Europe, white officers received staterooms, while their black counterparts had second-class lodgings. When the division assembled in France, 82 percent of its officers were African Americans. White officers pushed to replace them with white officers, and by the end of the war only 58 percent of the officers were black.

The 92nd Division received a particularly difficult assignment as the battle began on September 26. Planning for the advance had left a gap of some 875 yards between the westernmost unit in the American sector, the 77th Division, and the French 4th Army. The assignment to fill the gap and maintain communications with the French troops went to the 368th Field Artillery regiment of the 92nd Division. This poorly trained, ill-equipped regiment thus had one of the key assignments during the assault. This task would be its introduction to combat, as the division had had only patrol duty prior to the offensive. One of its responsibilities was to cut barbed-wire entanglements strewn across the battlefield, but the regiment was unfamiliar with the terrain and had no heavy-duty wire cutters. They had no American artillery support, and repeated requests for French artillery went unanswered, even though they were under heavy enemy fire. Despite these impediments, a portion of the regiment took the town of Binarville on the second day. After that accomplishment, the regiment began to break down. The regiment was still attempting to attack, but one battalion commander ordered a withdrawal and failed to specify where to regroup. Some German positions that had been bypassed began to fire from the rear. Communications broke down, and while one battalion advanced, others withdrew. The regiment lost unit integrity and was relieved on September 30. Despite a mixed performance, General Bullard condemned the entire mission. Others echoed his evaluation, and even General Ballou, who had been one of the least racist of the generals and who commanded the division, considered the mission a failure. The army used this case as evidence of the inability of black soldiers to perform under fire into the Second World War.

Although there is general agreement that the 92nd Division failed, there are mitigating circumstances in addition to poor training, lack of equipment, and the absence of artillery support. White units such as the 35th Division suffered a similar breakdown, but criticism of its performance was less vitriolic than the reproach of the 92nd. There is plenty of evidence of racism in the assessments of the 92nd. General Bullard had a long rivalry with General Ballou and used this event as a means to sanction Ballou as well as the 92nd. One of the white officers of the 92nd had demonstrable shortcomings in his own leadership of the division, yet his testimony became part of the condemnation of the entire division. The best historical study of the division's performance concluded that "comparison with the performance of and comments on white regiments shows unmistakably that the bitterness of the criticism was inspired more by the regiment's [referring to the 368th Regiment of the 92nd Division] color than by its failure."[3] Despite all the criticism, the division had experienced the trauma of combat and suffered 1,647 casualties.

In contrast, the four regiments of the 93rd Division performed with distinction, yet their record received little attention when the postwar debate began over the fighting ability of black soldiers. The army labeled the 93rd Division a provisional division, since it was

3. Arthur E. Barbeau and Florette Henri, *The Unknown Soldiers: African-American Troops in World War I* (New York: Da Capo Press, 1996), 152.

incomplete, composed of only four infantry regiments, the 369th, 370th, 371st, and 372nd Infantry Regiments. General Pershing was not sure how to use this partial division, but General Foch had been pleading for American soldiers to fill in for French losses. Pershing solved two problems by assigning the four regiments to Foch.

The 369th Infantry Regiment was the first of the African American regiments to arrive in France and the first to serve under French command. The regiment arrived in France in May 1918 and participated in the Battles of Belleau Wood and Château-Thierry. During an encounter in May, Sergeant Henry Johnson became the first American to be awarded the French Croix de Guerre when he and a private held off a German wire-cutting party, killing four and wounding thirty-two of the enemy. Both Johnson and the private suffered wounds, and because the private's injuries were more serious, Johnson handled most of the action. The regiment was in action on the front lines for 191 days, including the Meuse-Argonne offensive, and thus served on the front lines longer than any other regiment in the AEF. France awarded the entire regiment the Croix de Guerre, and individuals received another 171 awards. The other three regiments, while arriving later and not achieving the fame of the 368th, nonetheless acquitted themselves well and received praise and commendations from the French commanders under whom they served. French forces had used colonial forces, particularly from Senegal, so they were accustomed to operating with black soldiers and treated them with equality. The Americans had warned the French to use harsh discipline with the African American soldiers and to restrict their access to French civilians, advice that the French disregarded. The 93rd Division was on the front lines for many of the major battles of 1918 and suffered 3,534 casualties. Nevertheless, it was the failure of the 92nd that received all the attention.

ENDGAME: FROM THE ARGONNE TO THE ARMISTICE

By the end of September, Pershing's forces had yet to obtain all the objectives he had set for the first two days of the offensive. Transportation problems had proved vexing, and units were stranded in traffic snarls on muddy and shell-pocked surfaces. But the Germans had been plagued by similar problems and by influenza. Yet they had increased their forces to nine divisions and fragments of other units and were able to offer stiff resistance. Pershing would later reflect that the first eleven days of October caused "the heaviest strain on the army and on me."[4] The Americans were also suffering from the influenza, which began to wind down by mid-October, but in the week ending October 5, 16,000 soldiers were affected.

The French pressed Pershing to renew the attack, and he set the morning of October 4 as the time to do so. The goal was the Kriemhilde Stellung, which simply had to be penetrated. He and his staff agreed that the area near Romagne was the most susceptible target area along the long line. General Hunter Liggett, commanding the 77th, 28th, and 1st Divisions, had the task of taking the high bluffs in the Argonne Forest. General George Cameron's corps was to approach Romagne from the northwest and General Bullard's from the east. By the second day, it was clear that the attack had stalled, facing stubborn opposition from two of the best German divisions. But Liggett's 1st Division had penetrated with a wedge. Liggett and his staff devised a risky flanking movement that would leave infantry regiments exposed without artillery support during a critical portion of the advance. It also required rapid transit of the divisions involved. Pershing approved, believing that the gamble was worth the risk.

Two of the legends of the AEF experience in the war emerged out of the action that followed. The mission had been devised in part to rescue the "Lost Battalion," a portion of the 77th Division that had been stranded after penetrating German lines on October 2. Success in the rescue was a dramatic story in the American press, which had been closely following the fate of the Lost Battalion.

4. Cited in Edward M. Coffman, *The War to End All Wars: The American Military Experience in World War I* (1968; reprint, Madison: Univ. of Wisconsin Press, 1986), 320.

The second story was of perhaps the greatest American individual hero to emerge from the war: Sergeant Alvin York was a Tennessean who had been drafted into the army despite having applied for conscientious-objector status because of his religious beliefs. York, who hunted to help provide for his family, was an excellent marksman. As a member of one of the infantry regiments of the 82nd Division, York received orders to lead 13 privates in a raid on a German unit that had been harassing the division with machine-gun fire. York's team got within range, but the Germans opened up with their machine guns and killed 6 of the privates with York. Incredibly, York killed 28 Germans and brought in 35 machine guns and 132 prisoners. When asked how many he had killed, he replied, "General, I would hate to think I missed any of them shots; they were all at pretty close range—50 or 60 yards."[5] York received the Congressional Medal of Honor, and Hollywood produced a movie, *Sergeant York*, describing his exploits.

General Liggett's gamble paid off and earned the Americans leverage to drive the Germans from the Argonne Forest. By October 10, German forces retreated from the Argonne, and Americans moved in to occupy this crucial ground. Resistance was stiffer on the other side of the American sector, east of the Meuse River, where Germans held the high ground overlooking the Meuse and could fire down on American troops. Where the American sector ended, the French had two divisions. General Pershing reinforced the French forces, but the Germans also reinforced their forces and refused to give way. Germany was able to hold key positions along the Meuse River heights until the end of the war.

Nonetheless, the expulsion of the Germans from the Argonne Forest left the Americans in the western part of their sector near the formidable Kriemhilde Stellung, not far from Romagne, the objective set before the offensive began on September 26. Pershing conferred with his staff and decided to attack at Côte Dame Marie, a

5. Cited in ibid., 324.

ridge west of Romagne. The battle plan was to attack on October 14, the same date on which the French would attack farther west. The 32nd Division, which had been in place for three days in a stalemate with the Germans at Côte Dame Marie, attacked first as a diversion, three hours before the main attack. Then the 5th and 42nd Divisions launched their attack. The Germans defending the ridge seemed to be holding their own until an 8-man group was able to scale the ridge and fire rifle grenades into a key machine-gun nest, forcing its evacuation. The rest of the battalion followed later that afternoon and found that the Côte Dame Marie had been abandoned. The Kriemhilde Stellung had been breached, but the Americans were not able to execute the planned follow-up penetration, and Germany still held most of the fortification.

The Americans now paused to regroup and reorganize. General Pershing had decided earlier in October that he would divide the First Army, which now numbered more than 1 million men, into two armies, giving General Hunter Liggett, the army's best field commander, responsibility for the First Army and General Robert Bullard command of the Second Army. Liggett took time to consolidate control, bringing stragglers into the reorganized army, assigning new division commanders where others had done poorly in battle, and breaking up divisions to fill vacancies in other divisions caused by battle casualties.

In October the sheer number of American troops began to take its toll on the German army. It was becoming clear that although the Germans had fought valiantly, their effort was a holding action, trying to prevent the Americans from breaking through, but lacking the strength to launch an offensive of their own. And the situation was similar along the front in sectors where the French and British armies were also advancing. The Americans were taking prisoners in increasing numbers, and information taken from these prisoners pieced together a picture of decreasing morale on the German side.

In late October strains among the Allies emerged again. While some Allied field commanders praised the American effort, others sought to denigrate its performance. Most controversial was a letter from French prime minister Georges Clemenceau to Allied Supreme

Commander General Foch, complaining that the Americans had been marking time while the French and British forces were carrying the fight to the Germans in spite of their own losses and suggesting that Foch ought to appeal to President Wilson to override General Pershing. Military historian S. L. A. Marshall called the letter "venomous" and insisted that "there is no sensible explanation for Clemenceau's conduct."[6] Foch did not take Clemenceau's advice, recognizing that all three Allied armies had encountered similar problems and not wanting to cause further tension in the alliance. And for that matter, Clemenceau praised Pershing's contribution not long after writing the letter.

Pershing himself inadvertently caused dissension among the Americans. He had been pushing for a demand for unconditional surrender to end the war, but President Wilson had wanted a peace based on his Fourteen Points. Nonetheless, Wilson had told Pershing that he should speak freely about his ideas, which Pershing took as permission to argue his position before the Supreme War Council, exposing an unexpected division between American military and political leadership. Pershing backed off when he realized the implications of his statement and said that he intended it simply as military advice. Wilson accepted the apology, but it was an indication of some of the uncertainties not only among the Allies but also within American leadership as the end of the war approached.

The Allies, recognizing that the Germans were vulnerable, wanted to renew the offensive as quickly as possible. Liggett and Pershing agreed on October 28, but after Liggett conferred with the French commanders, who would again be advancing on the American left to the west of the American sector, he agreed to wait until November 1. This afforded additional time for Liggett to prepare, to be sure that everyone down the chain of command understood their responsibilities. The front was five miles narrower than it had been on September 26, so Liggett used only seven divisions instead of nine, although he

6. Marshall, *World War I*, 447.

9. American soldiers marching through the French village of Clermont on October 24, 1918, on the way to taking up a position in the Argonne region. Prints and Photographs Division, Library of Congress, LC-USZ62-71697. Copyright by Vergil J. Morris.

retained the overall organization in three corps. V Corps held the center and would lead the assault.

The Americans had gained invaluable experience in the previous battles and used it to good effect on November 1. Historian Edward Coffman gives an example of how the AEF had learned from the previous offensive. The 2nd Division and the 89th Division would be in the lead when the assault began, and each used tactics learned in the first offensive to outwit the Germans, as the Germans had done to the Americans in September. In the past, the Germans were able to gain an advantage by moving their machine guns closer to the American lines, so when the American artillery opened fire, German machine gunners were ahead of the area targeted by artillery and in position to confront the infantry when it began to advance. So the infantry withdrew five hundred yards behind the front, thus avoiding machine-gun fire, and the artillery fired into the closer area where German machine gunners waited. The 89th Division used a variation of this misdirection, sending the infantry under cover of darkness ahead of the edge of the forest, which was the logical place to initiate an assault. So when German infantry fired into the woods, the Americans already had the jump on the Germans and evaded German artillery.

When the Americans attacked, they found less resistance than they anticipated. The Germans had planned to retreat to the Meuse River, but the rapid advance of the AEF kept the Germans from executing an orderly withdrawal. The initial objectives of the advance were just north of the Kriemhilde Stellung, but as the Germans retreated, more distant objectives appeared within the reach of the advancing French and American armies. Foremost among them was the city of Sedan, twenty-five miles north of the Kriemhilde Stellung, which held historical importance for France. The Battle of Sedan in September 1870 was a humiliating defeat for France during the Franco-Prussian War; it resulted in the surrender of Emperor Napoleon III and marked the defeat of his Second Empire, the rise of Prussia, and a vital step in German unification. Understandably, the French wanted to take Sedan. But so did Pershing, who perhaps had had enough of French sniping at American military deficiencies and wanted to demonstrate what the AEF could do.

On November 5 Pershing had an order published under his direction as commander in chief of the AEF, stating that he wanted the First Army to take Sedan and that it should push through the night to do so. The order included an ambiguous instruction (regarding lines of separation between division assignments) that "boundaries will not be considered binding." General Charles Summerall, commanding V Corps, interpreted the statement to mean that Pershing was authorizing a race to Sedan, and Summerall was determined to win it. General Joseph Dickman, commanding I Corps, read the order to mean that he was to take Sedan, as indeed Pershing had intended. The result was indeed the race that Summerall anticipated, and the consequences of his decision could have been disastrous. A division of Summerall's command raced from a position seven miles from Sedan, in effect cutting in front of General Dickman's corps. Dickman was enraged and ordered Summerall's division (commanded by General Frank Parker) to clear the field. General Hunter Liggett, commander of the First Army, had never seen Pershing's order, which was another mistake in this confusing state of affairs. When he heard of it, he was as angry as he had ever been, saying that there is no way that the order could have been interpreted as allowing an American division to cut into the line of fire between another American division and the enemy. The French were equally upset for having been upstaged in the taking of Sedan, which surely meant more to them than it did to the Americans. Fortunately, the war was in its last days, and the "race" did not result in a catastrophe. Pershing brushed it off when he learned what had happened, but the careers of Generals Summerall and Parker suffered as a result of their actions.

All along the front, the Germans were in retreat. General Ludendorff had informed the kaiser as early as September 30 that the German army would not be able to withstand the Allied offensive, and Germany had sent peace feelers to the Allies in October. But the negotiations that led to the Armistice in France began when a German delegation crossed into French territory on the evening of November 7. The Germans met with Allied negotiators in General Foch's railroad car in the forest of Compiegne, forty miles northeast of Paris. (When France surrendered to Germany in June 1940 during World War II, Hitler forced French negotiators to sign the surrender documents in the same railroad car.) German representatives signed shortly after 5:00 a.m. on November 11, and the surrender became effective at 11:00 a.m.—the famous "eleventh hour of the eleventh day of the eleventh month."

Joyous celebrations broke out in cities around the world, and the coincidence of the decline in the terrifying influenza pandemic and the end of the war at the same time gave these festivities extra vigor. It was different along the front lines, where soldiers were generally more subdued. Some fighting continued past the eleventh hour where commanders had not received the news. And Pershing later expressed regret that he did not have a little more time to take more territory, since Germany was no longer offering much resistance.

For soldiers in the AEF, their military service did not end on November 11. At the time of the Armistice, there were nearly 2 million Americans serving in Europe: 1,037,000 in combat areas, 855,600 soldiers in reserve areas, and 47,700 civilians in support positions. General Pershing was willing to release all but 200,000 soldiers who would be used in the army of occupation in Germany, but there were few transport ships available to take the troops home. There also were tons of supplies and equipment to be shipped, including thirty thousand trucks, fourteen hundred heavy artillery pieces, and forty-five thousand horses. American ships available had a carrying capacity of only 100,000 to 150,000 soldiers, so delays were inevitable. Troops remaining in Europe continued military drills and took part in athletic competition while they waited for transportation home. More ships, including captured German vessels, became available as time went on, and the number of soldiers and sailors who crossed the Atlantic Ocean peaked at 350,000 in June 1919.

The Armistice brought an end to combat, but much remained to be done in addition to transporting troops. Treaty negotiations continued for more than a year and did not conclude until early 1920. American participation in the Allied victory earned a place at the table for President Wilson, and he used this opportunity to promote his Fourteen Points and especially his proposal for the League of Nations that he hoped could provide a forum for the peaceful negotiation of future international disputes.

SELECTED READINGS

Edward M. Coffman's *The War to End All Wars: The American Military Experience in World War I* (Madison: Univ. of Wisconsin Press, 1986) is a classic study of the preparation for war and the performance of the AEF in France, first published by Oxford University Press in 1968. Military leadership is the theme of Richard S. Faulkner's *The School of Hard Knocks: Combat Leadership in the American Expeditionary Forces* (College Station: Texas A&M Univ. Press, 2012). The books cited in chapter 8 by Robert H. Ferrell and Arthur E. Barbeau are also useful for this chapter, as is Robert H. Ferrell's *America's Deadliest Battle: Meuse-Argonne, 1918* (Lawrence: Univ. Press of Kansas, 2007). Douglas Mastriano's *Alvin York: A New Biography of the Hero of the Argonne* (Lexington: Univ. Press of Kentucky, 2014) tells the story of one of the most decorated soldiers of the war.

10

Plans for Peace, 1919

In September 1917, President Wilson began to consider his plans for postwar arrangements with the Allies. He asked Colonel House to form a committee to plan for negotiations. House assembled a distinguished group, chaired by his brother-in-law Sidney Mezes, the president of the City College of New York. Walter Lippmann, who was assisting Secretary Baker in the War Department, became the head of research for the group, which became known as the Inquiry. Nearly 150 people served in the group at one time or another, and 21 members later traveled to the Versailles Peace Conference with the president.

In December Wilson began to prepare for what he expected to be one of the most important speeches of his presidency. The work of the Inquiry informed his thoughts, but historians have disagreed as to how much the committee influenced what he said. As was his custom, he cloistered himself in his office, and when he completed a draft he shared it only with House and the first lady. The night before Wilson's anticipated appearance before Congress, Britain's prime minister, David Lloyd George, gave his own speech and used the term *self-determination*, a concept that became a core issue in postwar discussions in Europe. Wilson thought he had been scooped, but House convinced him that what he planned to say would supersede anything that Lloyd George had said.

On January 8, 1918, Wilson appeared in the chamber of the House of Representatives and presented what indeed was the most influential speech in his career. He set forth his goals for peace negotiations in a series of statements now remembered as the Fourteen Points. The first five points were general statements that reflected long traditions in American foreign policy and placed them in the context of current world affairs. The first point called for "open covenants of peace, openly arrived at," or an end to secret diplomacy. This point was a direct response to criticism of the secret agreements between European powers that were crucial in the outbreak of World War I, which entered anew into international debates after Bolshevik revolutionary V. I. Lenin opened the archives of the czars and exposed many of these agreements. The second point, "freedom of navigation upon the seas," had been an American goal since its colonial origins and was of current concern because of the submarine threat that brought the United States into the war. The third point called for the removal of "all economic barriers" to trade, echoing another long-held American quest for free trade. Fourth, in one of the most Wilsonian of the points, the president called for reduction of armaments.

The fifth point became a center of controversy in the months that followed. Wilson called for "a free, open-minded, and absolutely impartial adjustment of all colonial claims, based upon a strict observance of the principle that in determining all such questions of sovereignty the interests of the populations concerned must have equal weight with the equitable claims of the government whose title is to be determined." While Wilson did not use the term *self-determination* in the Fourteen Points, the fifth point became the definition of that term, which Wilson himself began to use not long after this speech. It inspired hope in colonial nations around the world, where people yearning for freedom expected that Wilson and the United States might bring an end to their subservience.

The next eight points dealt with the postwar adjustment of European and Eurasian (Russian and Turkish) borders and claims. These issues would be hammered out at the peace conference a year later.

Finally, the fourteenth point contained the core of what Wilson hoped to gain from American participation in the war: a "general association of nations" that would assure all nations, powerful and weak, large and small, of their territorial integrity and an opportunity to have their voices heard on the great issue facing the world—a means to solve international disagreements through negotiation rather than warfare. To Wilson, this League of Nations was the most important goal, one for which he would ultimately make compromises on other issues.

When Wilson concluded his speech, the war still had ten months to run. But the Fourteen Points became the most important document in defining the goals of the Allies, despite the fact that the European Allies would take issue with much of what Wilson said. Furthermore, when Wilson spoke in January, it was still not clear if the Allies would win the war and, if they did, what role the United States would play in that victory. Indeed, Wilson's role in peace negotiations was problematic until the war ended. In the meantime, his eloquence had served him well, and his ideas inspired people around the world to hope for a future in which they might have more say in shaping their own environment.

INTERVENTION IN RUSSIA

The Russian Revolution, coming as it did during World War I, posed challenges to the Allies in general and to the Wilson administration in particular. Ultimately, it triggered a series of events that led Wilson to support intervention into Siberia and the port of Vladivostok on Russia's Pacific coast, near Japan, an enterprise that had consequences for years.

Russia's revolution occurred in two phases, and they prompted very different responses from Russia's allies. The first phase, in March 1917, occurred a month before the United States entered the war. It toppled the czar and brought a liberal lawyer, Aleksandr Kerensky, to power. Kerensky seemed an admirable leader who might fashion a liberal democracy to replace the conservative monarchy that had been czarist Russia. Wilson and other Western leaders greeted this "provisional government" with enthusiasm, in part because it meant that all the Allies would now be democracies. These hopes faded as it became clear that Kerensky was no more successful than the czars had been in solving the problems that had marginalized Russia's participation in the war against Germany. Economic collapse, a breakdown in transportation in a country of vast geography, famine, and internal political opposition from the Right and the Left rendered the government ineffective. When the Bolsheviks, led by Vladimir Lenin, launched their October Revolution, they forced Kerensky from power easily. Kerensky had few supporters and little to show for his months in power.

The Bolsheviks posed several challenges to the West, and the United States, having declared war against Germany in April, felt these problems acutely. First, the communist ideology, soon to be molded into a doctrine called Marxism-Leninism, criticized the capitalism of the West and its accompanying imperialism. Second, in order to consolidate power in Russia, Lenin severed connections with the Allies and pulled Russia out of the war. Third, Lenin criticized the West on several grounds, most directly by exposing the nature of European diplomacy that had led to the Great War, particularly the way in which Germany, Austria-Hungary, and czarist Russia had carved up the Balkans in the aftermath of the collapse of the Ottoman Empire prior to the beginning of the war. Russia now became consumed by a civil war, with Lenin's "Reds" opposed by former supporters of the czar, the "Whites."

Matters became more serious for the West after Lenin sought to buy time to consolidate power before confronting Germany. He signed the Treaty of Brest-Litovsk in the spring of 1918, which surrendered vast Russian territory to Germany and took Russia completely out of the war, as Lenin had threatened. It enabled Germany to fight on only one front and transfer divisions to the western front. France had been advocating a joint incursion into Russia to shore up the front against Germany. Now, in the context of the Russian civil war, a Czech force of 40,000 soldiers trying to evacuate clashed with Bolsheviks forces and pleaded for Allied assistance. Wilson and British leaders consented to send troops.

Wilson dispatched 5,500 troops under British command to Murmansk in northern Russia and another 8,500 to Siberia, near Vladivostok, under the command of American major general William S. Graves. The Murmansk mission aimed to support anti-Bolshevik forces and clashed with Bolshevik soldiers, suffering 150 casualties. It was hard to find anything positive in this intervention, which had long-term consequences in Soviet-American relations. The Soviet Union could claim the moral high ground, since the United States had invaded its territory, whereas it had not invaded American territory.

Before leaving for Siberia, General Graves received instructions in an aide memoire that commanded him to avoid involvement in Russian politics. But the mission in fact was unclear and changed as the intervention progressed. Historians have offered several explanations for Wilson's decision to intervene, and the fact that they are still debating the reasons for the decision a century later is a good indication of how confusing the operation turned out to be. The Allies had been pushing for a joint intervention for some time, and Wilson resisted several appeals. Ultimately, he succumbed, despite contrary advice by Secretary of War Newton D. Baker. In an apt description of the operation, Baker had told Graves that he would be "walking on eggshells loaded with dynamite."

Confusion reigned not only because of the uncertainties surrounding the American mission. The Russian civil war continued apace, and while the Allies were inclined to favor the anti-Bolsheviks (the "Whites"), atrocities committed by both sides made it difficult to sympathize with either. Friction developed among the Allies. The French and British forces wanted to assist the Whites, and resented General Graves's insistence on following the aide memoire explicitly, and thus avoid involvement in the civil war.

Japan complicated matters further, sending troops to northern Manchuria and eastern Siberia ostensibly to aid in the Allied effort in response to Bolshevik entry into Manchuria. Wilson sought a pledge from Japan that their force would not exceed 7,000 troops, but Japan insisted that it would need at least 12,000. To this point, American relations with Japan had been cooperative. By August 1918, however, it became clear that Japan's intentions had little to do with Allied plans and centered instead on controlling Manchuria. Incremental increases in Japanese forces in Manchuria and eastern Siberia continued, and by November even the Japanese ambassador admitted that the troop level had reached 70,000. Wilson had no intention of sending more troops, since the mission was becoming problematic, so the Japanese were able to achieve their objectives with little more than diplomatic protests from the Americans.

The mission was a disaster; it had achieved little, and Wilson's opponents used it to criticize the League of Nations charter. Senator Hiram Johnson (R-CA) claimed that the Murmansk mission in particular demonstrated the consequences when the United States sent troops to a foreign nation at the behest of an international coalition and without consulting Congress, as he claimed could happen under Article 10 of the league's charter, which stated that the league's council would advise action by the league if one of its members were to be attacked. While this action was comparatively small in the context of World War I, involving only 14,000 American troops, its ramifications persisted for decades.

PREPARATIONS FOR THE PEACE CONFERENCE

The election of 1918, held just six days before the Armistice ending the war, became an early referendum on the League of Nations. As an off-year election (nonpresidential election), a third of the Senate and all seats in the House were at stake. Republican leadership had made clear its opposition to President Wilson's plan for the League of Nations, and he decided to take the issue to the people, asking for them to elect a House and Senate that would give him the political backing at home that would strengthen his hand in postwar negotiations in Europe. The strategy backfired, and the Republicans gained enough seats in both the Senate and the House to wrest control from the Democrats. Prior to the election, Democrats controlled the Senate by a 53 to 43 margin. Republicans needed to gain 6 seats in order to establish a 49 to 47 advantage, and they achieved exactly what they needed. It was a crushing defeat for Wilson, since it meant that Republicans would now chair Senate committees, and Wilson's archcritic, Senator Henry Cabot Lodge, would now chair the Senate Foreign Relations Committee, which would be critical in the debates over American approval of the League of Nations and the peace treaty itself. Democrats fared no better in the House, where Republicans picked up 25 seats to gain the majority, 240–192. The critical position of Speaker of the House, which scheduled debates and votes in the House, now fell into Republican hands, as did control of House committees.

Once the war ended, the victorious Allies began to plan for a peace conference, not only to determine the terms of the treaty officially ending the conflict, but also to make decisions related to territory, reparations, and the issues Wilson had raised in his Fourteen Points speech a year earlier. Switzerland and the Netherlands, both neutral nations, announced their willingness to host the conference, but France insisted on doing so, and its moral standing made a compelling case.

Wilson now had several decisions to make, and the response to his decisions gave him a foretaste of how difficult international negotiations would be. First, would Wilson himself attend, and if not, who would he choose to head the delegation? In the normal course of events, it was unusual for a president to participate in the negotiation of treaties, a task usually delegated to the secretary of state or even subordinate officials in the State Department. Nonetheless, for President Wilson, it was an easy decision. He had invested a great deal in the war and believed that he had earned a place at the table to determine the consequences of the peace that followed. Furthermore, France and Britain would be represented by their prime ministers, who would have outranked anyone other than Wilson himself, and there were intimations already that neither France nor Britain agreed with the implications for empires in the Fourteen Points. Many Americans also had reservations about Wilson leaving the country for an extended period of time; none of his predecessors had done so, and there were pressing issues—especially economic issues—that the nation faced in the aftermath of war. In the view of many within his own party, the results of the election of 1918 made his presence in Washington critically important.

Attention now shifted to the question of whom Wilson would select to compose the American delegation to the peace conference. His decisions have long been a source of controversy. Some decisions were obvious. Colonel Edward House, Wilson's closest adviser, would be a member of the delegation, although House was a better private adviser than public diplomat, and ironically their relationship deteriorated during the conference. Secretary of State Robert Lansing had to attend; Wilson did not rely on him, but it would have been a questionable breach of trust to exclude him. The other two appointments raised more questions at the time and among historians since. General Tasker Bliss was a member of the Supreme War Council, but there was no good reason to have him also serve as a peace commissioner. Most controversial was the fact that Wilson selected only one Republican—and a retired one at that—and no senators. Henry White, the sole Republican, had been a respected diplomat, but he had no current standing in the Republican Party and little influence to muster Republican support for the league or the treaty. Wilson's reasoning is not hard to fathom—he knew he would have plenty of challenges in dealing with foreign leaders and did not want to add to them by bringing a contentious group with him. But former president Taft had supported the concept of the League of Nations and might have mustered Republican support. A Republican senator, even the contentious Henry Cabot Lodge, would have served Wilson's ultimate goal better. Questions arose at the time, but they become even more troubling in retrospect, knowing the unfortunate fate of the League of Nations. And although some hailed Wilson as a prophet at the time, he could not have prophesied the battle with the Senate over the treaty. Europeans were grateful for the American role in ending the war, the Fourteen Points had received a positive reception, and Wilson had little reason to suspect how difficult the coming months would be. Historians, however, have criticized Wilson's decisions, and some have seen them as an early sign of Wilson's increasing rigidity.

Nonetheless, a distinguished group of advisers accompanied the commissioners. Among them were a future president (Herbert Hoover, who worked on issues related to food), two future secretaries of state (John Foster Dulles and Christian Herter, both of whom served under President Eisenhower), financier Bernard Baruch, and labor leader Samuel Gompers.

The president and his party sailed for Europe on the *George Washington*, a captured German ship that had been used to transport American troops (including Captain Harry S. Truman) to France. They arrived on Friday, the thirteenth of December. The next day, hundreds of thousands of people lined the Champs-Elysées to cheer him en route to a reception. The opening sessions of the peace conference were delayed until mid-January, so Wilson made visits to Britain and Italy in the interim. His reception in Rome rivaled the one in Paris, and Wilson had every reason to believe that he had a strong hand heading into the peace conference.

Expectations for what the conference might achieve were unrealistically high not just in Europe but worldwide. By the time delegates began to negotiate, Wilson's Fourteen Points and in particular the notion of self-determination had led people living in colonial status in Asia, Africa, and India and in conquered nations in Europe to believe that Wilson could be their savior. George Creel's Committee for Public Information, which had been primarily a domestic propaganda agency, had also been effective in publicizing Wilson's speeches in the colonial world. The enthusiasm emerging there resulted in what historian Erez Manela called the "Wilsonian moment," the notion that the American president would be able to convince—or force—the Allied leaders to grant nations the right to determine their leaders and their form of government. Many of these nations sent delegations or individuals to Paris to make their case. In retrospect, the most well known of these situations was the case of Nguyen That Thanh from Indochina, who petitioned the president in vain to hear his argument for independence. He would later be known as Ho Chi Minh and would lead Vietnam to independence against France and the United States. Among other petitioners were some of the great civilizations of the world: Egypt, India, and China, none of whom believed that they needed the tutelage of Western powers to learn how to govern themselves.

Americans, too, sought a hearing. W. E. B. DuBois organized a Pan-African Congress that held sessions in several locations to protest European colonization in Africa. Robert Russa Moton, who had taken

Booker T. Washington's position as the head of Tuskegee Institute, took part in one of these meetings. Samuel Gompers, the head of the American Federation of Labor, hoped to persuade Wilson to include guidelines for labor in the League of Nations.

THE PARIS PEACE CONFERENCE

The first session of the peace conference took place on January 18, 1919, at the Quai d'Orsay, the French Foreign Ministry, amid celebratory fanfare in spite of a rainstorm that hit Paris. French prime minister Georges Clemenceau hosted the assemblage of diplomats, and he and his delegation sat at the head of a long table, flanked by British prime minister David Lloyd George and the British delegation on his left and President Wilson and the American delegation on his right. Italian prime minister Vittorio Orlando, the other member of the conference's Big Four, sat some distance from the ceremonial center of power. These four leaders made up the Council of Four, and they would make the conference's most important decisions. In his introductory remarks, Clemenceau opened an issue that came to define the conference and the treaty—his demand for punitive reparations from Germany.

In subsequent meetings, the conference considered issues in plenary sessions, in which the Council of Ten, the major nations involved in making the decisions that would constitute the treaty, exercised its authority. Several constraints became clear during these meetings. First, the conference was handicapped from the start by the fact that Russia was not invited. The Bolsheviks had consolidated their control in Russia, and the major powers believed that their presence would be detrimental to the success of the conference. President Wilson tried to address this question in early sessions, but he had no support from other nations, especially given the fact that Allied troops remained in Russia. In fact, the Allies never did come to terms with the situation in Russia, and this point became one of the great failures of the peace conference.

Second, the "Wilsonian moment" promising self-determination quickly faded. Neither France nor Britain had any interest in relinquishing their colonies, and Italy and Japan hoped to add territory. Wilson had to make compromises in order to hold on to his dream of the League of Nations, and over and over he found himself backing down in order to preserve the league. Wilson made an eloquent statement defending the league on January 25, stating that the conference had two responsibilities, deciding on the terms of the treaty and preserving peace into the future by establishing the league. Wilson fought to keep the league as part of the treaty. He was able to do so, but only by giving ground to other Allied leaders on other issues.

Wilson had to return to the United States for the end of the congressional session in early March. It was a scheduled departure, but the conference continued to meet while he was absent. He attended a session on February 14 and then prepared for departure. He left Colonel House in charge of the American delegation.

Wilson crossed the Atlantic on the *George Washington* once again, arriving in Boston. The city declared February 24 a holiday in his honor, and a crowd of two hundred thousand cheered him. His reception in Washington was chillier. He met with members of the Foreign Relations Committees of both the House and the Senate and answered their questions at length. But it was clear that the line had already been drawn, and no one changed their position as a result of the freewheeling discussion. Senator Lodge allowed others to raise objections to the league, thus establishing that he was not alone in his opposition to the League of Nations. In a speech two days later, however, Lodge suggested that the treaty needed to be completed first, and then the league could be addressed as a separate issue—exactly what Wilson had been trying to prevent in Paris.

When Wilson returned to Paris, his goals came apart in pieces, and it was everything he could do to hold on to the league. The first fissure took place when he met with Colonel House. House explained that Clemenceau had been trying to separate the league from the treaty and was moving to establish a buffer state between France and

Germany. Wilson later told Edith that House had given away everything he had worked for, and he would have to start all over in order to correct House's actions. The relationship with House would never recover. Wilson had relied on him for years, and he felt betrayed. He relied more and more on Dr. Grayson, who became more than Wilson's physician.

After Wilson's return to Paris, the conference dealt with territorial issues that ran counter to Wilson's long-standing principle of self-determination. France and Britain both wanted to retain their empires, and both sought influence in areas where they previously had not dominated. Japan, which had been a British ally during the war, was beginning to extend its territory in Asia, a process that continued into the Second World War. Italy, which had joined the Allies late in the war, had its eyes on Fiume, a city on the Dalmatian coast on the Adriatic in the newly created state of Yugoslavia.

Japanese and Italian claims were both especially problematic. Neither nation had contributed significantly to the Allied victory, and their territorial claims rested on secret agreements made before the war, the very kind of agreement Wilson criticized in his Fourteen Points. The Treaty of London of 1915 had assigned Fiume to a new Kingdom of Croats, Serbs, and Slovenes, but in Paris Italy argued that it had a stronger claim because of the proportion of Italians living there. (Italy had the majority in the city, but Croats were the next most populous group and the largest ethnic group in the surrounding area.) Wilson refused to accept this logic, and Italy's Orlando was so upset that he left the conference in protest, although he later returned. After World War I, the territory became the Fiume Free State and ultimately part of Croatia.

The issue centered on a Japanese desire to lease the Shandong Peninsula from China. The Japanese claim came from Germany, but China insisted that it was historically Chinese territory and ought to be returned. China had signed an agreement with Japan extending the lease but claimed to have done so under duress. Wilson had to relent on this case and allow Japan to have the lease, but recent scholarship defends Wilson's statesmanship, which conceded to Japan in Paris but returned it to China in 1922.[1] Most observers at the time, however, condemned this decision as another instance of imperialism triumphing over self-determination and another betrayal of the Wilsonian moment.

Another secret agreement was at the foundation of one of the major decisions that became part of the Versailles Treaty. In 1915 and 1916, Sir Mark Sykes of Britain and French diplomat François Georges-Picot forged an arrangement that bore their names, the Sykes-Picot Agreement. The agreement stated that in the case of an Allied victory in the war, the two nations would divide Ottoman territories in the Middle East, with France taking the northern territory (the modern nation of Syria) and Britain taking areas to the south (including the modern nations of Iraq, Jordan, and Israel). The conference honored this agreement by assigning League of Nations mandates to France and Britain. A mandate was meant to establish supervisory responsibility to the two nations over territory with the intent of establishing independent nations once these areas were deemed ready to manage their own affairs. France thus received a mandate in Syria, and Britain received mandates in Iraq, Palestine, and Transjordan.

Other than debates over territory and the League of Nations, the most divisive issue on the conference agenda was the treatment of Germany. Clemenceau pushed for a punitive treaty at every opportunity, and elections in France and Britain demonstrated that such a treaty met the public mood. Advocates for a punitive treaty pushed mainly for four types of punishment: return of land that had previously belonged to France but had been seized by Germany at the conclusion of the Franco-Prussian War in 1871 (Alsace-Lorraine), high German reparations payments to the victors in general and to France in particular, French occupation of the Rhineland (the west bank of the Rhine River, an area also known as the Saar), and a "war guilt" clause in which Germany and its allies accepted blame for starting the

1. Bruce A. Elleman, *Wilson and China: A Revised History of the Shandong Question* (Armonk, NY: M. E. Sharpe, 2002), 5–6.

war. The first of these items elicited little controversy. Germany had taken Alsace and Lorraine from France after a war forty-eight years earlier, and France was now the victor and reclaimed its territory.

The remaining three items elicited spirited debate among the victorious Allies and great consternation from the Germans, who eventually had to sign the treaty. France's memory of the settlement after the Franco-Prussian War, when Germany demanded an indemnity of five billion francs and occupied much of northern France for two years until the indemnity was paid in full. So France now demanded establishment of a reparations commission that would determine the amount of the payment (eventually settled as a cash payment of thirty-three billion dollars and further in-kind payments of resources) as well as the occupation (with Britain) of the Rhineland, a prime industrial area. President Wilson had opposed a harsh settlement with Germany, and now British economist John Maynard Keynes weighed in with a scathing critique, calling the treaty a "Carthaginian peace." He argued that the severity of the treaty was such that Germany would not be able to meet its terms and that the result would be unpaid reparations and a German desire for revenge. Jan Smuts, a South African delegate, shared these concerns, and although he signed the treaty because it was necessary to end the war, he expressed serious reservations about its final form.

And there was more. Germany's military was to be dismantled, with limits placed on the size of its military forces and the weapons it would be able to develop in the future. Germany lost its eastern European lands, which became part of the reestablished nation of Poland. Poland also benefited from the establishment of the "Danzig Corridor," a strip of land that gave Poland access to the Baltic Sea at Danzig (presently Gdansk), and Danzig became a free city. Germany relinquished its African possessions mainly to France and Britain, which received the largest prize, German East Africa (now Tanzania). Japan received Germany's claim to the Shandong Peninsula. Germany protested but had no alternative but to sign.

It did so on June 28, 1919, in an elaborate ceremony in which representatives of twenty-one nations gathered in the Hall of Mirrors in the Palace of Versailles. The Chinese delegation protested the Shandong decision by refusing to attend the ceremony. If the treaty itself was not sufficient revenge, France arranged a symbolic reminder of the humiliation it had suffered at the hands of Germany in 1871. Germany now had to sign the treaty in the same room, and on the same table, that had witnessed France's surrender forty-eight years earlier.

France celebrated the treaty, and a crowd cheered Wilson, Lloyd George, and Clemenceau as they left the palace. The three men had battled for months, with Wilson often in the minority, but a mutual respect had developed nonetheless. Lloyd George told Wilson that he had done more than anyone to develop better relations between Britain and the United States. Clemenceau told Wilson that he felt as if he was parting with his best friend.

THE BATTLE OVER THE LEAGUE OF NATIONS

The trip home gave Wilson a welcome respite between the battles in Paris and the ones ahead in Washington, but the league was still very much on his mind. He planned to address Congress upon his return to Washington and began to write his speech and practice passages before members of the American delegation. Although speaking publicly was one of Wilson's undoubted strengths and he was accustomed to writing his own speeches, this one gave him trouble. He landed in Hoboken, New Jersey, to a celebratory welcome and then went on to Washington to confront the Senate.

President Wilson had preserved the League of Nations but at a cost. He agreed to the settlement of colonial claims that defied the principle of self-determination. Instead, France and Britain expanded their empires, gaining German colonies in Africa and mandates in the Middle East. Wilson now had to return to Washington, where he knew he faced another challenge in persuading the Senate to approve the treaty, which included the establishment of the League of Nations. He believed that the American people would support the treaty and the league, but it was the Senate that had to approve the treaty, and it had to muster a two-thirds vote to do so. The election of a Republican majority in the Senate in 1918 made this challenge particularly difficult.

Wilson's principal adversary was Senator Henry Cabot Lodge, a Republican from Massachusetts. He was a descendant of the wealthy Boston aristocracy on both sides of his family, the Cabots and the Lodges. Born in 1850, Lodge graduated from Harvard College in 1871 and earned both a law degree and a PhD in American history from Harvard, where he studied under Henry Adams. Like Theodore Roosevelt and Woodrow Wilson, he had written several books dealing with American history and government, including biographies of Alexander Hamilton and Daniel Webster and a two-volume biography of George Washington. Theodore Roosevelt was his closest friend. Like TR he was especially interested in American foreign policy, and in 1919 he chaired the Senate Foreign Relations Committee. As a result of the Republican victory in the election of 1918, he also held the informal position of Senate majority leader. (The Democrats formally established the positions of majority and minority leader in 1920, the Republicans in 1925.) Before Roosevelt's death in January 1919, the two men had shared a critical assessment of Wilson's foreign policy, particularly Wilson's reluctance to get involved in the war and his failure to prepare for the possibility of American involvement.

Wilson and Lodge shared a mutual contempt. Wilson had once canceled a speaking engagement when he learned that Lodge would be on the platform with him. Lodge had written to TR, "I never expected to hate anyone in politics with the hatred I feel toward Wilson." Even a rare light moment in their relationship reflected the mutual distrust. When Wilson appeared on Capitol Hill to give his speech presenting the treaty, Lodge and a few other senators accompanied him into the Senate chamber, and Lodge asked, "Mr. President, can I carry the treaty for you?" Wilson replied, "Not on your life," which elicited laughs from the escorting senators.

The much-anticipated speech, the one Wilson had labored over on the voyage home from France, proved to be a disappointment. Here was a key moment in his presidency, the kind of situation in which he usually was at his best. An eloquent defense of the treaty, the sort of speech people had come to expect from Wilson, might have given his defense of the treaty momentum at a critical juncture, but Wilson failed to seize the opportunity and delivered platitudes and generalities instead of a point-by-point response to his critics. Not only did the speech fail to inspire or win supporters, but Wilson's delivery was flat; he repeated sentences and missed others that were in his typescript. One senator, a fellow Democrat, commented that the senators "wanted red meat [but] he fed them cold turnips."[2] Wilson had experienced health problems while in France, including hypertension and headaches, sometimes so severe that he had to write in a cramped style with his left hand. His presentation before Congress exhibited similar symptoms, which may have been early signs of the stroke he would suffer that fall.

Lodge led the opponents of the League of Nations in developing and executing a strategy to deny Senate approval. With the League Covenant as part of the treaty, rejecting the treaty meant defeating the league. Lodge's approach was to defeat the league by delaying a vote and by presenting reservations to the league charter. In response to Wilson's Fourteen Points, Lodge offered his Fourteen Reservations. His principal concern related to Article 10 of the League Covenant, which stipulated that "the Members of the League undertake to respect and preserve as against external aggression the territorial integrity and existing political independence of all Members of the League. In case of any such aggression or in case of any threat or danger of such aggression the Council shall advise upon the means by which this obligation shall be fulfilled." Lodge insisted that that United States would not assume responsibility to protect the territorial integrity of any other nation or to commit its armed forces to any action unless specifically directed by Congress.

Two other articles presented similar concerns to Lodge and other league opponents. Article 11 stated that any "war or threat of war"

2. Henry Ashurst cited in John Milton Cooper Jr., *Woodrow Wilson: A Biography* (New York: Alfred A. Knopf, 2009), 509.

would be of "concern to the whole League" and that the league would have to take action in response to preserve the peace. Article 16 insisted that if any member of the league went to war without respecting the peace-preserving functions of the league, the action would be considered an attack against all members of the league and could subject that nation to trade or financial sanctions. League critics foresaw similar infringements on the responsibilities of Congress in these articles, and they insisted that the Congress of the United States would not relinquish any of its authority to an international body. Lodge expressed concern that the league might be able to make decisions that might even encroach on domestic matters such as immigration, the tariff, and labor issues. One of Wilson's goals in his own Fourteen Points was disarmament, but Lodge and other critics insisted that if the United States felt threatened, it could increase its arms without consulting the league. Nor would the United States accept any infringement of the Monroe Doctrine, and Congress would interpret the meaning of the doctrine.

Wilson responded forcefully to Lodge's reservations, defending in particular Article 10 as absolutely essential to the operation of the league, insisting that nothing in the League Covenant would threaten congressional power. In order to address the reservations directly, Wilson invited the Senate Foreign Relations Committee to come to the White House to discuss the League Covenant. In the August 19 meeting, Wilson described Article 10 as "a moral, not a legal obligation." When questioned further, however, he said that he considered a moral obligation to be superior to a legal one. He said that he considered the reservations "groundless." Wilson suggested that the treaty should be approved and that any reservations could be sent separately, an approach that Lodge and his allies rejected immediately. The meeting went on for three and a half hours, but it did not satisfy either side. It was clear that the Republicans would not accept any treaty that did not include reservations on the use of force. The debate continued into the fall.

By now the contours of the debate were clear, and the senators who had taken a position—and most of them had—fell into one of four groups. Approximately forty "strong internationalists," all but one of whom were Democrats, accepted the treaty as the president had presented it. Former president Taft led a small group of "limited internationalists" who supported the concept of the league but had concerns about certain provisions in the covenant. Taft worried that the United States might be drawn into another war, although he believed that the league's ability to declare a universal boycott against a nation would make a war unlikely. Next, there were approximately forty reservationists, which included so-called mild reservationists and strong reservationists. The mild reservationists included Democrats and Republicans in approximately equal numbers and constituted a swing group critical in the eventual vote on the treaty and the league. Senator Gilbert M. Hitchcock, a Nebraska Democrat, was the key member of this group, and he served as an unofficial liaison between the senators in the center and the administration. Hitchcock had Wilson's ear and tried to convince him of the need to compromise—to no avail. Henry Cabot Lodge headed the small group of Republicans characterized as "strong reservationists." This group, which included presidential candidate Warren G. Harding, opposed the League Covenant and had fundamental questions about the constitutionality for Americans of a body that could take power from Congress on a range of issues. And Lodge's influence extended beyond the strong reservationists because of his close relationship with Theodore Roosevelt, his reputation as a Republican leader, and his chairmanship of the Senate Foreign Relations Committee. Finally, the "irreconcilables" opposed the very concept of the League of Nations. There would be no compromise with this group, which included influential Republican senators William Borah of Idaho, Hiram Johnson of California, and Robert La Follette of Wisconsin.

This alignment was not rigid, especially in the center, and congressional vote counters and historians assigned different totals to each of the groups. But of course with the president needing two-thirds of the Senate, and his opponents needing only one vote more than a third (or thirty-three out of the total of ninety-six), the administration faced a formidable challenge. Without question, he needed to hold all the strong internationalists, win over the limited internationalists, and most if not all of the mild reservationists. By some counts, even if he did that he would still need some support from Lodge's strong reservationists. The situation seemed to dictate compromise, but Wilson refused to compromise. He faced a genuine dilemma. He had fought hard for the league in Paris, and the league he was able to achieve had already taken some hits. Now, if he had to go back to the Europeans with reservations, his vision of the league would fade still further. He believed deeply in the league and believed that some of the portions of the League Covenant that critics challenged were vital for the league to be successful. This conviction applied in particular to Article 10, which Wilson defended as essential. To his critics, he responded that no vote of the league would force the United States to go to war without concurrence by the US Congress.

President Wilson believed that a majority of the American people supported him and the league and that only a small group of willful men in the Senate opposed it. He had managed to keep the league as part of the Versailles Treaty and expected that there would be broad support for the treaty, which after all favored the victorious Allies. While there was significant support for the league and for the treaty, Wilson's assessment overlooked several factors that influenced popular opinion. First, while he had been in France defending the league, his opponents had an opportunity to formulate and publicize their opinions while the league's most effective advocate—Wilson himself—was out of the country. Second, the negotiations between the Big Four led many people to believe that the league would be controlled by the major nations, especially by Britain and France. The structure of the league indicated as much, since the power centered in the council, which was dominated by the major nations. The Sykes-Picot Agreement and the resulting mandates assigned to Britain and France also indicated that this setup would be the case, and the frustrations of colonies with the outcome of the Versailles meetings offered more confirmation. Immigrants to the United States from nations that felt excluded from the league, including people from Ireland, Germany, Russia, and China, had reasons for concern.

He also faced a formidable opponent in Lodge, who had both a Republican majority and several irreconcilables on his Senate Foreign Relations Committee. He, not Wilson, had control of the Senate agenda. Lodge was well versed in delay tactics. He conducted a reading of the entire 264-page treaty and held committee hearings on its content. He summoned sixty witnesses to appear before the committee, including known Wilson opponents such as William Monroe Trotter and members of the administration who had little responsibility related to foreign policy, but it all took time, and delay was central to Lodge's strategy. On August 19 Wilson took the unprecedented step of inviting the Senate Foreign Relations Committee to the White House. He gave a statement and then took questions for three hours, including challenging queries from irreconcilables Hiram Johnson and William Borah. Wilson held his own, although senators who had no reason to criticize suggested that the president had not been at his best.

Even without dealing with Lodge's antileague tactics, the summer of 1919 was a difficult period for Wilson. Several cities experienced racial riots, and domestic issues intruded on his single-minded concentration on the league fight. Postwar inflation threatened the economy, severe enough that it had earned the shorthand initials HCL (for "high cost of living"), and business leaders were calling for an end to wartime controls. A possible railroad strike threatened to paralyze the economy. The president held a series of individual meetings with senators, mostly Republicans, trying to persuade them to support the league. His increasingly persistent health problems continued to plague him.

Wilson decided that he was not winning over converts in the Senate, and rather than trying to compromise with Lodge, he would again take the issue to the American people. He had been rebuffed in this strategy in the 1918 election, but this time he would go on an extensive national tour to speak in defense of the treaty and the league. Dr. Grayson and Edith tried to persuade him not to go, and chief of staff Joseph Tumulty and even Bernard Baruch joined the chorus. But Wilson believed the trip was necessary. He had done all he could in trying to persuade senators and found that their positions were firm.

The schedule would have been daunting even for a healthy young person, which Wilson was not. Traveling by train, he would cover ten thousand miles in four weeks, and during one twenty-one-day period he would give forty speeches. He would speak in all but four of the states west of the Mississippi River. The train had accommodations for the president and first lady, and Dr. Grayson rode in a private car dubbed the Mayflower. Tumulty and a staff, including cooks, stenographers, Secret Service agents, and an entourage of twenty-one reporters, occupied other cars. There were accommodations for reporters to meet with Tumulty and the president. The train left Washington on September 3, seeming much like a presidential campaign.

The president's message was well rehearsed, and he remained focused on the League of Nations, saying little about other national developments. Press coverage kept the league debate in the headlines, as did Lodge's hearings in Washington. For the president, one of the most disturbing developments in the entire league debate took place just over a week into the trip. Appearing before the committee, William Bullitt, who had resigned in protest from the president's Paris delegation, testified that Secretary of State Lansing had said that the league in its then current form was useless and that if people understood the treaty, it would be defeated. Britain and France had gotten what they wanted in the treaty, and the league would not be able to change that fact. Lansing did not contact Wilson for a few days, and when he finally did so, he blamed Bullitt for the contretemps but did not really apologize.

Wilson soon had more to worry about than Washington politics. He started out the trip as healthy as he would be during the venture, but his health deteriorated as it progressed. The ride through Oregon and northern California provided a bit of a respite, and two nights in a hotel in San Francisco gave the most extended stop of the trip. The crowds in California sustained him, with ten thousand turning out for a speech in Berkeley, twelve thousand in Oakland, and thirty thousand at a stadium in San Diego. As Wilson's biographer John Milton Cooper observed, however, as the train headed back east, the president experienced "an ascent in altitude and a decline in performance."

Wilson's headaches returned, perhaps induced by the thinner air in the mountain West, and then coughing spells and asthma. At a stop in Salt Lake City, with a talk on a hot night before fifteen thousand people in the Mormon Tabernacle, Wilson stumbled through his remarks and sweated through his coat. The train went on to Cheyenne, Wyoming, and then Pueblo, Colorado, covering the vast distances in the West.

Those persons who accompanied the train had vivid memories of the Pueblo speech on the afternoon of September 25. Although no one knew it at the time, it would be his last public address of substantial length, and Wilson recovered his old eloquence. He stirred emotions in the audience and among his retinue when he spoke of the obligation to "the ranks of those boys in khaki—not only those boys who came home, but the ghosts that still deploy on the fields of France." He ended on almost a visionary note, saying that the truth "is going to lead us, and through us, the world, out into pastures of quietness and peace such as the world never dreamed of before."[3]

As the train headed east from Pueblo after the speech, Wilson told Grayson that he had been suffering from headaches all day, sometimes to the point that they blinded him. Grayson asked that the train be stopped, and he and Wilson took a walk for about an hour on a country road. Once back on the train, Wilson felt better, his headache gone. But shortly before midnight, he called Edith and asked her to summon Grayson. When the doctor arrived, he found Wilson nauseous, gasping for air, with his face twitching. After making Wilson comfortable, and once Edith resumed watch, Grayson went to talk to Tumulty about canceling the remainder of the trip.

The next several hours were agonizing. Edith later described the ordeal as the longest and most heartbreaking night of her life. When the president arose the next morning, having slept only since half past four, Grayson and Tumulty talked to him about canceling the rest of the trip. At first, he would not hear of it and worried that Lodge and the Republicans would call him a quitter and say that the trip

3. Ibid., 634.

had been a failure. Later, though, Wilson had to face the reality of what had happened, and he told Tumulty that he did not understand what had happened but that he felt like he was going to pieces. By the next morning, September 26, as the train passed through Wichita, he agreed to cancel the remaining stops on the trip. There really was no alternative.

It took two more days to reach Washington, and when they arrived Wilson retreated into the private rooms of the White House. On the morning of October 2, he had no feeling in his left hand and numbness in his left leg. Edith went to get Dr. Grayson, and in the meantime Wilson slumped to the bathroom floor. When Grayson arrived, he immediately suspected that the president had had a stroke. Grayson telephoned Dr. Francis X. Dercum, a neurologist with an appointment to see Wilson the following day, and asked him to come immediately. Dercum diagnosed what later came to be called an ischemic stroke, which is a stroke caused by a blood clot, develops slowly, and is seldom fatal, unlike a more serious apoplectic stroke, which is caused by a rupture and often leads to death. Wilson thus had been fortunate, but nonetheless he had suffered a serious stroke, one that left him with severe physical limitations for the rest of his life. His intellectual abilities were not impaired, but he had some paralysis, the left side of his face drooped, and he had sustained damage to his left eye.

Thus began one of the strangest periods in the history of the American presidency, as Wilson's biographers noted. A. Scott Berg considered it "the greatest conspiracy that had ever engulfed the White House" and "a power grab [that] enshrouded the Presidency in as much secrecy as possible." John Milton Cooper called it "the worst crisis of presidential disability in American history."[4] The inner circle surrounding the president shielded him in ways that would not be possible decades later. Edith later said that she had spoken with Dr. Dercum about the possibility of succession, of having Vice President

4. A. Scott Berg, *Wilson* (New York: G. P. Putnam's Sons, 2013), 644; Cooper, *Woodrow Wilson: A Biography*, 535.

Thomas Marshall assume the duties of the presidency. She claimed that Dercum had told her that such action would not be best for Wilson or for the country and that if he resigned, it would remove the greatest incentive he would have for recovery. So Edith Wilson, Dr. Grayson, and Joseph Tumulty controlled access to the president and issued only positive updates about his health and his abilities to carry out the duties of the presidency.

In Edith Wilson's recollections, Dercum's advice weighed heavily, but there were other factors that made possible this deception. The press was acquiescent, less eager to challenge the White House than it would be in later decades. There was sympathy for the president from the beginning, but even as weeks stretched into months, the president's inner circle was able to deflect pressure. Vice President Marshall did not aspire to take over as president and in fact expressed his hope that he would not have to do so. On the one occasion when Marshall went to the White House to see Wilson, Edith did not allow him to see the president and merely passed on his greetings. Marshall never again saw the president. Wilson himself made no move toward relinquishing the office and was complicit in the deception orchestrated by his inner circle. His supporters on occasion, when Wilson was having some of his better days, admitted visitors under controlled conditions.

Senator Gilbert Hitchcock, who represented Wilson's position on the League of Nations to his fellow Democrats, was one of those individuals granted such access. Hitchcock visited during the Senate's consideration of the Versailles Treaty and the League Covenant in November 1919. During the first visit, Wilson sat propped up in bed, unshaven, with his damaged arm hidden under the covers. During the second visit on November 17, Wilson presented a better appearance—shaved and sitting up—and seemed more in command. The gist of his message, relayed to the Senate through Hitchcock, was that there would be no compromise. Hitchcock left the White House impressed by the man he saw on this second visit. On November 29, however, Hitchcock requested to see the president again, this time as a representative of the Senate Foreign Relations Committee, to confer about the ongoing situation in Mexico. When he received a refusal from the

White House, he was upset, and Wilson's critics saw it as an opportunity to raise questions about the president's health. Dr. Grayson, who expected that such a situation might arise, prepared Wilson for a visit and on December 5 informed Hitchcock that the president could see them that afternoon. Hitchcock and New Mexico senator Albert Fall, dubbed the "Smelling Committee" by Wilson's critics, accepted and found Wilson propped up again, but with papers in reach of his good right hand and Edith beside him to take notes. Wilson was at his post-stroke best, and Hitchcock and Fall relayed a favorable impression to their colleagues in the Senate.

The only person to raise the issue of succession in a fashion that demanded some response from the president was Secretary of State Lansing. Lansing, of course, had his differences with Wilson, most recently aired before the public by William Bullitt, so he was not in a strong position with either the president or his palace guard. Historians have had mixed opinions about Lansing's motives, but he did take steps that no one else would. As the occupant of the senior position in the cabinet, he called meetings twenty-one times to discuss current business—certainly nothing approaching a coup d'état. Wilson reproached him severely. Lansing met with Tumulty and raised the issue of succession directly, citing Article II, Section 1, of the Constitution. Tumulty responded sharply that he did not need Lansing to lecture him on the Constitution and that he had no intention of bringing it up to the president. Ultimately, the relationship between Lansing and Wilson deteriorated to the point that Lansing resigned, an action that both men welcomed by the time it happened on February 13, 1920.

Wilson also broke with Colonel House, whose actions at Versailles the president believed undermined his arguments. House asked for an appointment in November 1919, and Wilson coldly refused. When asked about it, Wilson responded, "He's out of my life. That door is closed." House followed up with letters, but the president may not have seen them, and even if he did, he did not respond. House blamed Edith Wilson for the break, but it was the president's decision.

In the meantime, the Senate dealt with the treaty and the league. Wilson's stroke could hardly have come at a worse time, since matters were beginning to come to a head as he started back to Washington from Pueblo. Nonetheless, historians generally agree that in spite of some slips on the trip prior to the stroke, Wilson had made his case. But in the aftermath, there was no one to take on Wilson's role as the advocate for the treaty. Senator Hitchcock was thrown into the position of Wilson's spokesman, and he worked hard at arguing the president's position. But it was a difficult role, especially since Hitchcock and many other Democrats who supported the treaty had come to believe that compromise was necessary to preserve the treaty in some form, which left him in the unenviable position of arguing for a position he believed could not win against Lodge and his supporters, who had the votes to stop the treaty.

After Wilson and his entourage returned to Washington at the end of September, there was a lull before the debate resumed. The Republicans were in no hurry, since delay had been part of their strategy all along, and they could appear to be magnanimous, not pressing the issue in the aftermath of Wilson's stroke. The Senate had to act, and when it began to consider how to do so, it was clear that the strong reservationists were in control. Many of the Democrats who were loyal to Wilson had come to believe that compromise was preferable to defeat, and although they did not want to desert their ailing president, they did want to make an effort to salvage something out of the bitter struggle. Senator Hitchcock made another visit to the White House and informed the president of his conclusion that it was time to extend the olive branch; it was time to compromise. Wilson responded, "Let Lodge compromise." But of course Lodge had no need to compromise.

The issue played out in a series of three votes. The first two votes took place on November 19, 1919. The senators first voted on approving the treaty with the Lodge reservations. This version failed by a vote of thirty-nine yeas and fifty-five nays. On the same day, the Senate voted on the treaty as Wilson had submitted it, with no reservations. This version failed by a margin of thirty-eight votes in favor, fifty-five opposed. Then on March 19, 1920, the treaty came before the Senate for the last time. This version contained the Lodge reservations and an additional reservation supporting Ireland's independence movement. Twenty-one Democrats, hoping to get the treaty approved in some form, joined Republican mild and strong reservationists in supporting this version, but it too failed, forty-nine to thirty-five. This vote was the last; the treaty had failed.

In the aftermath of the great debate, there was substantial sentiment in favor of Wilson, who had sacrificed so much for a noble dream, only to be defeated by a small group of willful men in the Senate. Those people who sympathized with Wilson respected his commitment to principles. Some compared his battle to a religious quest, and Wilson himself, after Dr. Grayson informed him of the Senate vote, said, "Doctor, the devil is a busy man." Wilson's most recent biographer, A. Scott Berg, used this imagery for his chapter titles, using titles such as "Gethsemane," "Passion," "Pieta," and "Resurrection" for the section dealing with Versailles and the league fight.

But even Wilson's most vigorous defenders among historians in the century that followed acknowledge that Wilson bore much of the burden for the failure of the treaty in the Senate. Wilson's decision to go to Paris himself meant that he did not have the distance from day-to-day decisions that presidents have when they delegate this responsibility to diplomats, allowing themselves flexibility in the final negotiations. It also took Wilson out of the country while his opponents had direct access to the American electorate. He did take one Republican, Henry White, but White was a former diplomat who carried no weight with the Senate Republicans whose votes he needed. Wilson's decision not to take any senators left him to argue with a Senate that had no vested interest in the treaty other than the party loyalty of Democrats, who were in the minority when the treaty came to a vote. His decision to appeal to the American people in the off-year election of 1918, when the Republican Party remained the dominant party despite Wilson's two terms, backfired badly. Senators did not take kindly to this attempt to go over their heads and in their view to interfere in the politics of state electoral decisions. Wilson's refusal to compromise doomed the treaty, and soon after the debate began, the simple math of vote counting made it clear that he needed Republican support to reach the two-thirds Senate vote required to approve the treaty. As diplomatic historian Robert H. Ferrell put it, "It is clear that if the President had tried, even a little, to understand his opponents, the Covenant would have passed the Senate."[5] These decisions left Wilson with a desperate option, the speaking tour that he hoped would convince the people to pressure their senators to support the treaty.

So why did Wilson refuse to budge, to compromise, or even to understand the position of his opponents? He believed, and not without reason, that his opponents were out to destroy the treaty and the league. He had dealt in Paris with men with whom he had fundamental disagreements and had to give away a great deal to preserve hope for the league. Compromise would be a slippery slope—once begun, there was no telling where it might end. He detested Lodge and would not deal with him. Wilson had a low tolerance for people who opposed him, as the case of Colonel House illustrates. And House had been as close to him as any man, while Lodge was beneath contempt. Wilson was utterly convinced that he was right. To him, defending the league was a moral issue, and as he made clear in his discussion of Article 10, he believed that a moral issue was of a higher order than a legal one and thus not subject to compromise. Wilson also felt an obligation to carry out the agreements he had made in Paris, and he expected the Senate to cooperate in fulfilling those agreements. Of course, Wilson understood the Senate's responsibility in regard to ratifying treaties, but he believed that the league was something of a higher order; it needed to be confirmed in order to preserve the peace of the world.

Wilson's deteriorating health also influenced the outcome of the Senate debate. Many people with whom he interacted—friend and foe alike—noticed signs of his health problems even before he left on his

5. Robert H. Ferrell, *Woodrow Wilson and World War I, 1917–1921* (New York: Harper and Row, 1985), 174.

speaking tour in September 1919. Once he suffered the stroke, he was no longer able to carry on his battle with the Senate. His meetings with senators were infrequent, well-orchestrated affairs, not the kind of give-and-take that would have been required to negotiate. Historians who have studied the impact of the stroke on Wilson's behavior suggest that the stroke exaggerated characteristics of Wilson's personality that made compromise even less likely than it had been before. He had always made key decisions on his own, usually after consultation with others, but the final step in the process was usually taken in private. After the stroke, the circle of people with whom he could confer had shrunk, often to just three people: Edith Wilson, Dr. Grayson, and Joseph Tumulty. Of the three, only Tumulty had the kind of political experience that could be helpful and then only on explicitly political matters. Senator Hitchcock was the only senator who met with him on anything close to a regular basis, and Hitchcock was not able to persuade Wilson to take the necessary step toward compromise. In the crucial period after the stroke, Wilson was isolated and became even more rigid than usual. His health, not the best interest of the nation, was the principal concern of his inner circle; Edith Wilson acknowledged as much quite frankly.

The league and the treaty were not the only issues that suffered by the ad hoc decisions of Wilson's inner circle. When officials needed a presidential decision and sought access to the president, the inner circle often refused to let them see Wilson. Even the vice president was not able to see Wilson. Mrs. Wilson and Tumulty made decisions that were not theirs to make. They always tried to reflect what they thought the president would have done if he had been in full control of his faculties. But of course that is not the way the Constitution directs dealing with presidential incapacity.

So the United States had rejected the treaty and the League of Nations. In 1921 the nation tidied up the unfinished business of the treaty through the Knox-Porter Resolution that formally ended the state of war with Germany. The United States never did join the League of Nations, which proceeded without American membership. The United States did not ignore the league, however, and participated in several league meetings as an observer. Would it have made a difference if the United States had joined? Probably not. The league functioned relatively well during the 1920s, when its members were not burdened by war. But in spite of Wilson's vision of an organization that could resolve conflicts in a peaceful manner, the league did not have the apparatus or the will to deal with the kinds of crises that led to World War II. When Japan seized territory in Manchuria in 1931, the league protested, as did the United States. Japan ignored both protests. If the United States had been a member of the league, it's far-fetched to believe that Japan would have reacted differently. And this incident was the beginning of the end of the league.

History has rendered a critical judgment of the Versailles Treaty and indeed of the conference itself. The failures of the conference can be seen clearly in retrospect but, as is often the case, were not foreseen by the participants. These repercussions, however, affected international relations and the subsequent history of the United States for decades, even into the twenty-first century. Ironically, the failure of the United States to ratify the treaty or to join the League of Nations had much less to do with the impact of the conference than other decisions made by the conferees.

The most discussed ramification was the decision to structure a punitive settlement toward Germany in an effort to eliminate the threat of another major war. By requiring Germany to sign a "war guilt" clause accepting responsibility for the war itself, the treaty handicapped the fledgling Weimar government that had nothing to do with the war, making it difficult for this struggling democracy to establish credibility with the German people. By demanding unrealistically stiff reparations payments and allowing France to occupy the industrial area of the Ruhr, one of the most productive regions in Germany, the treaty created a system doomed to fail and to drive the German economy into bankruptcy. This collapse gave ammunition to German critics, among whom was Nazi firebrand Adolf Hitler, to attack the Weimar government and eventually to ignore the Versailles Treaty. In this sense, the treaty created the very situation its authors sought to avoid—a revitalized German nation whose people believed they had been victimized by the treaty and who sought revenge. Just two decades after the end of the Great War, Europe and the rest of the world plunged into the Second World War.

The conference, and especially the eloquent words of Woodrow Wilson's call for self-determination, raised the hopes for independence of people living in colonies of the world's major powers, only to dash them. Great imperial powers France and Britain saw the victory in the war as a vehicle to reestablish their empires. Japan, the rising imperial power in Asia, likewise seized the opportunity to justify its ambitions. While colonial nations looked to the United States as a great power that might support an end to colonialism, the United States too had its protectorates in Cuba and the Philippines and its spheres of influence in Latin America and China. League critics in the United States raised the Monroe Doctrine as one of the reasons they did not want to submit to the potentially arbitrary decisions by an international body. As the twentieth century unfolded, these decisions became the seeds for a great movement of decolonization that swept through Africa, the Middle East, and Asia.

The conference redrew territorial boundaries in a grand sweep, sometimes seeking to resolve ethnic conflicts, other times ignoring them. In the Balkans, where the war began with the assassination of the Austrian archduke, the conference had a challenging situation that had festered before the war began. As the Ottoman Empire retreated, ethnic minorities sought their independence. Drawing new borders to satisfy the people living in the Balkans proved impossible. Instead, the conference decided to create a new nation, the Kingdom of Serbs, Croats, and Slovenes, which became Yugoslavia in 1929. Although this arrangement lasted into the 1990s, it came apart in bloody fighting during that decade.

In the Middle East, the conference created Western-style nation-states where none had existed before and assigned the victorious European imperialist powers responsibility to assist them in the development of independent nations. This goal led to the establishment of League of Nations mandates managed by France in Syria and by Britain in Iraq, Palestine, and Transjordan (modern Jordan). The

British decision to relinquish its mandates after World War II led to the establishment of the State of Israel and the ongoing Israeli-Palestinian clash.

Ultimately, independence movements in India, Egypt, Algeria, and many African countries brought an end to the Versailles structure. Anticolonial nationalists in many of these nations found the Wilsonian concept of self-determination exhilarating and used it as a philosophical concept upon which to build their movements. Clashes between imperial powers and their colonial possessions seldom followed the peaceful course that Wilson had envisioned. And indeed Wilson's own vision was closer to the conception of the League of Nations mandates than it was to the aspirations of anticolonial nationalists. When speaking of American involvement in the Philippines and Latin America, he suggested that all nations—when properly directed—could assume the responsibilities of self-government.

American involvement in the decolonization movements after World War II varied but became intense in certain cases. Two of them in particular had long-term consequences. The Vietnam War grew out of support for a French desire to maintain its colony of French Indochina after World War II. And British revocation of its mandate in Palestine in 1948 prompted Zionists to declare the establishment of the State of Israel. The United States became the first nation to recognize Israel, a step that led to the close ties between the United States and Israel that have been crucial to American involvement in the Middle East ever since. Thus, in countless ways, the United States—and the rest of the world—has been dealing with the aftermath of Versailles throughout the twentieth century and into the twenty-first.

SELECTED READINGS

The previously cited Wilson biographies are excellent sources for the subjects addressed in this chapter, as is Clements's book on the presidency of Woodrow Wilson. All three discuss the battle over the League of Nations and the impact of Wilson's stroke. Robert H. Ferrell's *Woodrow Wilson and World War I, 1917–1921* (New York: Harper and Row, 1985) is an excellent analysis of Wilson's handling of all war-related issues, including the League of Nations. Erez Manela's *The Wilsonian Moment: Self-Determination and the International Origins of Anticolonial Nationalism* (New York: Oxford Univ. Press, 2007) deals with the dissemination of Wilson's ideas to the non-Western nations and their responses to these ideas. Margaret MacMillan's *Paris, 1919* (New York: Random House, 2002) is a detailed analysis of the peace conference that can be used to examine particular decisions and their impact.

11

After the War

The jubilation that swept the nation at the end of the Great War was short-lived. The high hopes that accompanied American forces to Europe had been fulfilled in the sense that the AEF had contributed significantly to the Allied victory. But that victory fell far short of expectations that it would make the world safe for democracy or that it would be the war to end all wars. Instead, the nation confronted challenges that few people had anticipated. The battle over the League of Nations and ultimately the Senate's rejection of President Wilson's vision demonstrated the deep political divisions that remained in American politics. Social and economic fissures also became apparent as the nation turned its attention back to domestic affairs.

Some Americans had benefited from the war. Farmers prospered, as the demand for food at home and abroad kept prices for agricultural goods higher than they had been before the war and higher than they would be afterward. Labor had done well, as government pressure and company profits from wartime production kept wages high and offered leverage for collective bargaining, both of which ended after the war. Women and minorities had opportunities to enter the workforce. But after the war, these advantages disappeared. Farm prices plunged, labor strikes proliferated, and employers gave jobs back to returning veterans, displacing women and minorities regardless of how well they had performed.

The United States entered the war in an era of domestic reform under the sweeping banner of the Progressive movement. The reforming zeal of the early twentieth century could not be sustained in the postwar years, crushed by repressive wartime legislation that restricted civil liberties under the Wilson administration and the return to "normalcy" under his successor, President Warren G. Harding. Civil rights and civil liberties suffered. African Americans had supported the war and expected that they would win support for the rights of citizenship by doing so. Instead, they encountered racism in multiple forms, including lynchings, the loss of jobs, and the continuing rise of the Ku Klux Klan. The Wilson administration was passive in reaction to discrimination against African Americans. It was aggressively hostile to radical labor unions, Socialists, and immigrants whom it believed supported political or ideological ideas that did not conform to the emerging doctrine of "100 percent Americanism."

There were positive developments that came out of the war. The United States emerged as a major power. The defeat of Germany, the devastation suffered by France, the losses suffered by Britain, and the calamities of war and revolution endured by Russia left the United States in a position to become the dominant power in international affairs. Its opportunities for economic expansion were unrivaled, although the nations that logically were its most important trading partners were the same nations that had experienced the most damage from the war and thus faced years of recovery to reestablish economies as vital as they had been before the war.

POSTWAR RECONSTRUCTION

When the war ended in November 1918, the United States was as poorly prepared for peace as it had been for war. While there had been little planning for war prior to April 1917, there was arguably less preparation for peace at war's end. President Wilson was consumed with the Versailles Peace Conference and his plan for a League of Nations and gave little attention to domestic affairs. From December 1918 until July 1919, he was abroad all but ten days, and when he returned to the United States in July, he faced a challenge from the Senate to his cherished League of Nations. Defending the League of Nations to the Senate and the American people consumed his energies from July until September, when he suffered the debilitating stroke that left him an invalid for the remainder of his presidency.

With no significant presidential input, plans for domestic recovery shifted to Congress, where they failed to get out of committee or ran into a political impasse of party rivalry. In May 1918 Wilson had appointed Grosvenor Clarkson, secretary of the Council of National Defense, to study the problem. Clarkson's research group gathered a wealth of information, but it had no authority to implement policy and closed down in April 1920. Early in 1918 Senator Wesley Jones (R-WA) proposed that President Wilson appoint a committee to study the issue, but the proposal did not clear the Finance Committee. In September Senator John W. Weeks (R-MA), one of the president's most vocal critics, proposed what would have amounted to congressional reconstruction, with a committee composed of six senators and six representatives with equal representation for Democrats and Republicans. Democrats refused to support a proposal that cut out the executive branch altogether. A week later, Senator Lee S. Overman (D-NC) proposed that the president appoint a committee to study reconstruction, but in the political environment just weeks before off-year elections, it predictably ran into Republican obstacles. Wilson weighed in, opposing Weeks's proposal outright and finding Overman's concept too broadly conceived. He suggested that he was not inclined to appoint such a committee.

With little central direction, policy developed in a haphazard fashion. Cabinet members carried on administration of their departments with little presidential guidance, and since some of them had presidential aspirations themselves, politics influenced their decisions more so than usual. Most wartime agencies had charters that mandated that they close down at the end of the war or shortly thereafter, so much of the structure of domestic administration during the war began to close shop after the Armistice. Even the superagencies—the Food Administration, Railroad Administration, Fuel Administration, and the War Industries Board, all of which had wielded enormous power during the war—began to shut down. Some thought the controls implemented by the Fuel Administration ought to continue for a transition period, but the agency ended most of its operations by March 1919. Herbert Hoover, who headed the Food Administration, carried on some relief work in Europe, but the Food Administration itself expired by July 1920. The War Industries Board was the most powerful of these superagencies, and several advisers, including Grosvenor Clarkson, recommended that at least some of its functions—especially price controls—continue until the postwar economy stabilized. But there were other authorities that wanted to end price controls and shut down the WIB. Included among these advisers was the head of the WIB, Bernard Baruch. President Wilson also opposed continuing price controls, so the WIB closed shortly after the end of the war.

The railroads—and the Railroad Administration—were another matter. The general director of the Railroad Administration was William Gibbs McAdoo, who was also secretary of the treasury and chairman of the Federal Reserve Board and the War Finance Corporation. He had demonstrated his undoubted abilities by finding ways to finance the war and had managed the railroads with efficiency. An ambitious man, he hoped to succeed Wilson as president, and of the members of the cabinet he had the best credentials. He was the senior ranking member of the cabinet, and while Wilson was at Versailles McAdoo was the most powerful man in the administration and in the country. His political situation was complicated by virtue of the fact that he was also the president's son-in-law, husband of Wilson's daughter Eleanor.

Government policies, or in many cases the lack of government policies, meant that the economy reverted to control by the private sector. With regulations lifted and wartime production shifting back to consumer goods, companies could chart their own course. Dollar-a-year men returned to their companies, taking with them the information they had acquired during their months of working with the government. Lifting government regulations also meant that government protection for labor unions, including support for collective bargaining, came to an end. Historians would later note that the postwar policies of the Wilson administration began to prepare the way for the economy of the 1920s, shifting advantages to management and voiding protection for labor.

THE POSTWAR ECONOMY

Images of the 1920s include the notion of the "Roaring Twenties," and much of that roar came from the economy. It took time for the economy to heat up, however, and in the immediate aftermath of the war, it staggered, stumbling into a minor depression by 1921. Several factors inhibited progress. The cancellation of wartime contracts hurt many businesses, and it took time for them to readjust to peacetime production. Prices, which had been held in check during the war, shot up quickly after the war ended. The cost of living increased dramatically. In 1919 it was 77 percent higher than it had been in 1914, and in 1920 it was 105 percent of what it had been in 1914. The price of clothing rose at such a rate that consumers rebelled, turning to overalls that were much less expensive than other new clothes, and the protest even reached the halls of Congress. In 1921 five million people were unemployed, 11.9 percent of the workforce.

There were both foreign and domestic reasons for the sputtering economy. The nations of Europe suffered from the ravages of war to a much greater extent, and it took longer for them to recover. But these nations were major trading partners of the United States, so their economic devastation slowed the American recovery as well. The punitive measures of the Versailles Treaty were so severe that it became impossible for Germany to pay postwar reparations, which in turn made it impossible for American allies to repay their debts to the United States—a truly international dilemma that further hurt international trade.

On the domestic front, strikes, unemployment, and checks on labor meant that workers and their families faced challenges that forestalled their recovery. But farmers were in even more dire straits. They had done well during the war and had produced surpluses, but after the war continued surpluses meant that the prices they were able to demand for their produce declined rapidly. And while the manufacturing sector recovered quickly, the agricultural sector did not. The situation for farmers got worse during the decade of the 1920s and then declined further during the Great Depression of the 1930s.

THE RED SCARE OF 1919–1920

Postwar tensions had severe consequences for American society, manifested in strikes, race riots, anti-immigration sentiments, and fear of Bolshevism. The federal government reacted to each of these perceived threats, particularly in response to the rising fear of Bolshevism. Even as the war came to an end, Bolshevism replaced German militarism as a lurking threat to American security. This fear had roots abroad not only in the Russian Revolution and the rise of Lenin to power, but also in the rise of leftist parties in western Europe, including Germany. But there were also domestic roots that included anarchist involvement in the labor movement, the rise of several Socialist Parties, the expansion of patriotic nationalism, the renewal of labor strikes after wartime labor-management agreements ended, and the repressive wartime legislation of the Wilson administration that framed opposition to federal policies as a national security threat.

A series of events in late 1918 and 1919 stimulated the fear that led to the Red Scare. In November 1918, Congress refused to seat Victor Berger, a Socialist elected to the House by Milwaukee voters. The following February a general strike in Seattle that involved some sixty thousand workers and unions that included the IWW and the AFL virtually shut down the city and led to renewed allegations against radical unionists. Postmaster General Albert Burleson, who had been a key figure in implementing the Wilson administration's wartime actions restricting civil liberties, charged before a congressional committee that the IWW was essentially a Bolshevik organization. More than thirty bombs were mailed to prominent politicians in April. The recipients and post office officials discovered most of them before they exploded, but when the secretary to former Georgia senator Thomas Harwick opened his mail, a bomb exploded and she lost both of her hands. Other bombing incidents (with no apparent link to the mail campaign) occurred in the spring, capped by the explosion of bombs in eight cities in seven states at approximately the same time on June 2. Strikes continued to erupt across the nation, and in September police in Boston went out on strike. Massachusetts governor Calvin Coolidge responded that "there is no right to strike against the public safety by anybody, anywhere, any time," a statement that gained him a national reputation that later carried him to the White House. Before the year ended, two crucial industries, steel and coal, suffered strikes. Steelworkers went out in September, and US Steel blamed the Bolsheviks. Two months later, the United Mine Workers went out on strike, and coal management, too, blamed the Bolsheviks.

It was a time fraught with danger, and it seemed that the country had ended an international crisis only to face an internal one. Industrial leaders and government officials had little trouble finding scapegoats and blamed radicals of all stripes: Bolsheviks, anarchists, Socialists, and the IWW. Congress came under pressure to do something to curb the strikes and end the violence and especially to deport radicals and limit immigration.

Attorney General A. Mitchell Palmer spearheaded the administration's response. To this point in his career, Palmer had been liberal. As a congressman from Pennsylvania, he supported the AFL and women's suffrage as well as child labor legislation. But several forces led him to adopt a vigorous conservative response to the apparent radical threat to national security. The pressure for some response from Washington was intense, and Palmer's own home had been bombed in the attacks that swept the nation on June 2. No one in the house was injured—apparently because the bomber tripped and the bomb went off prematurely, killing him—but the incident surely reinforced Palmer's belief that the threat was genuine. Furthermore, Palmer was ambitious and had his eyes on the Democratic presidential nomination in 1920. On June 3 Palmer announced that he was going to rid the nation of anarchists. In August Palmer began to organize his attack on radicals. He established a special division within the Justice Department's Bureau of Investigation and named twenty-four-year-old J. Edgar Hoover to head it. Hoover set up an index file on radicals and their organizations. The file became a database when the Justice Department moved against radicals.

Palmer struck on November 7, raiding offices of the Union of Russian Workers in New York, arresting more than a thousand alleged radicals, citing the bombings on May Day and June 2 as his justification. The Justice Department began to process those individuals seized for deportation. He next went after two of the most prominent anarchists, Emma Goldman and Alexander Berkman. Goldman had been released from prison on September 28 after having served two years for opposing the draft. Berkman, arrested on the same charges, was released three days later. Palmer referred to them as two of the most dangerous anarchists in the country, had them arrested, and on December 21 deported them to Russia, along with 247 others. The biggest of the so-called Palmer Raids occurred on January 2, 1920, with follow-up raids over the next few days. Justice Department officials, in an operation directed by J. Edgar Hoover, rounded up some 3,000 alleged radicals, many of whom were detained in unsanitary conditions or, in the case of those individuals held at Deer Island in Massachusetts, in freezing weather. Later, even Hoover had to concede that there were "clear cases of brutality."

At the time of the raids, Palmer's actions had general support among the public and in the nation's press. That support began to erode when the acting secretary of labor, Louis F. Post, criticized Palmer and the Justice Department for the tactics used during the raids, including allegations that the department had conducted illegal searches and seizures without the authority of a warrant and that in its sweeping arrest policy it had abandoned the concept of individual justice. The Department of Labor had responsibility for administering deportations, so Post used that authority to void some 2,000 of the Palmer arrests. Palmer fought back. In a cabinet meeting in April, he demanded that Secretary of Labor William B. Wilson fire Post. Wilson refused and backed Post's actions. Palmer now sought Post's impeachment, and Bureau of Investigation agents gave the process a nudge by leaking information about Post, including his association with Goldman and Berkman, to members of Congress who would sit in judgment during impeachment proceedings. The effort to impeach Post backfired on Palmer, for it gave Post a public forum in which he could elaborate the excesses of the raids and the illegal activities the Justice Department used in pursuing radicals. Furthermore, it offered an opportunity to others who had been offended by Palmer's tactics. Felix Frankfurter, the future Supreme Court justice, and eleven other prominent attorneys published a tract titled *To the American People: A Report on the Illegal Practices of the United States Department of Justice*, and the American Civil Liberties Union published a similar report. Palmer's star dimmed, and his intended candidacy for the presidency never recovered.

Palmer's antiradical campaign nonetheless had an enormous impact on radical organizations, since many of their leaders had been deported or arrested. The IWW never recovered, although it made an attempt to do so during the Great Depression. Goldman and Berkman were gone, and Bill Haywood followed them to Russia, where he lived his remaining years until his death in 1928. The Communist Party was also crippled. Some of the damage was self-inflicted, as the party split into two groups, the Communist Party, whose membership was overwhelmingly foreign born, mostly Russian immigrants, and the Communist Labor Party, whose leaders mainly spoke English. Both groups, of course, were targets of Palmer's Justice Department. The Communist Party also attempted a revival during the Depression. The Socialist Party also suffered from the government's postwar suppression. With its charismatic leader Eugene Debs in prison for a violation of the Espionage Act, party membership declined from 109,000 to 36,000 by 1920. Debs finally received a pardon from President Harding.

While the radical unions faded, the AFL fared well during the war and in its immediate aftermath. From 1917 to 1920, the AFL grew by 2 million to a membership of more than 5 million. Samuel Gompers, the union's founder, remained in power through the decade and increased its influence by cooperating with the government during the war.

With all the violence that had accompanied labor-management clashes during the decade, the final act of violence did not come until

10. A crowd gathers on Wall Street after the explosion of a bomb on September 16, 1920. Prints and Photographs Division, Library of Congress, LC-DIG-ds-07044.

just weeks before the 1920 election. It was not truly a labor issue, and in fact the perpetrators were never apprehended, or even identified, but the assumption and the trail of investigations led to suspected radical terrorism. On September 16, 1920, a horse-drawn cart full of dynamite and shrapnel exploded in the heart of the Wall Street financial district in New York City, across from the J. P. Morgan bank. The explosion killed 38 people, and the victims were more diverse than the likely targets of banking executives, as most were under thirty years of age, 5 were women, and 4 were teenagers. An additional 143 suffered serious injuries. It was the deadliest act of domestic terrorism until the Oklahoma City bombing of 1995. Subsequent investigations by federal agents and private parties persisted well into the 1920s, but failed to solve the crime.

THE QUESTION OF RACE

African Americans had supported the war effort. Their assignments during the war had been disappointing in the sense that opportunities for promotion and for a significant role had been denied to them; they believed that their service nonetheless merited an increase in opportunities in postwar America. In this hope they were to be deeply disappointed. Postwar America remained a racist nation, and African Americans confronted discrimination daily.

The African American diaspora, the Great Migration, continued unabated during the war, as industrial jobs opened for minorities both to replace white workers serving in the military and because of newly created jobs to service wartime production. The northern industrial cities attracted tens of thousands of African Americans during the war; Chicago's black population grew by fifty thousand in 1917 and 1918. When white soldiers returned home after the war, competition for jobs created a tense environment. When workers went on strike, employers often used African Americans as strikebreakers, exacerbating an already difficult situation. So while most African Americans who had migrated from the South to northern cities for jobs reported that conditions were better than they had been in Dixie, discrimination, racism, and violence were as prevalent.

From May 1919 to the end of the year, race riots occurred in twenty cities and small towns across the nation, from Longview, Texas, to Chicago and Washington, DC. In most cases the riots started with whites attacking blacks, and often the perpetrators were military men serving at bases in or near cities. Such was the case in one of the early riots on May 10 in Charleston, South Carolina, where sailors attacked and killed three black men and injured eighteen others, while five whites also suffered injuries. Labor violence taking place around the country inflamed the situation, with a rash of bombings on June 2 the most dramatic. James Weldon Johnson, an African American writer and a major figure in the Harlem Renaissance a decade later, coined the term *Red Summer* to describe the racial riots.

Racial hatred in Washington erupted in a riot after the *Washington Post* ran a series of articles claiming that African American men had been attacking white women. For three days, from July 20 to 22, white soldiers attacked and beat black men and drove through black neighborhoods shooting at them at random. Blacks retaliated. According to the NAACP, police intervened only when it appeared that whites were losing and that at times they assisted the soldiers. Six people died, and more than two hundred were injured. Afterward, the *Post* admitted that the "attacks" it had described that had precipitated the riot had been verbal, not physical.

The worst of the riots took place in Chicago. The city had been reeling from a series of strikes affecting city employees, including garbage collectors and clerks in city hall. The trial of Tom Mooney, a radical labor organizer implicated in the San Francisco Preparedness Day bombing, further inflamed protesters nationwide. Whites had threatened African Americans before the Fourth of July, but the holiday passed without violence. On July 27 a young African American boy swimming at a Lake Michigan beach crossed a line delineating the black from the white sector, and whites stoned him, killing him as a policeman watched without interfering. A white gang entered a black neighborhood and fired at African Americans at random. Blacks retaliated, touching off a riot that lasted for five days. Ultimately, fifteen whites and twenty-three African Americans died, and as many as five hundred people suffered injuries.

Racial violence continued into the fall. Seventy-six African Americans were lynched in 1919, the highest total since 1901. In 1918 Congressman Leonidas Dyer of Missouri introduced an antilynching bill in Congress, which became known as the Dyer bill. Although the House of Representatives passed the bill in 1922 and it won approval in committee in the Senate, a filibuster by southern senators defeated it. Antilynching bills introduced in later years consistently met effective southern opposition and never became law.

The postwar racial violence stimulated the growth of the Ku Klux Klan, which reached its peak of membership in the mid-1920s, when it claimed to have more than four million members. Originally rooted in the South, the reborn Klan spread across the nation, particularly to the Midwest. It continued to target African Americans, but also attacked Catholics and Jews, especially recent immigrants. The Klan was a proponent of the restrictive immigration laws passed in the early 1920s. The Klan intimidated African Americans, and the threat of violence was one of many tools used to suppress the black vote. A singular victory for the African American right to vote in this era was the 1915 Supreme Court decision in an Oklahoma case (*Guinn v. United States*), but it made little difference because of a variety of means still legal to deprive blacks of the vote.

The frustrations of the African American community created a need for new leadership. Leaders such as W. E. B. DuBois and the other members of the NAACP appealed to African American elites and to those individuals looking for a legal solution to the problems African Americans faced, but to the majority of blacks these solutions were insufficient to confront the full tide of racism they faced in their daily lives. The leader who offered the greatest appeal to the African American masses was Marcus Garvey. Garvey's newspaper, the *Negro World*, offered news but also Garvey's opinions, which sought to instill pride. He argued that moderate leaders such as DuBois were too willing to settle for amalgamation with white America. Garvey wanted to demonstrate that African Americans were capable of managing their own affairs. His United Negro Improvement Association was doing that very thing. In June 1919 the UNIA had established the Black Star Line and purchased its first ship. He sold shares at five dollars each and raised a half-million dollars to capitalize the line by selling one hundred thousand shares. He claimed that in June, the UNIA had two million members, and even if this figure was exaggerated—as critics then and since have argued—there was no question of his mass appeal and no doubt that the *Negro World* had the largest circulation of any African American newspaper. Within years Garvey's enterprises would run into financial and legal trouble, but by the end of 1920 he had established himself as one of the foremost leaders of the African American people.

THE ELECTION OF 1920

The election of 1920 was a defining conclusion to the policies of the Wilson administration. President Wilson hoped that the election would be a referendum on the Versailles Treaty and on the League of Nations, and indeed it became just that, although the outcome was not what he had hoped. Remarkably, Wilson believed that he had recovered sufficiently to seek reelection, although his inner circle discouraged him from doing so. The election was a decisive defeat for Wilson's dream. Former president Theodore Roosevelt was an early front-runner for the Republican nomination, but his health failed and he died in 1919, leaving the Republican nomination an open issue with a long list of qualified contenders.

The Republicans met in Chicago on June 8–12. The party had a strong field of candidates that included Governors Frank Lowden of Illinois, Hiram Johnson of California, and Calvin Coolidge of Massachusetts; Major General Leonard Wood; Senators Robert La Follette of Wisconsin and Warren Harding of Ohio; and Nicholas Murray Butler, the president of Columbia University and the Republican candidate for vice president in 1912. At the outset, it appeared that there would be a battle between Frank Lowden and Leonard Wood, and in the early balloting that was indeed the case. They were the only candidates to receive more than 200 votes, and by the sixth ballot they were in a dead heat, each with 311.5 votes. In the next ballot, things began to change, as Senator Harding's campaign manager, Harry Daugherty, maneuvered Harding into contention. The legend that emerged from the convention was that party bosses met in a "smoke-filled room" where they debated, looking for a compromise candidate. Lowden's support wavered on the next ballot, and Harding, an undistinguished senator but the compromise choice of the party bosses, emerged as a contender. It took ten ballots, but Harding won the nomination. Governor Calvin Coolidge won the vice presidential nod in convincing fashion.

The Democratic Party held its convention in San Francisco, convening on June 28 and continuing until July 6. Secretary of the Treasury William Gibbs McAdoo, a dominant figure in Wilson's cabinet and the president's son-in-law, appeared to be the favorite for the nomination, but Wilson refused to support him, hoping that the convention might be deadlocked and turn to him in desperation. Wilson's delusions probably cost McAdoo the nomination, and no one ever placed Wilson's name in nomination. Another cabinet member, Attorney General A. Mitchell Palmer, also wanted the nomination, but the excesses of the so-called Palmer Raids during the Red Scare earlier in the year had damaged his reputation irreparably. The party's only recognition of the Wilson legacy was a statement of support for the League of Nations in its platform, but even that endorsement was tempered by reservations. Balloting made the ten ballots of the Republican convention appear to be a quick decision; it took forty-four ballots before Ohio governor James Cox emerged as the Democratic nominee. Delegates expected a drawn-out battle for the vice presidential nomination, but Cox expressed his preference for the former assistant secretary of the navy and a rising star in the party, Franklin D. Roosevelt. Delegates acceded to his request and nominated FDR by voice vote.

The only significant third-party candidate was the Socialist Eugene Debs, the much-admired labor leader. Debs, still in prison as a result of his opposition to the draft in 1917, nonetheless was able to win more votes than any Socialist candidate had achieved in prior elections, a total of 913,664, or 3.4 percent of the total.

The two major-party candidates ran contrasting campaigns. Harding ran a "front-porch" campaign from his home in Marion, Ohio. Reporters came to Marion to hear what Harding had to say, which was carefully noncontroversial and thus not very interesting. He called for a return to "normalcy," a term that he never clearly defined, although voters seemed to know what he meant—essentially a rejection of everything Wilsonian and of the turmoil of the war and Progressive reforming zeal.

In contrast, Cox ran an ambitious campaign, traveling around the country making speeches and meeting with people. He met with Wilson before launching his campaign and seemed to have pledged support for the League of Nations. He backtracked once he began to campaign, however, when he saw how unpopular the league was, even among Democrats.

The election was one of the most decisive in American history. Harding received 16.1 million votes (60.32 percent) to 9.1 million (34.15 percent) for Cox. Harding won the electoral vote even more decisively, 404–127. Much of the explanation for the landslide was that the country was still predominantly Republican and would remain so until the Great Depression. But it was also an overwhelming rejection of the Wilson presidency.

The country was headed in a new direction, less eager for reform, tired of war and of American involvement in foreign affairs in general. The election marked a clear break from the activist policies of the first two decades of the century, and the American people set out to find out what normalcy was all about.

SUGGESTED READINGS

Burl Noggle's *Into the Twenties: The United States from Armistice to Normalcy* (Urbana: Univ. of Illinois Press, 1974) examines the complex of social, economic, and political issues that the nation faced after the war. David Pietrusza's *1920: The Year of the Six Presidents* examines an election in which party conventions were far more dramatic than the subsequent campaign.

Index

ANDREW J. DUNAR is professor emeritus at the University of Alabama in Huntsville. His books include *America in the Fifties* in this series, *Building Hoover Dam* (with Dennis McBride), and *Power to Explore: A History of Marshall Space Flight Center, 1960–1990* (with Stephen P. Waring), which won the History Book Award from the American Institute of Aeronautics and Astronautics in 2001.